LAMENT FROM EPIRUS

LAMENT FROM EPIRUS

CHRISTOPHER C. KING

An Odyssey
into Europe's
Oldest
Surviving
Folk Music

W. W. NORTON & COMPANY

Independent Publishers Since 1923

New York London

An earlier section of Chapter 5 appeared in the *Oxford American Magazine*.
An essay that became a section of Chapter 5 appeared in the *Paris Review Daily*.

Translation of "Anathema Se Xenitia," "Samantaka," and traditional *mirologi*
courtesy of Demetris P. Dallas. Translation of "Panegyri of Kastritsa" courtesy of
Jim Potts. Translation of "The Bridge of Arta" courtesy of Thomas Scotes.

For information about permission to reproduce selections from this book, write to
Permissions, W. W. Norton & Company, Inc., 500 Fifth Avenue, New York, NY 10110

For information about special discounts for bulk purchases, please contact
W. W. Norton Special Sales at specialsales@wwnorton.com or 800-233-4830

Manufacturing by LSC Communications, Harrisonburg
Book design by Chris Welch
Production manager: Beth Steidle

Library of Congress Cataloging-in-Publication Data

Names: King, Christopher C., author.
Title: Lament from Epirus : an odyssey into Europe's oldest surviving folk music /
    Christopher C. King.
Description: First edition. | New York : W. W. Norton & Company, [2018] |
    Includes bibliographical references and index.
Identifiers: LCCN 2018001031 | ISBN 9780393248999 (hardcover)
Subjects: LCSH: Folk music—Epirus (Greece and Albania)—History and criticism.
Classification: LCC ML3604.7.E65 K56 2018 | DDC 781.62/804953—dc23
LC record available at https://lccn.loc.gov/2018001031

W. W. Norton & Company, Inc., 500 Fifth Avenue, New York, N.Y. 10110
www.wwnorton.com

W. W. Norton & Company Ltd., 15 Carlisle Street, London W1D 3BS

1 2 3 4 5 6 7 8 9 0

For Charmagne

"Listening to the phonograph record is like eating with false teeth."

—KAMIL AL-KHULAI, 1904

CONTENTS

LIST OF ILLUSTRATIONS

LAMENT FROM EPIRUS

CURIOUS BLACK DISCS AND DEAD ENDS

A TIME-TRAVELER, A PERSON FROM THE TWENTY-FIRST CEN-
tury, stands on a cliff overlooking a mountain pass in southern
Europe, in northwestern Greece, a few thousand years after the
end of the last Ice Age, having traveled back in time by way of
some technology unknown to us. This traveler is observing human
beings while they interact with one another in this challenging,
remote environment.

Something is happening among these proto-Europeans. One
person places a long wooden shaft, holes bored along the side, to
his lips, producing sound. Other sounds exit the mouths of the surrounding people. The collective sound appears fragmented to the
listener—the time-traveler—standing above. At times the voices
and the flute notes appear smooth, mellifluous, but then disjointed
and abrupt. During this flood of sound, members of this group
move in cryptic yet intentional ways. When this lush cacophony
ceases, so too do the movements of the people.

What is going on down there?

Any of us could be this time-traveler. And any of us would
realize—based on our observations—that these people are com-
municating. We perceive sound and movement, assuming cause

and effect. The question that should linger in our minds is this: are we observing a use of language, a use of music, or something else— an alien and impenetrable behavior?

There was a time in our distant human past when we were cold, hungry, and fraught with anxiety. In order to live we had to communicate with one another. Language is a very powerful tool to exchange meaning. It is necessary for cooperation within a species; it is a tool for survival. Music, too, is a potent means of exchange. But have we ever considered music—long thought of as a form of entertainment or of symbolic expression—a tool for survival?

ҩҩҩ

Music is as universal and as primal as language. There is evidence of musicality from every culture—both preliterate and literate— known throughout the world.

Music permeates our lives: listening to it, making it, judging it, or collecting it. Practically every day—sometimes several times a day—we hum a melody or repeat a line from a song that has unconsciously become embedded within us.

Language itself is intertwined with music. We often describe the sonorous qualities of the human voice and of nature with musical terms such as "melodious" or "rhythmic." The tonal properties of instruments are likened to the sounds of humans: "The violin pierced the air like a woman's voice" or "The trumpet wailed as the drums growled." Likewise, it would be impossible to describe music without the lexicon of human emotion—*sad, happy, unhinged.*

Our earliest form of communication may have been a blending of the melodic with the spoken, much like a birdsong. Few would argue that birds communicate *nothing* with their patterns of tones. And most would agree that avian utterances are arrangements of sound with an aesthetic dimension: they are musical.

Our early ancestors may not have recognized a binary, the verbal and the musical. As humans evolved, perhaps linguistic expression and melodic expression bifurcated. Like a vestigial part of our anatomy, music may have mutated or atrophied, obscuring its original purpose.

Toddlers, before they form words and sentences, often communicate with a mixture of the verbal and the musical. My daughter Riley—before she uttered her first sentence, "Angels eat babies' eyes"—expressed herself with piercing melodic lines that sounded like the cries of a pterodactyl sweeping across the sky. My wife and I inferred from these sounds that she wanted to be fed. This was the language-song of a hungry child.

Epic poetry—among the earliest artifacts of our propensity for storytelling—was musical. Many have theorized that repeated phrases and tonal patterns helped the ancient poet-singer recall the verses—an early mnemonic technique. Listeners were pleased to hear melodic refrains punctuated with action and meaning. When these rhapsodic songs were captured in writing by pressing a stylus into a substrate, we preserved the words along with trace elements of their musicality.

But evidence of music's origin is fragmented. Humanity is a careless time-traveler. We rarely mark our passage through the millennia in a conscious way. Evidence has been lost, leaving an incomplete trail of artifacts—of clues—about the origin of this universal human activity, music making. Often we are left wondering what music actually is.

John Blacking proposed that music is "humanly organized sound," a pat yet inclusive definition. Blacking was a pioneering ethnomusicologist who contrasted the folk music of central and southern Africa with the classical music of Europe. In his book *How Musical Is Man?* Blacking advanced the notion that listeners are just as musical as performers in traditional folk economies. In cultures that do not write down their music but rather transmit their songs and dances from one generation to the next, the ability to critically listen to and appraise a traditional folk performance "is as important and as much a measure of musical ability as is performance, because it is the only means of ensuring continuity of the musical tradition."

In Blacking's view much of Europe and the West's classical or art music is preserved differently: it is written in standard musical notation. A proportionally small number of people know how to read music. Those who assess a given performance in the West—for instance, an opera critic—belong to an exclusive clique. Therefore Western culture sees musicality limited to those who are trained to perform or who are educated in aesthetic criticism or music theory.

Blacking and I would agree that music is universal and primal. But he avoids confronting the notion of functionality. If music is humanly organized sound, the question drifts unanswered, "organized to *what end*?" Why is sound organized as music in the first place?

Like Blacking, I am fascinated with folk music that thrived in societies where songs were passed orally from one generation to the next. In such traditions lyrics were occasionally written down, but this was not the main form of transmission. The process of learning how to play an instrument was likewise a craft that was taught by an older group of musicians to a younger group within the context of their culture. The transmission of this cultural asset sounds simple. It is not.

Documenting folk music generates complications. For instance, who ought to explain the phenomenon of an indigenous music? Should they be *insiders*, such as native performers who craft the songs, or could they be *outsiders,* such as anthropologists using tools from their discipline? Can these perspectives be traversed somehow? The answers to these questions have eluded me for over thirty years.

A written description aims for precision. An instrumental phrase aims for impressionistic ambiguity. These two modes of communication, the verbal and the musical, appear to pull from two different parts of our psyche. Verbal communication has a definitive, logical vocabulary—a lexicon. Musical language possesses a slippery tongue changing shape from one region or historical context to another—a palimpsest. You simply cannot use words to describe music any more than you can play a sentence on a violin. These two modes just do not correspond. Or so I thought.

༄ ༄ ༄

I am a record collector. The type of disc with which I am obsessed, the 78 rpm phonograph record, is made of slowly decaying organic materials,* bound together and coated with synthetic compounds. Like most of the music that Blacking studied in the 1950s, it is a relic of the past, a fossil.

These curious black discs are all that connect us with the best part of our musical past, with the rapture that we were once able to convey through deep song and dance. These records are fragile, yet they were the dominant medium of auricular permanence and commerce for roughly the first fifty years of the twentieth century.

When I was young, I discovered that 78 recordings—unlike so many other parts of contemporary culture—needed no outside validation, just an attentive, appreciative listener. I was the listener and the artists that made them were my friends. They were constant. People would betray you, institutions would fail you, but this, *this* old music, a music lacking all pretension, would never change.

Old performances on 78s transformed me. They become a singular point of reference: I understand my musical surroundings, perhaps even my physical and cultural environment, through this antiquated medium. These recordings form an aperture through which I make sense—or perceive the senselessness—of the world.

In my view, classical music is cerebral and aspires to a lofty

---

* Unstable substrates melted together: shellac, clay, cork, horsehair, bovine bones, and tree resin, to name a few.

yet groundless culture that few can enter. Contemporary popular music, which permeates every aspect of life from eating out to shopping for shoes, is over-researched, mass-marketed vacuous tripe—a dulling, inescapable, even sinister noise. I understand many people have strong attachments to contemporary music, but I cannot deny what I hear. In modern music, I hear self-centeredness, a constant referencing of individual artistic expression. It is all about the "me." But in the old music that I love, I hear selflessness, continuity, and communal expression. It was all about the "we."

These vessels of sound—the 78 rpm disc—harness something transient and sacred: vibrations in the air. The instantaneous and the inexplicable—a halting breath between bow strokes, the whispers by a musician in the studio that "time is up," a train whistle etched in the grooves in a studio too close to the tracks, ghost echoes—were captured on this nascent technology. Real culture is etched within these recordings: artifacts of the way we used to navigate the world and of how we used to interact with music. They are vehicles of something fleeting but also something that begs you to follow, a Siren in a paper sleeve.

These discs loom before me like the black monoliths in *2001: A Space Odyssey*. I am one of the groping, awkward hominids and the disc is the mysterious source of knowledge. Despite my undying affection, the phonograph disc is simply a tool to capture vibrations in the air: a record of humanly organized sound.

In this phonographic-cinematic metaphor, both the mint 78 and the stone monument possess an aura of perfection and potency to me. The grooves of the 78 disc may seem to contain flaws, but the flaws are in us, not in the music contained therein. The imperfection is in the exchange: we cannot see the musicians or shout encouragement to them while dancing. We cannot live within the disc. We can only listen. The crude technology distances us from the context that first prompted and then nurtured these musical activities. Without the context, one loses touch with the original intention of the music.

Whatever Kubrick was conjuring with the first act of his film, "The Dawn of Man," I am confident that he intended the metaphor to be both universal and specific: universally applied to our ceaseless quest for explanation and specifically applied to the resolution of his film, "The Jupiter Mission," where the tool of our creation, HAL 9000, turns against its human progenitors. A tool that we created becomes an instrument of our own destruction. And in truth, the phonograph record all but killed the authentic folk music that I love.

Travel back in time to early-twentieth-century southwest Louisiana, to the small town of Basile. This is before electrical lines stitched across the backs of prairies from the big cities into the woodlands. There is a house dance—a *bal de maison*—on the outskirts taking place on a Friday night to celebrate a rice harvest. A clapboard farmstead is lit with rush lamps and kerosene burners. Rugs and roughly hewn chairs rest outside in the smoky, humid air so dozens of farming families can dance inside to the music of Denus McGee—a white fiddler—and Amede Ardoin—a black accordionist. Everyone, including the musicians, speaks a French dialect. They are Cajuns.

There is moonshine here. And steaming kettles of gumbo set outside over fire pits. Oldsters are showing youngsters how to dance the cotillion, the mazurka, and the waltz in double-time: they glide to melodies that traveled from France to Nova Scotia to Louisiana. The secret, the old men say, is for everyone to move in perfect unison around the musicians as if they were gears within a clock.

Folks from across this parish have been anticipating this event all year long. They will dance practically without rest until Sunday mass. Young men flirt with the women. McGee and Ardoin play an especially sorrowful tune, "La Valse de Amitiés" ("Love

Waltz"). Hearing this song sparks a collective memory, a feeling of regret and desolation among the dancers: a story of heartbreak and longing. The musicians' voices do not need amplification—they cut through the wet night air and straight into the hearts of the listeners. Old men shout encouragement to Ardoin. Ladies in white petticoats cry. Everyone who has anticipated this *fête* feels an emotional release that spreads over the crowd like a cool, balmy wave.

At this moment in the early twentieth century, this sort of social gathering—in which music profoundly transformed whole communities—was happening all over the world. Musicians lived next door, not in a jukebox. Sure, at the house dance Ardoin and McGee would have received cash in the hat, food, moonshine, maybe more. But their function as music makers was more essential than air and therefore more valuable than money. They were vital to their community. And they were treated as musical royalty.

A decade or so later, in 1934, McGee and Ardoin recorded "*La Valse de Amitiés*." Jukebox wholesalers in Texas and Louisiana would have collected 35 cents for each disc sold in Texas and Louisiana—cash in the bank during the Great Depression. But by 1934, Ardoin and McGee's music was antiquated, resulting in minuscule sales. By then, most beer houses and juke joints wanted amplified, *modern* Cajun dance pieces infused with electric lap steel and drums.*

Music—at least in terms of how we understand it—has always involved a dimension of exchange, of money. In the United States, record labels saw profits in folk music starting in the 1890s with "ethnic" recordings, followed in the early 1920s with black blues and white country music. Phonograph companies released folk music from virtually every ethnic and racial enclave in America and across the planet.

---

* Christ, drums *and* electric guitar.

Terry Zwigoff—film director and 78 disc collector—called these diminishing regions of folk artistry "pockets of eccentricity." Commercial recording companies captured songs from some of these isolated regions precisely at the time when such music was becoming less central to the culture. And it was commercialism, along with pressures to assimilate, that nearly wiped out living folk music.

⤸⤸⤸

At the beginning of the twentieth century, most places had some degree of contact with the outside world—nothing was left untouched by wars, colonialism, and the reach of religion or governments. But as we can see through certain photographic archives, like the images Albert Kahn produced for his *Les archives de la planète*, the Earth once contained a bewildering diversity of people and of music.

However, when mass commercial recording began, almost every ethnic and rural musical expression commenced an accelerated process of homogenization, a sad urgency toward bland uniformity. During this short span of time everything started to fall apart, or fall together, as it were. Regional styles, repertoires, and, perhaps most crucially, interactive and contextual functions went from being a central component of a culture's music to a quaint, antiquated notion—quickly forgotten. Everyone wanted to sound like those heard on the most recent technologies: disc and radio.

Pressures from within the ethnic communities and cold business logic from the record companies encouraged the annihilation of regional sounds. Communities wanted to assimilate, to become modern. Record companies wanted to make bank, implying a tacit mandate to record palatable, easy-to-market music. Musicians had to satisfy the aesthetics of the artist and repertoire middlemen who decided who and what would be recorded. Back porch hayseeds would have to slick up their sound, straighten out their crooked tunes, and shorten their natural performance time to conform with the constraints of the disc. If they failed, they would not record more than once.*

The explosive growth of the phonograph and jukebox business would all but eliminate the need for live, native folk music. Between the two world wars we had discovered our dual nature to both preserve and destroy culture. One of our tools—the phonographic recording device—both documented and poisoned authentic rural music. Raw folk music would practically vanish by the time the 78 rpm record format had run its course.

໑໑໑

Before music became a commodity, it was nourishment: food for the soul. Communities needed music; therefore musicians were esteemed. When I listen to an especially fine recording from some isolated place, I hear the connectedness underneath the music: the artist's connection to the village and the song's connection with the past, with memory. I hear authenticity, what *was*. When I hear music from the present and the not so distant past, I perceive a pale derivation, a whimper, of what once existed. I hear *what was lost*.

There is an inexact metric to my judgment of folk music, and I parse my appraisal in terms of authenticity—a loaded term if there was one. First, I understand traditional folk music as humanly organized sound produced by distinct groups of people who are geographically, linguistically, religiously, and ethnically unified.[1] Second, the behaviors and beliefs within a folk tradition retain their purposes when they are passed down from a parent to a child, a mentor to a docent. This act transfers culture. Authenticity, as I understand it, measures the transmission of practices (including music) within a folk tradition. When a practice is handed down from one generation to the next, authenticity of that practice is

---

* Of course it would help if they added drums and electric guitar.

preserved to a high degree. When a practice is disrupted or devalued, then authenticity is lessened.

You may ask, "Well, what about this string band from Brooklyn? I just saw them at the farmer's market when I picked up my kombucha. These younger guys learned from older guys who in turn learned from 'authentic' southern fiddlers in the 1960s."

I would say that this music is less authentic. Why?

Let's take a break and visit my record room. First, I need to turn on my equipment to warm up. OK.

Do you want a drink? It helps. Do you want to get high? Fine.

Right now I'm playing for you a 78 recorded in 1927 by Da Costa Woltz's Southern Broadcasters called *John Brown's Dream*. Nice copy, right? Pretty rare. The fiddler is Ben Jarrell, from a small town called Toast, North Carolina. He's playing in an idiosyncratic style with his strings tuned up high, heavily syncopated bow strokes, lots of embellishments. Ben is playing just like his father and his father before him. Ben Jarrell had a son named Tommy born in 1901 who fiddled just like him. Tommy was "rediscovered" in the 1960s and made hundreds of recordings. He taught musicians—mainly guys from the Northern states—how to play fiddle and banjo. Tommy had a son but his son died before passing on Tommy's music. Some local musicians learned from Tommy, but not many.

Most of these young Northerners who learned from Tommy moved away but continued to play Tommy's tunes, copying his style. What they didn't have was the context—the unique social cohesion—that nurtured this music in the first place. Tommy learned from his father but he also played for house parties and corn-shuckings. The particular type of rural, isolated lifestyle that Tommy and his community lived informed his playing just as much as the lessons that his father gave him on fiddle.

I can't say that the recreations—the contemporary interpretations of traditional music—are inauthentic. But I can say that those who learned this repertoire and style from rural Toast,

North Carolina, without living the same kind of life as Tommy are playing a *less* authentic music. Revival musicians simply do not convey the deep web of cultural bonds and nuances that existed when the music was captured on 78. Even though the rural eccentricities may have started to degrade earlier, to become faint when they were recorded decades ago, the intensity was still there. What existed then was an apex of expression. What exists now is a nadir of imitation.

What is etched within these curious black discs no longer exists in the world. Or so I believed.

✎ ✎ ✎

Sometimes having an artifact is not enough. I yearned for music that was not a dead end on my record shelf, something vital. In my studio, thousands of black discs in tan sleeves stood—row after row of memorials to dozens of deceased or dying musical traditions. I believed that there was no music existing in the world with an unbroken connection to its original context, its culture.

I was wrong.

In the twenty-first century, I discovered the unimaginable, a land and music that time forgot. The music thrives in an isolated part of the Balkan Peninsula, a literal and spiritual gateway between the East and the West: *Epirus*.

Here in a corner of northwestern Greece is an area suspended in time, negotiating the influences of modernization yet possessing the necessary components for a robust musical life. Witnessing the music of this region, I realized that folk music, like all organic things, requires a biosphere. The elements for life and for music mirror one another: there must be a protective atmosphere, a source of nutrition, and a purpose for existing.

Epirus exists within such a musical biosphere. In this place, dance justifies life, songs affirm death, and the great mystery— "What is the purpose of making music?"—is answered. By traveling to this place, I was able to traverse the perspectives of insider and outsider and to understand how the expressions of language and music are unified as one mode.

⬥⬥⬥

When I listen to a 78 or a contemporary field recording of northwestern Greek music I discern these four characteristics: the music of Epirus has ancient, continuous roots; emotional intensity; an inextricable bond between the soil and people; and an ineffable dimension that speaks profoundly about the human condition.

Longevity is critical. There are celebrations and songs in Epirus that are undoubtedly rooted in the pre-Christian past, preserved— as if in amber—for hundreds, possibly thousands of years. But what initially seized me was the intensity of the music, *the best I've ever seen.*

To explain what I mean by intensity, here is a cinematic metaphor from the nihilistic crime drama *The French Connection.* In it, countercultural chemist Pat McDermott tests the purity of heroin smuggled into New York City. In McDermott's economy, purity is the same as intensity. Setting up a glass beaker apparatus, applying a sampling of said heroin to a solution, McDermott then fires up his Bunsen burner. As the temperature rises, so too does McDermott's evaluation of the qualitative merits of the opioid sample:

> Blastoff!
> 180–200—Good Housekeeping Seal of Approval
> 210—U.S. Government Certified
> 220—Lunar trajectory—Junk of the Month Club Sirloin Steak
> 230 Grade "A" Poison—Absolute Dynamite! 89% pure junk
> *The Best I've Ever Seen*

When I listen to a 78 recording, my appraisal of its merits is like McDermott's grading of heroin. We perceive the temperature rising based on the purity or intensity. Our metric for evaluation is not grounded in academic thought. McDermott and I are outside the fray: we have an intimate knowledge of and interaction with the phenomenon because of our obsessive devotion to it. Just as McDermott knows how to judge a drug's power based on his own personal use, I too can grade the intensity of music based on my lifelong worship of these curious black discs.

Intensity is a result of the interconnections between a place, its people, and its music: a localized vitality. In Epirus the music is purposeful: it is a tool for survival and communal healing. A symbiosis exists between the artists and the people, where the nourishment being shared *is* the music.

∾∾∾

Like most life-altering experiences for a sheltered, misanthropic record collector, my first exposure to the music of Epirus came from several battered and beat-to-hell 78s. But these recordings only served as a gateway to the living music of northwestern Greece. Every visit to the region led to a greater discernment of the mechanisms at play in this music. I discovered that in Epirus, music contains a curative, healing function.

This discovery led to an epiphany, a revelation about how we, as modernized Westerners, have a simplified if not fundamentally flawed misconception about the origin and purpose of music. When one understands the purpose of music in Epirus, one discovers an alternative view.

Epirotes say they need this music because "life has always been hard in the mountains, everything has always been uncertain." Music here is a balm—a curative—for the unknowable and the inevitable. There are threats to all cultures at all times, but in northwestern Greece they have a name for the ultimate threat, *Charon*—ferryman to the underworld, aka Death, the one who collects the last ticket.

Like other odysseys into the unknown, this book will not follow a single thread but rather multiple strands forming a polyphonic tapestry of a place—Epirus. This is a story about a very specific music. But this is also a story about deciphering a larger enigma: why we make music. It is a story involving a murder mystery, a humble artist, a vast landscape and an impenetrable soundscape. It is a story about longing, memory and regret. It is a story about Epirus.

1

A STREET OF GRAMOPHONES

The utter loneliness, and the gates of mystery opening, inviting,
the dark abyss . . . temptation—ah, it's only human! Understandable!
And what is curiosity? The first reflex of a newborn baby,
the most natural of impulses, the primal wish to find the Cause,
the Cause of the Effect, the Effect that in turn causes Action, and
so a continuity is established . . . the chains that bind us . . . and it
all began so innocently!

—STANISLAW LEM, *MEMOIRS FOUND IN A BATHTUB*

ISTANBUL FROM THE SKY AT NIGHT PRESENTS ITSELF AS A VAST, teeming organism, undulating with life and shimmering with fractured points of light. Osman, the first sultan of the Turks, dreamt that out of his navel would grow a tree from which the world would find sustenance, shelter, and identity. According to his soothsayers, this tree would become the Muslim Ottoman Empire. Istanbul, the city the Greeks founded as Byzantium—later named Constantinople—can be viewed as the shade and the shadow cast by this tree of Ottoman rule.

Osman would not live to see Constantinople conquered by the Turks in AD 1453 or watch his empire seize most of the territory controlled by the Christian Byzantines. Prior to Turkish rule, from AD 330 to 1453 the Greek Orthodox Church was the spiritual force that held Byzantium together.

The combined rule of the Greeks and the Turks of this city, ending with the establishment of the modern Turkish Republic in 1923, was almost 1,600 years. Istanbul witnessed nearly two millennia of

A STREET OF GRAMOPHONES

The utter loneliness, and the gates of mystery opening, inviting,
the dark abyss . . . temptation—ah, it's only human! Understandable!
And what is curiosity? The first reflex of a newborn baby,
the most natural of impulses, the primal wish to find the Cause,
the Cause of the Effect, the Effect that in turn causes Action, and
so a continuity is established . . . the chains that bind us . . . and it
all began so innocently!

—STANISLAW LEM, *MEMOIRS FOUND IN A BATHTUB*

ISTANBUL FROM THE SKY AT NIGHT PRESENTS ITSELF AS A VAST,
teeming organism, undulating with life and shimmering with fractured points of light. Osman, the first sultan of the Turks, dreamt
that out of his navel would grow a tree from which the world would
find sustenance, shelter, and identity. According to his soothsayers, this tree would become the Muslim Ottoman Empire. Istanbul, the city the Greeks founded as Byzantium—later named
Constantinople—can be viewed as the shade and the shadow cast
by this tree of Ottoman rule.

Osman would not live to see Constantinople conquered by the
Turks in AD 1453 or watch his empire seize most of the territory
controlled by the Christian Byzantines. Prior to Turkish rule, from
AD 330 to 1453 the Greek Orthodox Church was the spiritual force
that held Byzantium together.

The combined rule of the Greeks and the Turks of this city, ending with the establishment of the modern Turkish Republic in 1923,
was almost 1,600 years. Istanbul witnessed nearly two millennia of

bloodletting—grotesque carnivals of invasions and retreats, flexing of muscle and atrophy.

But history and ancient agonies were far from my mind when my wife, my daughter, and I first arrived in Istanbul in 2009. We had to leave our home to clear our heads. Weaknesses from within me and forces from outside were dismantling my life, eroding and fracturing the core. I had lost my father and my younger brother. During this upheaval I nearly lost my wife and daughter. There was no time to mourn, since I was too busy counting my losses. Almost everything was uncertain and unstable in my life except for my sense of hearing and my instinct for collecting.

Earlier that year my wife Charmagne mentioned, as if she were sleep-talking with a stranger, that she had always wanted to see the Hagia Sophia in Istanbul. Life had removed the option of travel. She was too busy raising our daughter and I was too consumed with producing collections of old music to think of a vacation. Our choices insured that we could happily get by in life but little more than that. However, the word "Istanbul" carved a stubborn impression.

A week later Charmagne read aloud from *The New York Times* that Leonard Cohen would be performing for two nights in Istanbul. The intricate tapestry of memories and regrets in my mind registered a completed circuit and I recalled "Istanbul." But I had never heard of this Leonard Cohen and was immediately apprehensive of bringing him into my life.

When I asked who he was, she replied, "You know, 'Bird on a Wire' . . . 'Chelsea Hotel Number Two'?" I shrugged this off as esoteric knowledge, but the next day I secured a flight to Turkey for us and our three-year-old daughter Riley. An acquaintance provided concert tickets after I booked a hotel room in a repurposed nineteenth-century sanatorium flanking the Hagia Sophia.

⋘

Traveling on the western side of Istanbul is like maneuvering through any grotesquely commercialized and overpopulated city—

everything and everybody demands your attention and your money. Over the course of our two-week stay I would be stalked by a particularly sadistic, single-minded shoeshine artist who set up his enterprise outside the hotel, seemingly just for me. After our first encounter where he demanded five Turkish *lira* to spray ammonia on my shoes, I took to wearing open-toed sandals and checking all egresses before fleeing the hotel. Inevitably he would be at every exit and entry point, fully prepared to accommodate my Nazarene footwear.

We intended to be tourists, to consume sizzling kebabs, salty *kaşkaval* cheese, freshly shucked clams for male potency, and confusing iterations of baklava emerging from clouds of powdered sugar. But every traveler wants to walk away with a special experience, a rare trophy to prove the importance of their visit and—most selfishly—their own singularity, something no other visitor has sullied. My family's desires were modest, pedestrian. An "authentic tribal rug" would fit our budget and linger after our death, providing evidence of our exotic travels.

Most rug stores on the European side of Istanbul touted gaudy floor coverings suitable in my mind for Arabian pimps and hustlers of other nationalities. We wanted something that spoke of authenticity—grit. The hotel staff told us we only needed to walk a few minutes through a crumbling alley that meandered asymmetrically from the sanatorium-hotel toward a rose park. Here— they assured us—we would find rugs documented with Facebook images and Twitter accounts of the bent and hobbled female weavers from the Anatolian countryside.

#authenticity

The evidence of a cruelty-free floor covering might have been alluring to certain Brooklynites or academics from Oberlin, but this type of validation did nothing for me—I wanted a rug woven with suffering and humanity but without the cross-stitch of social media.*

We arrived at the hole-in-a-wall rug shop, established extemporaneously, changing locations as the supply of textiles and the flow of tourists saw fit. Within ten seconds of entering, my eyes shifted from the elaborate patterns of *Türkmen* textiles and evil-eye motifs to a dark, moldering cabinet in the corner of the shop: a veneered, windup gramophone player from the earlier part of the last century.

Seeing an old phonograph in the wild, possibly untouched and virgin, implies that the contents of its chamber, the shelves within the cabinet, could contain discs that hadn't been played in 90 years. It may hold music unheard since the day the engineer captured the sound in his cramped studio. For a collector like me, this realization is simultaneously a pornographic and a spiritual moment, akin to encountering a salacious peep-show after entering a *sanctum sanctorum*. There is unspeakable lust and reverence. Opening the sealed doors of such a cabinet releases the heavy odor of aged paper enveloping the rare musk of shellac—an odiferous marriage resulting in the second most arousing smell in the world.

Every time I come across such phonographs, particularly in the hidden recesses of a home or a shed, I vividly recall my first

---

* It occurs to me that I'm a living fossil—a rare sapient hominid without a cellphone, a Facebook account, or a Twitter handle. For thousands of years we have gotten along nicely without instantaneous long-distance communication devices conjoined with a camera and portals to entertainment and data. As a species, we've excelled at fashioning objects into tools that serve a meaningful purpose—improving the general quality of our survival. However, the Smart Phone has transformed *us* into tools of these devices. We have become slaves to technology and the concept that "technology makes things easier." Perhaps many human activities were not intended to be easy—maybe the complexities of actual human interaction are richer, more valid when taken along with the attendant messy difficulties.

good score at the age of fifteen. I was just emerging from puberty when my maternal grandmother, Mimi, died. My grandparents' farm was built on several hundred acres of land deep in the Highlands of southwest Virginia. The interwar years had whittled down their farmstead to only a few dozen acres. After the stock market crashed, the imagination of the middle class crashed as well. Panic and desperation seized everyone, including my grandparents, who had never even deposited money in a bank in the first place.

My grandfather took on itinerant sharecroppers and transients to work the farm. Tarpaper shacks skirted the acreage surrounding their house. Only one of these shacks remained at the time of my grandmother's death.

One morning in August—erroneously termed "Indian summer" in this part of Virginia—my grandfather asked me to clean out this last shed before he burned it to the ground. Air at this time of the year was thin and raspy dry. The only detectable moisture was trapped within the spidery chestnut brown trickles of tobacco juice glistening at the corners of his mouth. One thin arm hefted a coffee can of kerosene while the other pointed at the shack.

The structure smelled like cancer, wrapped as it was in peeling creosote paper and topped with a rusted tin roof. Using a crowbar, I plied open the door. In the center of the room—still wallpapered with printed reportage from the 1930s such as "BEARS IN RUSSIA DIG UP GRAVES FOR FOOD"—was a windup Victrola falling in upon itself. There was a gaping hole in the galvanized roof above the phonograph. Decades of melting snow and dripping rain had reduced the machine to a swollen, pulpy mess of wood and pot metal. Several hornet's nests clung to the ceiling above. The colonies buzzed in unison, angry at my entry.

Next to this decaying machine was a tightly lidded box. Dragging the box outside and twisting off the lid, I found that it contained almost two dozen old 78s, nothing of which was recorded after 1930. These were "holy grail" records—prewar blues, gospel, and Cajun 78s that I would again encounter later in life. There were ethereal songs by Washington Phillips, gravelly gospel tunes by Blind Willie Johnson, and plaintive ballads by Cajun musicians Joe and Cleoma Falcon.

To this day, I have no idea who had owned these records that I salvaged from this shack or what happened to the ghosts who once owned them. Not twenty minutes later, my grandfather burned the shack to the ground.

Shaking off the fever of this recollection, ignoring the Turkish rug merchants, I half leapt, half levitated to the cabinet. First I tilted the hinged lid of the phonograph, revealing a void where the machined parts—the tone arm and turntable platter—had once been. Then I opened the front doors, only to expose another gaping emptiness. The vendor, Ishmael, but preferring the name "Izzy," stood behind me laughing. In perfect English he said, "It is an ornament, a prop . . . you like? Would you like to buy?"

Holding my lust and disappointment in check, I asked Izzy if he knew places in Istanbul that sold the old discs played on these machines. Some careful negotiation of meaning and idiom yielded this: the European side of Istanbul where we stood had been completely westernized. Little remained that was not intended for the global tourist. No places here sold *kil plaka*—literally a "clay plate" containing music.

But Izzy said that on the Asian side of Istanbul, across the Bosphorus, I could find "very many" old records and the phonographs that played them. I scoffed at this notion of plenitude. But then I realized that we were not here for me: we were here for this Leonard Cohen and the happiness Charmagne would derive from hearing him. We were also here to buy an authentic tribal rug.

Saturated in sweat, we spent several hours scrutinizing stacks of *kilims*—thin wool rugs with meandering patterns of azure, oxblood, and saffron. We decided upon one rug that spoke of hardships through its coarse Oriental weaves of mustard and sage thread. Our responsibilities as global tourists came to a close. We decided to cross the river by ferry the next morning so that we could see this part of Istanbul that time had forgotten.

❧ ❧ ❧

Most urban Americans would view the barges traversing the Bosphorus as deathtraps. But that morning's panicked flight from the imploring shoeshine artist, running in my open-toed sandals, proved more hazardous than these boats. I escaped from his narrow alleyway, taking the tram to the quay. There we boarded a Cold War–era iron craft with a suspicious lack of lifeboats and preservers.

The spray hit the glass of the ferry as I stared across the profiles of my daughter and wife, my gaze fixed on the Asian shore. Air rushing inside the open cabin carried with it the heavy smell of sturgeon and diesel. The wet heat was already oppressive by nine o'clock that morning. In my entire life I had barely spent more than a few weeks outside my native Virginia, and I found the unfamiliar combination of Mediterranean sun and humidity stifling, crippling movement, even inducing hallucinations. I had convinced myself early in life that blended with my mongrel Scots-Irish heritage and other questionable scraps of genetic code was an unhealthy dose of Neanderthal ancestry. Here in the cradle of humanity I realized that this is what killed the Neanderthal—the heat. The heat was killing me.

There was no functional dock where the barge landed. We staggered onto the gravel of the blinding sun-swept shoreline, heading to the edge of the area said to contain relics from the past. Dehydration from brined cheeses, brain fever from the sweltering sun, and favism from subsisting on falafel and hummus for days—all of these factors contributed to my delirium as we entered a cobblestone street leading south through the district of Kadıköy.

The directions we received on the European side of town did not correspond to the maze of back streets and dead ends. Unlike in the European district of Istanbul, few people here spoke English. We communicated slowly with drawings and gestures. I was ready to surrender—to either expire altogether or curl up in the gutter for a siesta until the coming of Leonard Cohen—when she found it. Charmagne said, "Look, it's a street of gramophones!"

And it was.

Shops filled both sides of this sprawling road. Phonographs budding with Victorian floral tinhorns lined the tables in front of each storefront. These were not props. These were the remains of early-twentieth-century cosmopolitanism and affluence—evidence of the cultural crossroads that existed in Istanbul.

Phonographs also signified a transformation, a globalizing force that Turkish journalist Refik Halid Karay detected when he wrote in the early 1920s:

> Listening to a song from a phonograph, which I assume Edison simply invented as a new year's present for his grandchild, was as difficult as swallowing honey from a carob. Then the gramophone arrived with its flat, hard records, and the Americans' sound machine became cheaper and easily available, drowning out the world with blabbing, loud music, and din. What a state Istanbul was in! On streets lined with coffee houses, the cacophony of forty-odd gramophones playing at once will gnaw at your ear, scratch your heart, and blow your head up.

Surveying these machines, I found that some were crafted in Russia before the revolution. Most, though, were branded with the ubiquitous and metaphorically rich "Nipper" logo. His Master's Voice, one of the dominant recording companies in Europe, manufactured these phonographs. With his head cocked gently to the phonograph's horn, this embossed terrier adorned sound equipment in countless homes throughout the world in the earlier part of the twentieth century.

As our daughter skipped in the street, we wove from one shop to the next, sorting through towering piles of 78s. The surreality of the scene wore off quickly. I realized that practically every record was of American and British pop and dance bands from the late 1930s and early 1940s—a vacuous, mediocre, and sucking time period for all music. Instead of unheard village music from Europe and Asia, we saw hundreds of discs labeled "Swing And Sway With Sammy Kaye," and possibly the complete discography of Tommy Dorsey and Glenn Miller And His Band. Everything had been picked over for decades—all the good records taken and replaced with soda jerk music. We were abandoning the Street of Gramophones.

I could hear the dying gasps of culture behind me when I noticed a shop window displaying a hand-painted banner, *Gramofon Antik*. As I peered through its nearly opaque window, a man sitting next to the barred door told me in broken English mixed with Turkish— through pulls and puffs on his water pipe—the owner would be back in an hour after the Muslim midday prayers had ended. I was craving a slice of salty country ham and several gallons of water, but we decided to have tomato salad and anchovies across the street. We waited for him.

Strolling up the alley, Mustafa, the owner, was a giant of a man. He had a chiseled mustache and immaculately groomed black hair. Through a rough exchange of Turkish and English, he understood that I wanted to look through some records. Unchaining the door to his office, he sat down behind an enormous mahogany desk topped with glass. From behind this desk he produced a stack of fifteen discs and slid them to me as if he were dealing cards and I was cutting the deck.

None of these records had sleeves to protect them from the elements, from wear, from one another. I pawed through them as he studied me. Sounds of the street drifted through the slightly open door, filtered through the heat and the airborne dust. My daughter laughed as my wife chased her in front of the store. Mustafa told me he got these discs just yesterday.

They were curious. The 78s in my hands were made before the Second World War. Any decent collector can glimpse at a disc and tell before the first blinking of an eye if something was pressed before the 1940s. The thickness of the shellac, the presence or absence of a "start groove," the heft, the aura—all of these elements contribute to dating the object.

Stranger still was that these discs were labeled in Greek, but the text made no linguistic sense. A few lessons of Greek yielded a basic understanding of grammar and common words. These discs before me were indeed foreign, alien—enticing.

They were also well loved, trashed by time. Dull steel needles dropped at particular passages of music gouged the surface of these discs. Deep scratches left by an errant tone arm slashed across the grooves. Here was evidence of repeated listening. Points of wear ran perpendicular and parallel to the music—the pitted and scarred surfaces resembled a lunar landscape. Outer edges of the once vibrant green and black labels were muted from constant shuffling.

These discs—like those that I had junked throughout the rural American South—suffered from the passage of time. Records were expensive. Needles were reused until the grooves were played to death. Paper sleeves decayed. These records had the same aura as those I've found of Delta blues or Kentucky mountain music.

What was trapped inside of these grooves?

I looked up at Mustafa, asked for a price. "Two Turkish lira per disc if you take everything," he replied. That was around twenty dollars, a safe gamble. I handed him the cash, asking him if he had a box. I added, "Do you have other 78s for sale?" He looked at me—perhaps through me—as he rose calculating. He asked "You . . . collector?" I said "Yes, big-time collector."

Slapping his desk with the cash I had given him, he said, "You, wife, child, come upstairs!" I motioned to Charmagne to fetch Riley from playing across the alley with some children. Mustafa led me out the door, leaving my purchase on the desk. With a twined knot of keys he locked the door to his office. To his right, he opened a thick wooden portal with an ancient hammered-copper latch. We were led inside.

Not a sliver of light penetrated the curling stone staircase that we climbed. Mustafa shuffled his fist full of keys, unlocking a towering door at the landing. This released a wave of sunlight over us as we entered a high vaulted room, lit from the west through narrow stained glass windows. We were bathed in an orange and yellow glow.

Two walls, the western and the northern, had shelves from the floor to the ceiling packed vertically with old 78s in sepia-toned factory sleeves. Facing the western wall was an overstuffed sofa from the 1930s. At a right angle to the edge of the sofa, running the course of the southern wall to the entryway, was a bookcase latched shut with lead glass doors. Its shelves overflowed with catalogs of early-twentieth-century Turkish and Greek music. In the center of the room—supernatural in the golden light of the tinted windows—was a brass-horned windup Victrola.

We sat on the couch while Mustafa flung open a pocket window. He called out into the street for a vendor to bring coffee, tea, milk, and a plate of *lokum*, Turkish delight, for the little girl. Before we drank our coffee Mustafa poured rose water over our hands. Charmagne and Riley demonstrated something akin to martyrdom as they sat for three hours, watching Mustafa pull armloads of 78s from his wall. After cranking the handle on his phonograph, he would slide the heavy tonearm gently onto these discs. Soulful *oud* solos, clarinet *taksimler*,* and *zeybek havasis* from Anatolia filled the room. During this listening session, Mustafa and I craned our heads together, tilting our ears into the brass horn of the phonograph. At the end of one record Charmagne said, "You collectors all look alike. You could be brothers—crazy brothers!"

Charmagne cautioned me to ration my cash unless we wanted to be stranded in Istanbul. I only bought the curious Greek discs from downstairs along with a few records from his collection. Mustafa packed the records inside of one smaller box, surrounded by balled-up newspaper, and then nested it inside of a slightly larger box like a Matryoshka doll. Everything was sealed tight. Everything was in order. We returned to the western side of Istanbul.

⌒⌒⌒

For the collector, there are few miseries greater than having a stack of mysterious 78s without the ability to play them. The box sat on the hotel nightstand across from my pillow and my gaze for ten days. I fought the urge to open it again to examine the discs.

Two days before leaving Istanbul, we attended the Leonard Cohen concert. It was staged in an open-air faux Roman amphitheater bordering the Bosphorus under a clear sky patched with a full moon. Charmagne, loving the Luddite that dwelled in my soul, had mended and reinforced a 1930s double-breasted white linen suit, the "Palm Beach," so I could wear it to this event. Even a hayseed from the sticks of Virginia knows when not to dress as a rube.

During the intermission between sets, while I carefully counted my pocket change three times, I asked Charmagne why they didn't have muscular handlers on stage to assist Cohen every time he

---

* *Taksimler* are improvisations based on ancient notions of how certain musical notes affect the psyche. They are extemporaneous, without meter, and intended not for dancing but for contemplation. Earlier in history, Greek, Turkish, and Arabic musicians were judged primarily by their ability to perform a *taksim*.

dropped to his knees for his low, soulful bellows. She suggested that the backup singers were likely trained for this task.*

Our minds drifted from the music. Charmagne was anxious about Riley and I wondered if the babysitter had touched my box of records.

We left as he sang "Chelsea Hotel Number Two."

⁕ ⁕ ⁕

At home, I didn't even stop to brush my teeth before I sliced open the box that had sat on my lap for the fourteen-hour flight to Virginia. After I unpacked the records, washing them with 99.44% pure Ivory soap and a beaver-hair shoe brush, I crept into my record room and began to play the 78s. Charmagne and Riley had collapsed from jet lag.

The first disc I played was unlike anything I had ever heard. It was a dissonant instrumental played with an uncontrolled abandon. The clarinet sounded as if it were in the throes of death—bent, contorted, and skirting along the margins of control. But it was the next disc that changed everything. Insistent droning voices and instruments merged, clashing against each other. One vocal threaded its way between instruments while another voice mirrored the lead singer an octave below. The music reached a crescendo, crashed, and repeated. From the sweet spot in my record room it sounded like a massive coffee can of angry bees had been shaken and released in front of me.

One disc after another spiraled me into aural disorientation. Decades of listening to unvarnished prewar music—Delta blues by Charlie Patton and fiddle records by the Carter Brothers and Son—did not prepare me. I was being swept away and I didn't—couldn't—resist. It was like the first time I heard the doomed Cajun

---

* Indeed, he would collapse onstage less than a month later in Valencia, Spain, on Friday, September 18, 2009, after suffering from a case of food poisoning or possibly favism.

accordionist Amede Ardoin. His tortured voice grabbed me by the neck and dragged me through some wilderness of emotion. But it was pleasurable—a necessary catharsis.

A subset of these records was different from the rest. The repertoire was similar but the ornamentation, the approach to the melody, and the "touch" were distinct. This smaller group of discs had the name of a single artist—Kitsos Harisiadis—printed in Greek on the label. Whereas one group of records had a forceful, violent tone, the discs by Harisiadis possessed a hypnotic and peaceful balance, an area between the carnal and the spiritual. The structure implied yearning, sadness, and more yearning. A stark violin fluttered in and out of the phrases and a strummed stringed instrument kept a steady and thoughtful time, like a pulse.

Sitting in my record room, listening to these discs, I lost all sense of time. These records that I stumbled across in Istanbul triggered a mechanism inside me. They had aspects of the early rural music with which I was familiar but they also possessed *something behind the sound*—an unknown intentionality, a function. At this point, I had no clue what this music was or even where it came from. And like the stack of records that I junked on my grandparents' farm, I wondered who the owners were, why they brought their records to Istanbul, and what ever became of them.

A few days later I teased the best possible sound out of these battered discs onto CDs and sent them to friends. I transcribed the master numbers that had been pressed into the "dead wax"— the region that exists between the run-off groove of the music and the edge of the paper label. Then I started my investigation.

The internet was useless. In a thoroughly analog manner, I sent letters to collectors. However, most of my collector friends specialized in American blues, hillbilly, or jazz. They had little to offer other than condolences for this new-found obsession and the inevitable, deadly precipice to which it would lead.

Fortunately I knew some specialists in ethnic music from the region, in particular a discographer and retired professor of Turkish and Greek language, Hugo Strötbaum. I sent him the CDs and the information. He replied that some of these discs were Albanian issues produced with Greek labels, likely for southern Albanian immigrants working in Greece. The 78s by Kitsos Harisiadis were from the region of Epirus, an area that straddles northwestern Greece and southern Albania. In the early twentieth century, the areas above and below the demarcation between Albania and Greece contained speakers of both languages.

Once I located Albania on a map, it was easy to trace out the area of Epirus that is currently governed by Greece—just 3,600 square miles, one and a half times the size of Delaware. In antiquity, Epirus was a geographical area shared between Albania and Greece. Today Epirus is a prefecture, a modern administrative region in the northwestern part of Greece.

What drove my pursuit was this question: what caused the music from this small region to be so different from the musical expressions surrounding it? I needed evidence—more artifacts. Like a sonic archaeologist, I needed to gather clues. Then I could map the culture. I had thought that the sounds contained in these old 78s, like virtually every deep folk record that I owned, represented a dead end—musical fossils of a people long assimilated into the Monoculture of the West.

For instance, in 2008 I wanted to find a *bona fide* Ukrainian fiddler to play at the Richmond Folk Festival in Virginia—an event for which I help program and select artists. In the 1920s and 1930s dozens of Ukrainian violinists cut 78s in New York and in Chicago. Most of these musicians were first-generation immigrants from cities of Odessa and Lviv as well as one-horse villages scattered throughout the countryside.

But so many skilled musicians sailed over the Atlantic to the United States that the population left behind in the old country collapsed, unable to transfer their musical heritage. With the introduction of the generic, soul-sucking polka craze from the Midwest in the mid-1930s, most of these exceptional first-generation musicians were left holding the bag—a bag containing the violin that had little use next to the trendy, louder piano accordion. Within two generations, Ukrainian-American fiddling heard during the golden age of 78s would be extinct.

Now there are no traditional fiddlers who play in this antiquated style. They are a dead end on my shelf.

The evidence I needed—more phonograph recordings from this region of Epirus—was hard to get. Collectors of foreign language discs cautioned me that these records from northwestern Greece rarely appeared in printed auction lists. These auctions, typically typewritten in a microscopic font, photocopied, and staple-bound, were mailed to collectors who, like myself, sat anxious for their arrival and consumed them in pained isolation. Like printed pornography, most of these lists were sent in nondescript brown envelopes, and such literature could lead to financial ruin, the destruction of one's sweet home life.

The internet has gradually replaced the printed word, both sacred and profane. The worlds of collecting and of pornography have exploded (if not merged) online. In this sense, eBay provides a shocking panorama of material items to satisfy—or to starve—the collecting impulse. But online, 78s from southern Albania and Epirus were almost nonexistent. Except for one fortuitous instance.

☙☙☙

A few months after returning from Turkey I noticed two discs for sale online in the obscure "expatriate" Columbia series, the same numerical run of the discs that I'd bought in Istanbul. The Columbia-GG series had labels printed in Greek and were intended for Albanian, Turkish, and Greek purchase within Greece. The prices were steep, a few hundred dollars per disc, and the sellers were in Athens. I sent an email inquiring if they had more discs like these. I received a reply in perfect English that yes, they had a few more for sale. The message came from two brothers, Vasilis and Elias Barounis.

Both men were well connected to the world of record hunting in Athens. While in the United States antique records could be found practically anywhere, in Greece most old phonograph records were located in the urban center of Athens. Some discs would turn up in bazaars. The best records would surface when itinerant workers emptied a building of its contents. House cleaners, mainly Gypsies, would contact the Barounis brothers and a transaction would occur. This is how you built a collection and also how you dispersed records to other collectors.

Elias was born in 1956 and his younger brother Vasilis in 1965. Like many Greeks, they were originally from a rural area—in their case, a village called Velanidia in Messenia, Peloponnese. They grew up listening to the family windup phonograph and traditional music performed live. There was no electricity in their town. Like many Greeks from the countryside, they were bound up in the traditional lifestyle.

Elias's obsession with phonograph discs struck early. He tried to buy a gramophone and a stack of records from his aunt when he was twelve but she refused to sell. This left a scar of longing on a young Elias. It wasn't until he moved to Athens at the age of twenty-three that he acquired his first phonograph player and built his collection. Elias wanted to share: he wrote and published over thirty articles on traditional music in as many years, appeared on television and radio, and lent his discs for reissue on CD. Like me, Elias heard something pure, something intense and lost, in these curious black discs that is no longer heard among living artists.

Vasilis was consumed with collecting the same 78s as his older brother, but their endeavor was collaborative, not competitive. Vasilis was an English teacher in the public schools of Athens and also developed computer skills that Elias lacked. In this way, he became one of the first Greek collectors to make contact with foreign collectors.

Together they built one of the finest collections of *demotic*, or Greek folk, 78s that exists outside of a public institution. *Demotic* music can be understood loosely as a category of rural songs and tunes, whereas *laïki* music contains songs and tunes popular in the city. When one hums the melody from *Zorba the Greek* or one closes one's eyes and imagines a troupe of bouzouki players, one is imagining *laïki*, or city music. What I stumbled across in Istanbul, capturing my imagination, was *demotic* music. It was hill country music for hayseeds like me.

I agreed to buy a few discs of Albanian music. There was only one Epirotic disc—another Kitsos Harisiadis. This was all they had to offer. Vasilis said, "This music of Epirus, it is very rare."

Like the Barounis brothers, I wanted to share what I had discovered. One crucial factor that I had discerned with southern Albanian and northwestern Greek music was that it steadfastly resisted assimilation—it shunned outside influences and seemed to only reference itself. This was a clue as to why the music from this area was unlike the music of its neighbors.

Therefore I titled the first collection of music that I assembled *Don't Trust Your Neighbors*. As in previous collections that I had produced, I sought to explore a philosophical concept alongside or through a musical one: a marriage of ideas. If we can explore the philosophical through literature, such as the existential fiction of Camus or Sartre, what prevents us from exploring the philosophical through music, an expression that is just as powerful as the written word?

The theme of this collection was one of self-reference, confidence. When we seek approval, we have a despicable tendency to change ourselves—to assimilate. This music from southern Albania and northwestern Greece maintained profound disinterest in the opinion of outsiders. Following the cultural message derived from these discs, we should trust ourselves and our perceptions of the world. We ought to do this if we do not want to be defined by another, to be altered by outside influences—people, cultures, the Monoculture.

I sent a copy of *Don't Trust Your Neighbors* to the Barounis brothers. Elias replied a week or so later. Vasilis had died. Elias was shattered. He said, "At least I have this old music to listen to." Elias then did something unprecedented among collectors: he offered to sell me his entire Epirotic archive—almost one hundred discs, a large number considering that less than three hundred discs of Epirotic music were issued. He did this out of an impulse to honor his brother and to disseminate the music. I would go from a paltry few to a plenitude. It was at this point that I acquired a staggering responsibility as a caretaker of this region's ancient musical legacy on the 78 rpm disc. I became bonded to Epirus, loyal to its sounds.

Boxes arrived. Charmagne would call me at work, sometimes twice a week: "There's another box from Elias here on the porch. I hope there is a pair of shoes inside." There were never any shoes, only enigmatic discs that—upon listening—posed arrays of questions about the origin and purpose of music. As this collection grew, it became less of a passive object stacked on my wooden shelves and more of an active entity with which I engaged—a cipher that I desperately needed to explore. With music like this, why would anyone need shoes?

The instrumental tunes from Epirus took me to places similar to two other prewar records that I had owned for years: "Happy One-Step" by Denus McGee and Sady Courville, and "Indian War Whoop" by Hoyt Ming and His Pep-Steppers. Both were fiddle-led dance tunes from isolated pockets in the deep South recorded in the late 1920s. I sat in my record room playing these two discs shuffled between those from Epirus. The experience was hypnotic: the asymmetrical rhythms and the unfamiliar scales meshed perfectly with records that I had lived with for decades.

The difference between these prewar southern recordings and the early music of Epirus was more of a veneer. The music from Greece just took me to a darker place—a place that I did not believe that I had within me. Upon listening, a discrete emotional space opened, embracing pain and longing from an alien land. There was tranquility in my thoughts after a long listening session, as if I had returned from an internal retreat. I began to wonder why this altered state of perception came from this music. Why did it have this effect on me, and could it have a similar effect on others?

Elias provided me with the names of the musicians and rough translations of the titles. I discerned patterns from this large sampling of Epirotic records. Many of these discs were from families with the last name "Halkias," "Harisiadis," and "Harisis." Cryptic words appeared frequently but with sparse meaning. For instance, Elias translated *mirologi* as "dirge," *skaros* as "shepherd's song," and *xenitia* as "migration." I knew that these were rough approximations. To penetrate the enigma of this music, I needed context.

᠙᠙᠙

One day in the middle of receiving this deluge of records, I discovered a book published in 2010 called *The Ionian Islands and Epirus* by Jim Potts, in a series named *Landscapes of the Imagination*. I was particularly intrigued by the author's observations of cultural continuity found in the mountainous areas of Epirus, especially in a place called Zagori—that the music reflected a degree of freedom from outside influences. These statements were all couched in the present tense, implying that this cultural continuity was ongoing.

I wrote to the author, explaining my obsession, expressing admiration for his work, and requesting any photographs of musicians from Epirus. Within a few hours I received a detailed reply, including an essay written by Potts on Epirotic folk music that echoed our shared sentiments:

> Deeper than the deepest blues, more profoundly moving and full of yearning than the *rebetika*, with roots in the years of slavery under the Ottoman Empire (1430–1913), Epirotic folk music ("*ta demotika*") has grown on me over the many years I have listened to it.

With this first exchange of communication I had found someone who heard in Epirotic music what I heard, and who felt a similar urgency in comprehending it.

Jim was British-born, Oxford-educated, and a retired cultural diplomat who had worked in, among other places, Greece, Ethiopia, and Czechoslovakia. He was a published poet, and since the 1960s he had been, like myself, an unrepentant 78 record hound. He had once served a post in Thessaloniki, and was married to Maria Strani, a Greek writer originally from Corfu, an island off the coast of Epirus and Albania. They lived in Dorset, England, but they also had a home in Vitsa, a village located in central Zagori, Epirus. They were coming to America in December to visit their daughter, who worked in Washington, D.C., a short drive from our home. Jim proposed a visit, and we enthusiastically agreed.

Meanwhile the records flowed from Athens, Greece to the tiny hamlet of Faber, Virginia. Establishing connections with more collectors and dealers, I was now intent on building a world-class collection of Epirotic music. But nearly all the boxes from Greece arrived brutalized, packed with only a handful of padding—scant protection for such rare and fragile artifacts.

I created and sanctified Saint Victrola, the miraculous protectorate of 78 discs facing the peril of a transatlantic voyage from

Greece. I began to imagine these collectors—none of whom I had met—sealing the box and then offering a prayer to Saint Victrola.

Before the Pottses' visit they introduced me to their friend Demetris P. Dallas via email. The collection of Epirotic music that I was putting together—*Five Days Married and Other Laments*—included songs in Greek that needed translation. Both Jim and Maria found the idioms on these old recordings too difficult to comprehend, and so they recommended Demetris. Like Jim, he was a poet. Demetris struggled to understand the words to some of the songs but rendered rich translations and annotations despite the difficulties.

Demetris was educated in English at Athens College and the University of Athens. His ancestral village of Elafotopos in central Zagori was not far from the Pottses' village of Vitsa. Demetris, like Jim, insisted that the musical culture—the role of dance and the repertoire of the local musicians—was largely intact and vital in Epirus. I should come and see for myself, they said.

Another thing happened before the Pottses visited us. It came in a package from Elias. He had asked earlier if I had heard of an old Epirote musician named Alexis Zoumbas. When I replied that I had not, he wrote back, "He is deep. I think you will like him."

ຄຄຄ

While I was in the midst of finishing up the writing and remastering for *Five Days Married*, a fourteen-by-fourteen-inch box as thin as a pizza delivery carton arrived on the front porch on a Saturday. Two corners of the box were crushed flat, while the middle was caved inward as if it had received a drop kick from a sadistic mail handler—in my mind one of the thugs in Sam Peckinpah's film *Straw Dogs*.

Carrying the box like it was a broken child, I felt the contents shift inside. I imagined a shower of fragments sliding out of the box followed by a wisp of tissue paper. Miraculously, both discs were fully intact and glistening in the light. A single wadded ball of newspaper fell out of the mangled box.

I lit a candle to Saint Victrola.

After I washed the discs, I scurried back to my record room. Most commercial 78s from the 1920s and 1930s were pressed as 10-inch discs. This gave the artist three to three and a half minutes to tell their story. These two discs by Alexis Zoumbas in the package were 12-inch discs, allowing an extra sixty to ninety seconds for the musician to express themselves. I would learn that every solo disc recorded by Zoumbas was of the 12-inch duration, even after such a format had become antiquated.

No artist needed that extra time more than Zoumbas.

"Epirotiko Mirologi"—"A Lament from Epirus"—was the first side that I played. As the stylus slid into the start groove, a dark, low series of repeating phrases from Zoumbas's violin descended to an even darker, lower note echoing from a bowed contrabass. They then became the same tenebrous note. As the violin fluttered and cried—posing pregnant questions and stillborn replies—the bow of the contrabass never left the strings.

Later, when another 78 collector, Sherwin Dunner, heard the record, he said to me:

> His music is so heartbreakingly sad that if I listened to it all at once I'd jump out a window. That's the ultimate compliment. We all know the meaning of the words "forlorn" and "despondent," but no one takes these words and expresses them as music with such unabated intensity.

As the needle tracked out into the dead grooves, I felt as if I had been taken apart and rearranged.

I needed a smoke.

The next three sides that I played convinced me that Zoumbas was a folk musician of the highest order. The expressiveness that he brought both to the *mirologi* and also to the last side that I played, "Tzamara Arvanitiko"—"An Albanian Shepherd's Tune"—communicated something ineffable—an emotion grafted onto a sound. What he played translated into a distinctly recognizable sense of loss. It was as if Zoumbas had peered into the abyss and this is what echoed from within the chasm.

The first disc that I played for Jim Potts when he and Maria visited was not "Epirotiko Mirologi." I played instead a record that I knew Jim adored but likely had never heard directly from the phonograph disc: "Fixin' to Die Blues" by Washington "Bukka" White. Born in 1909 on a farm in rural Houston, Mississippi, White was a consummate Delta blues guitarist, just as Zoumbas was a highly respected Epirote violinist. The commonalities between White and Zoumbas did not end there.

Zoumbas's "Epirotiko Mirologi" follows the patterns of all traditional Epirotic *mirologia*. These pieces are based on the graveside laments sung for thousands of years throughout what was then the Greek-speaking world. Zoumbas transposed the insistent female keening of the *mirologi* to his violin. Its melody parallels the bitterness of a traditional song from Epirus collected by A. Giankas:

> *What shall I send you, my dear one, there in the Underworld?*
> *If I send an apple, it will rot, if a quince, it will shrivel;*
> *If I send grapes, they will fall away, if a rose, it will droop.*
> *So let me send my tears, bound in my handkerchief.*

Bukka White's "Fixin' to Die Blues" expresses similar regret and surrender:

> *Just as sure as we living, just as sure we born to die, sure we born*
> *   to die*

Just as sure as we living, sure we born to die
I know I was born to die but I hate to leave my children crying
So many nights at the fireside, how my children's mother would cry,
How my children's mother would cry
So many nights at the fireside, how my children's mother would cry
Cause I told the mother I had to say goodbye.

White's relentless guitar figure—a one-chord bottleneck phrase—mimics the ostinato, the obsessive repeating of notes characterizing the *mirologi*. As Bukka White hammered through this song, I could see Jim's eyes light up behind his spectacles.

Jim is a tall, lean man who carries himself with relaxed, unpretentious dignity. However, his external comportment breaks down when he hears the blues. He saw many of these musicians, including Bukka White, in the 1960s. He knows how to enter into a séance with these phantom voices, channeling their spirits.

A veiled lust spread across Jim's face while listening to Bukka White as he began to survey my 78 collection. This gaze, this longing for curious black discs, marks him as a fellow obsessive.

Jim and Maria invited us to visit them in Greece, where I could hear Epirote songs performed in the villages. Although I disbelieved that this music could still exist in the world unchanged, the thought of being in the place that at one time produced the music was thrilling. We decided to visit, in a few months.

Maybe I could find the abyss where Zoumbas sourced his *mirologi*.

❧❧❧

It's only a few hours by ferry from the island of Corfu to the shore of Epirus. The port of Igoumenitsa, our gateway to northwestern Greece, lies across a short span of saltwater. The island is near the coastline of Greece and Albania—one reason why many nations battled to control this rocky mass in the middle of the Ionian Sea.

The cancer on Corfu is the horde of *Homo sapiens*, an invasive species of which sadly I was one. The island's natural beauty and contour is stressed under the weight of urban sprawl and garbage. The universal vileness of humanity was on full display upon our arrival. Maria Strani-Potts's cautionary and horrific parable, *The Pimping of Panorea*, paints the avarice and thoughtless havoc visited on this fragile island environment. People appeared innocently by the side of the road next to the beach, upturning their trash while smiling at us.

Standing on the beach with Jim, I shook off my repulsion. Epirus loomed just across the water. I felt an urgent need to verify the reality of the place. Jim said, "You're not going to try to swim are you? Plenty of people have tried . . . and failed."

I imagined a solid layer of skeletons between Corfu and the coast of Albania. Jim was an excellent swimmer. Had I have tried to swim, I would have panicked and turned back after going two or three feet in the water, thinking about all those whitewashed bones.

After my three guilt-ridden days in Corfu, the Pottses told me they had planned a small party in our honor at the Dassia Beach Hotel, the old-school hotel where we stayed. Demetris Dallas— the man who had recently helped me with translations and with whom I had corresponded extensively but whose face I could not conjure—would be there.

Maria Potts also had news. Prior to our arrival in Corfu, she had circulated a note—in essence a "wanted" poster—in Vitsa. I had written the text. It read:

> *I am seeking any information on Alexis Zoumbas, a violinist from the village of Grammeno who recorded in the 1920s and may have played in Vitsa earlier.*

It didn't occur to me until later that I was soliciting details about a man who may have last performed in this village over ninety years ago.

Maria had received a response. A villager from Vitsa had an

uncle who lived in Grammeno and who knew two of Alexis Zoumbas's nephews. Upon hearing this, I felt lightheaded, unreal. Was
it possible that I could meet those who had known Zoumbas? I
spent the next few hours rereading the folder of notes—a very thin
dossier—I had gathered about him.

Among the contents of this folder was a document implicating
Zoumbas in a murder before he moved to the United States. My
notes also suggested that he may have been shot dead in the United
States. What started as an odyssey to understand the function of
this music acquired another dimension, a homicide. It was at this
moment that Alexis Zoumbas became a stubborn apparition—a
perpetual presence—accompanying me. At times I would see Epirus through his eyes.

Charmagne had lovingly re-stitched the "Palm Spring" linen
suit—the one I had worn in Istanbul—before traveling to Greece.
Before heading downstairs to meet the Pottses, I stood smoking—
shirtless and vital—with only suspenders and trousers on a bal-
cony above the beach. Eventually I put my shirt and jacket on even
though the heat was stifling.

At a long table by the beachfront a dozen of Jim and Maria's
friends stood to receive us. Presidents, prime ministers, and dic-
tators of major and minor nations have never been greeted so
warmly. I took off my glasses and everything took on the hue and
movements of a grand *fête* captured on newsreel footage from the
1930s. If only a brass band would march out of the sea.

Demetris Dallas, *phile mou*—my friend—and his wife Maria
arrived. As he sat across the table from me, I put my glasses back
on and our eyes met. If a mirror had been placed opposite me, it
still wouldn't have corresponded with the exact reflection that was
Demetris. I was slightly wider in discrete regions; otherwise we
could have been identical twins, even down to our Neanderthal-
like hands.

Out of a smooth ivory cloth bag, Demetris slid a perspiring bottle. Grabbing me by my arm he said, "*Phile* Chris, here is some *tsipouro*, let's drink!"

Tsipouro is the *de facto* drink of Epirus, northwestern Greek moonshine. Clear as water with an elusive sweetness, it is the most powerful and transcendent of all intoxicants.

We poured one another shots while trading stories. Demetris produced a gift and handed it to me gingerly. Fidgets in our limbs and faces indicated that the alcohol was working through our bodies and taking over our brains.

The gift was five CDs of recordings of Demetris's favorite clarinet player, Gregoris Kapsalis, who came from an illustrious line of Gypsy musicians in Epirus. The music spanned over forty years of village performance. One of Kapsalis's teachers was Kitsos Harisiadis, the same musician who recorded those discs from 1930 that I had junked in Istanbul. I would learn that Harisiadis, although born at the end of the nineteenth century, had learned his repertoire from another musician who was almost one hundred years old at the time. Here was evidence of over two hundred years of unbroken music, transmitted from one man to another and then another. I wondered to myself if Harisiadis had known Zoumbas.

Demetris included a handwritten note with this gift. I was too inebriated to examine it, but the next morning before we embarked to Epirus I read and then reread the letter outside the hotel by the beach. Demetris thanked me for including him in the credits for *Five Days Married* and for focusing on "our small patch of land," adding: "It was a great pleasure to meet you—therefore to know that there's substance to the man in front of the email keyboard."

Holding the letter, I felt unsteady, disorientated—as if I were peering into some dark abyss along with Zoumbas. I knew that Alexis had left Epirus to sail to America from Corfu. And here I was, retracing his steps but backwards in space and time. Here too I was heading toward the soil that Kitsos Harisiadis never left. I was embarking on an odyssey, a séance with these two ghosts as my guides.

Two thoughts simultaneously emerged as the wind picked up over the sea. First, I was going to a place where music existed independent of the medium—the disc. Would I be able to comprehend its power without the mediation of the artifact to which I had grown accustomed? Second, the generosity of Demetris, Jim, and Maria implied a profound degree of trust. Music is the highest cultural asset that a people can share. Soon I would have unfettered access to such wealth. Would I live up to this notion of trust?

As we set off to Epirus, I wondered how much substance there was to myself—an outsider, a man behind the keyboard.

2

THE BLACK EARTH OF EPIRUS

The Earth is insatiable. It will never be satisfied.
Insatiable Earth, how many people have you eaten? You will never let
*   me go.*

This Earth which fed you shall also eat you.

My name is Black Earth, my name is Black Tombstone,
And I make mothers part from their sons and wives part from their
*   husbands,*
I make poor sisters part from their brothers.

—TRADITIONAL LAMENTS FROM GREECE

THE OIL-STREAKED DOCK ADJOINING THE QUAY FOR FERRIES
and barges in Igoumenitsa, the main port of northwestern Greece,
could not stand in greater contrast with the imposing peaks rising
from the shore of Epirus. The panoramic flatness of the sea behind
us to the west crashed abruptly, almost violently, against the staggering gray-brown mountains ahead of us to the east. At our landing, we stepped onto a pier once painted blue but now scarred
rust-red across its iron skeleton.

Lush greenery, olive and fruit trees, rose slightly above the shoreline, gradually surrendered to rolling vistas of scrub, patches of wild
thyme and sage, and thickets of stunted pine and oak. In this over-
whelming August heat, the dust rising from the crowds of people
and vehicles, the din of a thousand voices and the oily smell of boat
fuel put me in mind of the amphibious landing on Omaha Beach.

Igoumenitsa was a frontier garrison, an ominous aperture to a mythical land that lay hidden behind this swelling mass of machinery and iron. As my eyes gazed past the foothills to the terrifying white peaks of the Pindus Mountains, I was humbled by my placement in the low-lying gray gravel washes.

The earliest descriptions of Epirus from Greek and Roman writers began with an accounting of the terrain. They were aghast at the endless frontier. Indeed, according to one explanation among many for the name *Epirus*, *aperos* meaning "infinity" and *gaia* meaning "land," Epirus is the "infinite land."

Among the first books written in English about the history of northwestern Greece was R. A. Davenport's *The Life of Ali Pacha, of Janina, Vizier of Epirus*, published in 1822. Davenport described the ancient Greeks' view of Thesprotia, the area of Epirus that included Igoumenitsa before it became a modern port: "Civilization first commenced among the Thesprotes, who were nearest to the sea. The mountains of ancient Thesprotia were considered by the Greeks as the extreme confines of the world, the land of darkness, the region of night, the kingdom of inexorable Pluto."

If the unending terrain so impressed early writers, consider how these educated elite regarded the people inhabiting this land. They were hardly civilized and barely Greek. Outliers did not live in a *polis*—a city-state—and they rejected many social conventions of the time. Sleeping in huts and herding thousands of sheep, the wool-clad inhabitants of Epirus guarded a sacred land. This lifestyle was incomprehensible to most urbanites in Athens and in Rome. The Greek historian Thucydides and the Roman Strabo viewed the Epirotes as uncultured outlanders—"others"—but Herodotus and Pausanias saw them as Greek.

In his *Meteorologica* Aristotle confidently asserted that Epirus was the source of the ancient Hellenic race, the original location of the pure Greeks referred to earlier as the *Graeci* and later as the *Hellenes*. However, the dialects, tribal affiliations, and customs of

Epirotes must have seemed otherworldly to these elite men writing for the affluent in Athens and Rome.

To be honest, I also exoticized this land and its people before setting my feet on the soil. Who could embrace such feral music? What feeds this harsh landscape of sound? I knew that this region produced Alexis Zoumbas and Kitsos Harisiadis and yet I was largely ignorant of *what* nurtured their music. The answer, I was told, was found within the phenomenon of the *panegyri*.[2]

As Jim, Maria, and Demetris had explained, the *panegyri*, or feast dance, was *the* defining event connecting this music with the soil. Throughout Greece, *panegyria* are held to commemorate the saint identified with a specific village or a particular Orthodox calendrical event. Every year, people would travel back home to their ancestral villages—sometimes hundreds if not thousands of miles. The traditional song, "Anathema Se Xenitia"—"Damn You Foreign Lands"—captured several times on 78, conveys this sentiment:

> My migrant birds, scattered across the world,
> Your beautiful youth has grown old in foreign lands.
> A curse on you, foreign lands, your towns and cities too,
> No wife and children, nor parents by our side.
> Day and night young maidens are expecting you at home
> Who've yearned for years to set their eyes upon your manly faces.
> Let there be weddings at the villages, let festivals get started,
> Let joyful bells ring out in monasteries afar.[3]

I understood *panegyria* as similar to the homecomings that I attended with my parents at their ancestral churches. After a tedious service, dozens of old ladies in their Sunday best, their hair arranged in inflexible beehives, carried platters of country ham and cold fried chicken to tables set underneath towering oak trees. Sugared ice tea was poured. A group of old men including my grandfather would open their instrument cases and start playing old familiar tunes—dark murder ballads such as "Pretty Polly," historical songs like "White House Blues"—commemorating the assassination of President McKinley in 1901—and frolic pieces like "Granny Will Your Dog Bite." The sweet smell of chicken fat mingled with the damp earthiness of the oak leaves as the fiddle and banjo spun a tune in the dappled shade. And then I would lie down, surrounded by a pile of chicken bones and empty instrument cases.

By the time I woke to adulthood all of this was gone—the secret music of my valley, the mysteries of fried chicken. Everything special had surrendered to the forces of modernization and creeping suburban blandness.

In Epirus, I was told, it was different. While the region was unified by a culture and a sound, each Greek village was isolated, and the music played at such events reflected its own idiosyncratic sounds and dances. If you traveled over a mountain range in mainland Greece in the early twentieth century, the music and the instrumentation would be distinct from the place you'd left, even though the distance was only a few miles.

The *panegyria* of northwestern Greece are more deeply felt by the people and more steadfastly preserved here. Much of Greece, like the rest of Europe, has succumbed to globalism. But the local festivities in Epirus and other remote areas of Greece have retained a purity of purpose. I had to understand why.

☙☙☙

Driving out of Igoumenitsa, negotiating the traffic of fleeing humanity, my eye, your eye, the attentive and curious eye seizes upon imposing limestone structures crowning certain mountain passages overlooking the road. Mountain peaks throughout this lower region of Epirus are studded with *kastra*, castles or defensive positions overlooking the valleys and passes.

The intentional ordering of these rock piles suggests an ominous warning from both nature and man. A few thousand years ago there might have been smoke rising from these outcroppings, severed heads impaled just within sight of the narrow passage and a young Joseph Conrad channeling the palpable fear through the voice of Charles Marlow:

WE SEE YOU AND YOU ARE HELPLESS.

There is archaeological evidence of culturally unified tribes traveling north from the Ambracian Gulf to coastal Igoumenitsa and Sarandë in Albania at the end of the last Ice Age, over 10,000 years ago. These people would have been nomadic hunters or proto-shepherds, not settlers eager to stake a claim. After the close of the Pleistocene Epoch—as the ice shrank back from the sea—and the beginning of the Neolithic period, distinct groups formed territories throughout southern and central Epirus. At the highest point of diversity among these groups, around 1000 BC, there were fourteen tribes throughout this frontier speaking a general form of the Greek language.

If spirits inhabited the stone structures above our car, then they were likely Thesprotian ghosts, the earliest of the Greek clans inhabiting this particular region. In truth, the Illyrians—the tribe inhabiting most of Albania—were more mercurial than the Thesprotians. An ancient stock of warriors appearing in Homer and Shakespeare, they were regarded as non-Greek, savages and barbarians. To educated Greeks and Romans, the other tribes of Epirus had Mycenaean influences and elements—they had culture.

The Greek geographer Pausanias and the Roman natural philosopher Pliny the Elder were among the first writers to visit Epirus, reporting on the geography and customs. Although Thucydides, Strabo, and Herodotus wrote about this frontier land, there is little evidence to suggest that they actually placed their feet on the soil.

But Pausanias and Pliny were here. They wrote about the Thesprotians that ruled the southern coastal region of Epirus until about 370 BC, when another tribe, the Molossians, overpowered and, in effect, unified the Epirote tribes. Epirus became a vast region bent upon guarding its treasures after this Molossian unification.

But what was within this territory that was worth protecting? To both the ancient Greek and modern Western visitor, the land of Epirus was and is agriculturally poor. The mountains made for hard traveling and harder living. A glimpse out the car window catches a wild stunted rosemary shrub contorting itself to seek water where there is none. With little mineral wealth, scarce arable land, and torturous topography, why was this land so fiercely prized?

As you drive northeast inland from coastal Thesprotia to the mountainous Zagori and Pogoni areas, you witness the shrinking vegetation and paucity of life. The sheer verticality of the crumbling mountains and jagged cliffs is unrelenting, the summer sun unforgiving. These same mountains are nearly impassible in the winter, locked in ice under several feet of snow. As I survey the landscape, I am reminded of the spaghetti westerns of Sergio Corbucci—bleak and hostile but with a high lonesome clarinet solo by Kitsos Harisiadis.

To any traveler, the extreme contrasts contained within the landscape of Epirus are perplexing, begging the question of both how and why people live in such a seemingly inhospitable location. The answer is slippery and only fully articulated once your feet are on the soil and you are among the villagers, who, within themselves, contain staggering contrasts and paradoxes.

Jim slid a CD into his car player. I was in the passenger seat and we were booking it toward the city of Ioannina. Emanating from the car speakers was "Fixin' to Die Blues," not the Bukka White side that we had heard in my record room a few months earlier but a rollicking, syncopated version by a much younger Jim Potts— "Memphis Jim" from the late 1960s. Jim's slide guitar mirrored the funky figures played by White. Instead of the gravelly Mississippi voice percussively stressing the vowels as they elided to the next verse, Jim's polished English accent distinctly emphasized the consonants:

> Look over <u>Y</u>onder, on the <u>B</u>urying <u>G</u>round, on the <u>B</u>urying <u>G</u>round
> Look over <u>Y</u>onder, on the <u>B</u>urying <u>G</u>round
> Yonder stand <u>T</u>en <u>T</u>housand, standing still to let me <u>D</u>own

I looked over yonder as his station wagon left a haze of dust. We were steadily ascending the mountain passes out of Igoumenitsa.

Over yonder were burying grounds.

All of rural Greece is a burying ground. As far back as the songs of Homer (if not earlier), Greeks practiced an elaborate ritual of preparing their dead for their dark passage. In antiquity, this transition led to the underworld and, after Orthodox Christianity became general, this portal was to the afterlife.

When someone died, the family cleaned and purified the body with wine. The body was put in repose and visited by members of the village and their kinfolk. Women sang lamentations around the departed. These songs of mourning—literally "words of fate"—are known collectively as *mirologia*.

For thousands of years the basic structure and function of *mirologia* have changed little. They are the oldest musical forms in continuous use known in Europe.

In book 24 of the *Iliad*, Achilles declares a temporary armistice with the city of Troy so that Hector—the defender of Troy who is slain by Achilles—may receive a proper lamentation and burial. Hector's mother, Hecuba, laments alongside Hector's daughter Cassandra and his wife Andromache. The hard business of caring for the dead appears to have been always women's work.

> And they brought him home and laid him
> On a corded bed, and set around him singers
> To lead the dirge and chant the death song.

They chanted the dirge, and the women with them.
White-armed Andromache led the lamentation
As she cradled the head of her man-slaying Hector.
The women's moans washed over her lament,
And from the sobbing came Hecuba's voice:
Hector, my heart, dearest of all my children,
The gods loved you when you were alive for me,
And they have cared for you also in death. . . .

Nowadays, village or regional customs dictate the form of the lamentation. *Mirologia* can be vocalized, metered lines of recollection and regret or they can be nonverbal keening—a controlled musical wailing with no discernable words or syntax. The *mirologia* of the *Iliad* are the former variation. The latter—the melodic cries that come before, outside of, and beyond words—were likely a byproduct of legislation of Athens in the latter years of the sixth century BC prohibiting irrational expressions by women during funerary rites. As described by Plutarch, the statesman Solon created laws against the rending of hair at funerals and of "reciting set lamentations"—*mirologia* with words—at ceremonies for the dead. Words added power to a woman's voice, and men like Solon sought to limit such power.

In contemporary Epirus, the closest female relatives keen and lament all day over the body. The women closest to the deceased— the mother, sister, wife or daughter clothed in black—tear at their hair during the *mirologi*. Mourning continues as the body is carried to the village burial ground in a thin wooden coffin. After the grave is filled with dirt, the oldest or the closest female relation returns to the deceased every morning before the sun rises and every evening after the sun falls to tend to the lost one.

In the early 1960s, Australian playwright James McNeish captured on a hidden reel-to-reel recorder a traditional graveside lament in central Zagori, the region to which we were traveling:

Where are you going, my dear, dear one . . .
Where are you going, my fresh sprig of basil
To lose your bloom? You are not meant to descend into the black
    earth . . .
You will repent, my boy, a thousand times an hour
For the decision you have made to die.

Candles, bread, wine are laid out at the grave. On the third, the ninth, and the fortieth day after the death and on the third-month, sixth-month, and one-year anniversary after the death, a special ceremony is held at the site. This rite is then repeated annually. But for the truly devout, lamentation may continue every day for years.

The soul of the deceased needs comforting. In this dark, unfamiliar place the *psyche*—the free breath of life imagined as the seat of consciousness—is unaccustomed to being free of a body. This lamentation, this remembrance, soothes the wandering soul of the departed.

Maria, sitting in the back of the car behind Jim while we drove to Ioannina, told me that she once walked by a woman keening in a village burying ground and heard her song. It was the saddest sound she had ever heard.

The tradition of the area determines when the body will be exhumed. It could be three, five, or even seven years until the bones are carried into the light of the day. When the remains are dug up, all of the kinfolk and friends—the whole community—turns out. After a blessing by the priest, the family washes the bones in wine and places them in the village ossuary. The process of mourning, of remembering the dead while taking care of their transition from this world to the next, is complete.

The classicist Margaret Alexiou describes it best: "This expression of the irrevocable finality of death performs a vital function . . . the mourner gains an assurance that the dead has accepted his lot and will never return, either to help or to harm the living."

Both the soul of the deceased and the soul of the living are at peace, as they have found their place.

The ossuary holds great power over the villagers. One's home soil is the last thing that one would want to surrender. Only when a settlement is threatened with annihilation by invasion, famine, or drought will the people of the town relocate themselves. But they bring the bones of their ancestors with them. You cling to your soil as long as you can, but if you leave, you bring the generations with you.

This ancient form of mourning implies that our corporeal husk is a temporary manifestation before our eventual return to the soil. Everything in life is a preparation, a fixin' to die.

In northwestern Greece the attentiveness given to death and the deference bestowed upon mourning is fundamental. "This is a serious thing that must be done and we must understand why it is done." We come from the earth and we return to the earth. But this is not the pedantic notion of "ashes to ashes, dust to dust" followed by rapid, meaningless genuflections and a quick planting in the ground. Mourning in Epirus is not rushed or superficial. The agony of the living while lamenting the dead bestows character on the next generation. The increasingly common Western practice of maintaining a Facebook profile of a deceased person, a digital legacy, as a memorial to the dead, would be an affront to common decency here.* In this part of Greece, taking care of the dead requires the protracted investment of the living.

Death imparts meaning to those still living. Writing in 1885, the English Grecophile J. Theodore Bent said of the Greeks living in the Cyclades, a chain of secluded islands in the Aegean,

> The idea of death in the mind of a Modern Greek is distinctly
> pagan: death to them is solely the deprivation of the good things

---

* #deadlinks

of this life: their minds do not seem to be capable of looking forward to a future beyond the "dark grave" and the "black earth." Hades is the destination of the dead, Charon is their ever-watchful guardian; punishments for sin are carried on in Tarturus, in the fiery river, the Phlegethon of antiquity. Christian teaching has adapted to itself rather than obliterated ancient myths.

Many Greeks, especially those in the cities, have cast aside what they see as superstitious and backward views. But in the rural areas, such as Epirus, these changes have been slow, gradual.

Unique to Epirus, the vocalized lament, the *mirologi*, became an instrumental tune played at the *panegyri* and by the graveside. A public and a private musical *memento mori*, it is a calculated wailing through an instrument such as the clarinet or the violin. I had only ever heard these *mirologia* on 78s. And we were on our way to hear them played on the soil from which they grew.

This Earth which fed you shall also eat you.

⟆⟆⟆

"Jim! Jim! Use *both* hands, Jim!" Maria admonished from behind the driver's seat as we twisted through the mountain passes toward Ioannina. Maria's voice was normally calm and measured. Her dignified English accent was contoured with Greek Corfu lace—aristocratic to my ears. However, the hard angular turns coupled with the early Epirotic music from my collection on the stereo elicited from Maria a high, desperate plea—not quite terrified but more of an urgent, cautionary command.

Corfiotes such as Maria—Jim pointed out—do not care much for the heavy tones of the clarinet and violin from Epirus. In retrospect the music added unnecessary tension to the trip, what with the low, dark clarinet phrases punctuating our conversation. Every five minutes or so Jim would take his right hand off the steering wheel to point out a village, bridge, or archeological site that *I must visit*. Every time he did so I sensed Maria's eyes widening behind her glasses. Her brows would knit as her fingers dug deep into Jim's headrest. "*Both* hands, Jim!"

I felt unreasonably safe next to Jim. One can tell when a driver is intimately familiar with the curvature of a crooked, lethal road. Imagine a potter throwing his clay onto a rotating wheel. He knows how to apply a subtle pressure with his thumb to a spindle of clay such that it results in a graceful concavity on the neck of a vase. All this while the platter spins faster than the eye can see. Such is Jim's way behind the wheel of the car. However, this does not mean that I didn't fear Charon's grasp at every turn of the road toward Ioannina. The whole drive felt like a close, dry shave with a straight razor.

The roads throughout Epirus are marked every few hundred feet by *eikonostasia,* "icon stands"—also called *ekklisakia,* "little churches." Out of ignorance I at first called them "death houses," and that meaning resonates with me still. Everything displayed within the environment of lower Epirus—both man-made and God-given—appeared to be an insistent reminder of death. Signs and symbols acknowledging the dead were everywhere.

These memorial structures are miniature metal or wooden shrines in various stages of decay. Behind their glass doors are oil lamps or *kandylakia,* "little candles," in front of icons, sun-muted photographs, handwritten notes, or maybe small bottles of *tsipouro.*

We stopped often to examine these *eikonostasia.* I peered through the opaque glass windows and the sky behind the shrines would turn black and bruised. The wind would pick up, leaving a chill across my body.

There is an organic symmetry between these dilapidated hand-made structures and the harshness of the surroundings. It is perfectly consistent with what I heard in the music. The heavy despair of the clarinet and the sad avian mimicry of the violin mirror the environment. Nature, sound, and death—they all contour and color one another in Epirus.

The thin atmosphere dropped deep around me as I gazed into an *eikonostasi* containing a cloudy snapshot of family, a mother with her hair modestly contained in a kerchief, a father with a thin mustache, both proudly holding their two babies, all of them lost at the bottom of this switchback in 1989.

Unexpectedly, I learned Greek drivers erected *eikonostasia* to mark a spot where someone had survived an accident as often as they did to mark a fatal spot. Nevertheless, I thought of death the whole ride to Ioannina and further into the heart of central Zagori.

The serpentine road toward Ioannina was leading away from the two spiritual centers of Epirus. The Oracle of Dodona and the Acheron River were religious sites that had drawn outsiders to this region for centuries. These two places figure prominently in classical literature and in the mystery cults that thrived prior to the dominance of the Orthodox Church. After the religion of Jesus arrived, these religious practices went underground.

The oracle of Dodona is the oldest soothsaying shrine in mainland Greece. Stones may have been set on this location 2,000 years before the birth of Christ. Plutarch and Pausanias wrote about the oracle and its centrality to the various tribes of Epirus. It was originally a place of veneration for those who worshipped Gaia, the Earth Goddess. After the glaciers surrendered their icy territory, Gaia emerged as the preeminent deity throughout the Balkans, which were known in antiquity as the Peninsula of Haemus. Ultimately she was no match for Zeus and his more cultured, less frenzied followers.

When the Molossians conquered the region encompassing Dodona, the central deity became more Hellenic, a natural move to align Epirus with the rest of mainland Greece. People then venerated Zeus here, and this shift in worship elevated the oracle of Dodona to the second most important shrine, only behind that of the Oracle of Delphi, Apollo's seat of power.

Our understanding of a worshipper's visit to ancient Dodona is as follows: A devotee of the oracle either asked a question verbally or else etched the question on a scrap of metal or potshard. These questions were presented to a soothsayer born within a lineage to serve the shrine. Such inquiries would range from the mundane to the profound. "Am I to have children?" or "What am I to do?"

Depending upon the stage of construction under the sacred oak grove within Dodona—its stratigraphy is every bit as marked by progress and regress as the Parthenon—one's fortune could be read by the sound of oak leaves crackling in the wind or from thin copper chimes suspended from said oak branches moved by a sudden gale. The diviner constantly listened and translated the sounds of nature.

If the oracle of Dodona was a place of hope—hope for a prosperous life or for a change in fortune—then the River Acheron was a place where there was no hope, where everything was resigned to the Fates. Here, every departed soul was ferried to the underworld by Charon—Death himself. The world above and the world below merged into one terrestrial and spiritual entry point from which there was no exit.

By the banks of the Acheron was another oracle, the Necromanteion—the Oracle of Death. Greeks journeyed here to communicate with their lost loved ones. Below this sacred ground, Hades and his perpetually youthful and doomed wife—pale Persephone—ruled over all dead souls.

The ritual purpose of the Necromanteion was quite different from Dodona. The collective Greek belief at this time maintained that the dead were powerless above the ground once they were properly mourned and buried. However, the dead became potent after they were consigned to Hades. Specifically, the deceased had deep precognitive abilities that could be channeled by the oracle after certain rites were practiced.

Based on archaeological reconstructions and literary accounts from the eighth to the fifth century BC, the supplicants of the oracle of Necromanteion consumed a special diet to prepare them for their encounter with the dead spirits. Afterwards, they would be led through several subterranean chambers, each one of which was darker, more disorienting. The passage to the gates of Hades could take two or three days. Ruins of machined pieces found here—wheels and geared parts—suggest the oracles may have employed mechanisms to create visual effects that would influence pilgrims' perceptions during their journey, creating an inversion of sorts to Plato's Cave.

Darkness and light, silence and chaos, a gathering together of primal elements under a purposeful arrangement—here was an early attempt to "move the mind." When one's senses are manipulated, the immersion of oneself in the world of the dead can put one in a different psychological place, an altered state of consciousness. Maybe this altered state was a tacit aspect of Greek popular religion.

Clairvoyance led believers to Epirus: the ghosts of Alexis Zoumbas and Kitsos Harisiadis drew me here. Would I emerge just as transformed as these ancient supplicants?

࿐࿐࿐

"A keep is meant to keep things *in* just as much as it is meant to keep things *out*," I repeated to myself as my eyes scaled the *kastro* of Ioannina, its stone rampart like the flinty skin of a Titan scarred by musket shot. The enormity of the *kastro* hypnotized me, both the thickness of the walls and the vast infrastructure sprawling within. Here, lodging for concubines was segregated according to gender or the blurring thereof: eunuchs were a common sight, hermaphrodites, less so. Sexual playthings were housed and subdivided by preference of deviance and perversion. Armories, troop quarters, mosques and minarets crisscrossed the interior.

Like a mote of dust settling on a sill in the blinding sunlight, I stood minuscule by the western wall of the keep, standing on the curb parallel to Karamanlis Avenue in old town Ioannina. The *kas-*

Kastro of Ioannina and Lake Pamvotis, circa 1850s.

tro is a brooding, vast organism teeming with dark recollection—
its magnitude dwarfing the other monoliths of Epirus.

For almost 500 years, the *kastro* was the center of Ottoman
power in this part of northwestern Greece. Recently uncovered
fortifications suggest that this site was a stronghold in the Hellenistic period, from around 400 to 200 BC. This castle saw sustained
conflict and bloodshed—a towering stone witness to carnage for a
combined two thousand years.

I felt like I had stumbled across some prehistoric megafauna in
a remote jungle, our jaws open and our minds working to size one
another up.

I was not the first to be overwhelmed by the *kastro* of Ioannina.
Recounting his travels in 1812–13, the English physician Sir Henry
Holland wrote of his approach to Ioannina from the south:

> At length, when little more than two miles distant, the whole
> view opened suddenly before us; a magnificent scene, and one

that is still almost single in my recollection. A large lake spreads its waters along the base of a lofty and precipitous mountain. . . . Opposed to the highest summit of this mountain, and to a small island which lies at its base, a peninsula stretches forwards into the lake from its western shore, terminated by a perpendicular face of rock. This peninsula forms the fortress of Ioannina; a lofty wall is its barrier on the land side; the waters which lie around its outer cliffs, reflect from their surface, the irregular yet splendid outline of a Turkish Seraglio, and the domes and minarets of two Turkish mosques, environed by ancient cypresses. The eye, receding backwards from the fortress of the peninsula, reposes upon the whole extent of the city, as it stretches along the western borders of the lake.

Nearly two hundred years after Holland's description, old town Ioannina was now brimming with activity in August as all the migratory birds—expatriated villagers—returned to their home soil for *panegyria*. Baring bright toothy grins in the intense sunlight, pedestrians mingled alongside the *kastro* as Jim approached me. "Imagine two hundred years ago . . . along this wall all the torture and executions by the Ottoman troops. It's not like that now!" he said crisply.

As Jim spoke, his eyes cocked gently toward the castle's wall. A man with an ample black mustache beneath his aquiline nose, wearing a loose loam-green short-sleeve shirt, reclined on a bench. He relished his pistachio ice cream unaware that below him thousands of souls were consumed by Hades—an earthly, fleshy gift from the ruling *pasha* to the underworld. While the Turks were here, from 1430 to 1913, most of northwestern Greece[4] was controlled by overlords—*beys* and *pashas* appointed to their territories by the Supreme Porte in Constantinople. Most Greeks were essentially slaves with little recourse for justice. Outside the castle walls it would have been common to encounter a hanging, crucifixion, impalement, flaying, beheading, or the Turkish specialty, *falaka*, in which the victim was suspended upside down with his feet pinched between two rifles while his captors beat his feet with a rod.

The first stones were likely laid for the *kastro* with the Molossian unification of Epirus under Neoptolemus I, anecdotally referred to as the first king of the Molossian dynasty. King Pyrrhus—famed for the eponymous equivocation of victory at the price of defeat— and Alexander the Great—the principle disseminator of late classical Greek culture by the edge of a sword—descended from Neoptolemus.

This dynasty gathered the tribes under an early constitution. Epirus's bonds with Athens and the Macedonian Empire were strong until 167 BC, when the Romans sapped the power from the Greeks. But the Romans could not sustain their presence in Greece: their empire was crippled by its own failing infrastructure.

By the sixth century AD, Ioannina was an established Byzantine outpost. Slavic, Florentine, and Neapolitan rulers then invaded *en masse* over the next few hundred years, unraveling the ties between it and Constantinople, Rome, and Athens—a slow bleeding that left this remote countryside weak. But the *kastro* survived: built in stages, it grew from a stony child to a hulking fortress while consuming the lifeblood of fallen foreigner and native alike.

But the blackest, most brutal epoch for Epirus occurred when the Ottoman Turks captured Ioannina in 1430. This, the longest, most continuous imperial subjugation of Greece, would also be its most horrific. The occupation reached its violent crescendo with the man who made Ioannina the "Diamond of Epirus"—the Albanian-born Ali Pasha.

No man left a greater legacy, ambiguous as it is, on the cultural and physical landscape of Epirus: his governance indelibly shaped the collective memory of this region.

Many songs performed in the villages today celebrate his exploits. Alexis Zoumbas recorded "Ali Pasha" in 1927. Kitsos Harisiadis's grandparents would have been subjects under Ali's rule. Musicians thrived in his court. Most importantly, Ali Pasha's story and the brutal narrative of Turkish rule are woven inextricably with the songs of Epirus. To appreciate the sentiments of the Epirote song-book, one needs to understand life during the time of Ali Pasha.

Ali was a cultivated ruler. He hosted the British poet Lord Byron along with dozens of European intellectuals and generals. Among his achievements, he—unintentionally perhaps—precipitated the creation of the modern Greek state.

He was also a vengeful, calculating berserker who took every-thing personally. Those he deemed to be with him and those he thought were against him changed just as suddenly as the crooked flight of a *pelargos* or white stork* skimming across Lake Pamvotis in Ioannina. Yet his uncompromising rule was not unprincipled. The elemental source of his political vision was his mother's curse, stated simply as "Avenge me."

The bitter venom coursing through Ali's blood did not come from his mother's milk: it was spoon-fed to him after weaning. The

---

* Rare nowadays here, this species of white stork, the *Ciconia ciconia*, darkened the skies of Epirus in the early nineteenth century. Historically, the stork nested in the seventeen minarets of Ioannina of which only three remain. This bird had two names in Epirus: the neutral *pelargos* or "stork" and the more incendi-ary *tourkopouli* or "Turkish bird." The Turks loved this bird and after the end of the Ottoman occupation, Greeks delighted in killing them whenever they could. This practice has stopped but the storks learned their lesson—they were not welcomed here. With the rapid decline of an ecological element—the minaret—and an open hatred for their kind, this avifauna no longer has a home in Epi-rus. Complex organic systems like this stork and cultural assets like folk music can be compromised and threatened when their native environment is set off kilter—such systems must either adapt or perish. Just as we can understand the decline or extinction of a species due to drastic alterations in their environ-ment, so too can we understand the weakening or disappearance of a folk music by similar alterations within the location of that cultural asset.

Ali Pasha of Ioannina.

closest reckoning for the year of his birth, 1740, saw Ali's family in fairly good straits. Ali's father, Veli, was a high-ranking functionary in Tepeleni, in southern Albania. However, Veli was soft. He failed to execute the wife and children of an official that he replaced in Tepeleni. Like many Albanian officials, he was murdered by a neighboring rival after he was demoted. Veli died penniless when Ali was thirteen.

Veli's second wife and the mother of Ali, Khamco, descended from noble Albanian stock. She did not accept her husband's insolvent demise. Taking up arms, Khamco recruited bandits—known in Greece as *kleftes*—and raided villages throughout Epirus. In

short order, she controlled a number of towns that feared annihilation at the tip of her sword. Her swift acquisition of power also
provoked the suspicion—justified in her case—of almost everyone around her. After brutalizing villages and collecting taxes, it
is said that she would retire to her bed with several of her faithful
bodyguards, believing that the nonexclusive sharing of her body
guaranteed something resembling fidelity. This belief proved to
be unfounded.

Khamco's abuse of Albanian villages through provincial graft
followed a well-worn path. Throughout the Ottoman Balkans, the
Turks and Albanians excelled at collecting taxes and tributes from
the local *beys* and *pashas*. The efficiency of collecting such goods—
money, humans,[5] raw resources—and the size of the tributes sent
to the Ottoman sultan often resulted in commensurate grants of
desirable territory.

For hundreds of years during Turkish rule and up until the end
of the Greek Civil War in 1949, Albania and northwestern Greece
had enclaves on both sides of the porous border. Some villages contained exclusively Greek Orthodox and Greek-speaking people.
Other towns held only Bektashi Muslims and Albanian-speaking
populations.[6]

It was reported in legend that Khamco secretly wanted to control a small Greek village called Khormovo within Albania. In her
bed, she expressed this desire (as well as probably others) to at least
one (but likely many) of her bodyguard lovers. One male concubine
may have been from Khormovo. Another guard may have been
from nearby Gardiki—an Albanian Muslim village that had grown
wary of Khamco. The towns of Gardiki and Khormovo were neighbors. Don't trust your neighbors.

On the day Khamco rallied her troops to seize Khormovo, the
Muslims of Gardiki lay in ambush. Villagers of Gardiki captured
Khamco, young Ali, and Khamco's only daughter, Shainitza. The

family was imprisoned in Gardiki. Village men took turns raping Khamco and Shainitza. This savagery lasted several months until a Greek merchant paid for their release.

As described in an Albanian song, Khamco mounted her horse, pained but defiant, with chin lifted high in the custom of women from these parts. She was met by Ali and Shainitza. Leaving Gardiki, tossing her untamed hair from her slightly unhinged right eye—damaged and drifting from her ordeal—Khamco vowed that only dust would be found in these villages.

Ali had a sacred obligation to annihilate the villages of Gardiki and Khormovo. But first he needed some blood training. The environment of near-anarchy—clan feuds, executions, and punitive rape existing in northern Epirus—was Ali's school ground.

A gang of raw Albanian youths assembled with Ali as captain. They started to rampage towns previously seized by Khamco, consolidating her holdings. Now confident, Ali attacked Khormovo. But at fourteen years of age, he was quickly deflected from Khormovo's walls.

The humiliating tongue-lashing Ali received from Khamco was likely more painful than his defeat at the hands of the Khormovo militia. It is said that his mother told him that he would be better off serving as a passive whore in a pasha's harem—a *poustis*—or spinning wool behind a train of asses than attempting the more masculine activity of avenging the insults to his family.

Ali skulked away to another territory, determined to gain his mother's respect. He took up with another gang of thugs. After a while Kurd Pasha of Berat, a town in southern Albania, captured him. Kurd—or "The Wolf"—was a distant relative of his mother's: he spared Ali's life. This, of course, was a mistake.

Ali desired two things that the Kurd had: his power and his young daughter. Kurd would yield neither. Ali took up arms again in the forest outside of Berat, preventing commerce with surrounding villages. Kurd offered an enormous bounty on Ali's life. Two friends conspired with Ali to present a bloody, bullet-ridden cloak to "The Wolf." It was Ali's garment full of musket shot and stained with the blood of a slaughtered sheep. With the money that they collected from this subterfuge, Ali built an outstanding wild bunch of mercenaries.

This simple act of calculation—a mapping of logical outcomes and potential permutations to obtain a finite end (in this case, money)—was a profound lesson for young Ali. He uncovered this discrete truth: the end *is* the end, damn the means. Unlike tragic Shakespearean characters, Ali had no conscience. He raced toward his goal, soaked in gore and eyes agog, blind to all external principles.

Strategically avoiding "The Wolf" while residing in the nearby town of Delvino, Ali married a woman of considerable social position, Eminé (even more sensual to one's ears is her Albanian pet name, Umm-Gulsum). With this marriage he sired two sons, Mukhtar and Veli. The year was 1767 and Ali was twenty-seven years old. His ambition was to rule all of Epirus and Greece.

Ali perfected a pattern of calculation, deception, and murder that would repeat to the point of absurdity until the end of his very long life. Even more absurd was the gullibility of those who fell for his snares. Sometimes you feel sorry for the rabbit, or, in the case of Ali's schemes, the tens of thousands of rabbits. However, one thing that you can be certain of: Ali never felt sorry for the rabbits.

He first designed a plan to rid himself of his newly acquired father-in-law, Caplan Pasha, overseer of the Delvino region. Ali hoped to be appointed *pasha* in his place. On Ali's advice, Caplan Pasha delayed the punishment of some villages provoking the ire of Constantinople. Simultaneously, Ali sent word to Constantinople that Caplan had a secret pact with these villages. Predictably, Caplan's head was severed from his body and sent to the Ottoman leaders. Much to Ali's chagrin, Caplan's son, another Ali, was ceded the territory of Delvino.

Ali, conspiring with his mother Khamco, made arrangements to have the other Ali, Caplan's son, marry his sister Shainitza. Ali then convinced another brother-in-law, Suleiman, to commit fratricide in exchange for the wealth now held by Shainitza.

William Plomer—one biographer of Ali—clarifies succinctly, "It was a pretty arrangement: a brother was to kill a brother, while another [half] brother was to reward this deed by encouraging his sister's marriage with her deceased husband's brother, who was at the same time her deceased husband's murderer." Suleiman shot his brother Ali dead and then, on the command of his half-brother Ali, Suleiman consummated his new marriage on the floor with Shainitza, their bodies coupling next to her recently departed husband.

Ali gained the title of Pasha of Delvino, but only after coolly eliminating three more claimants to the position. Next on his agenda was controlling the roads that connected Epirus with the interior of mainland Greece. This was an easy task once Ali realized that he could pay off robbers and *kleftes* when he needed peace and, in turn, ask for kickbacks from said thieves when a village refused to pay for protection. It was a perfect racket. The *kastro* of Ioannina was now within Ali's sight.*

The year was 1787. With Russia at war against the Ottoman Turks, Ali was appointed his own command at the age of forty-seven. Seeing an opportunity to further his own powers, he met on amiable terms with Russian General Potemkin, who himself

---

* Key to Ali's success was his flair for morbid showmanship. Returning from scouting expeditions with his Albanian troops, Ali is said to have had bags of decapitated heads, collected from raids, swinging on either side of donkeys in his cavalry train. Ali's collecting habits impressed his peers in Constantinople and, more importantly, the wealthy and powerful of Ioannina.

aspired to conquer Constantinople. Ali returned to Albania knowing he had powerful allies.

Summoning several thousand Albanian soldiers, he occupied the
countryside around Ioannina. An initial battle led to a stalemate.
Ali, resourceful as always, fabricated a document from the Sultan
of Constantinople granting the rule of Ioannina to himself. When
the sealed scroll was presented to the city's *beys*, they all swore
their obedience to Ali. Within a year even the Sultan recognized
Ali's official title as if he himself had signed the royal appointment:
Ali Pasha of Ioannina.

৯৯৯

If there is one string of incidents that best explains Ali Pasha's
patient vindictiveness, it is his annihilation of the two villages that
defiled his mother. Early in 1787, Ali received word that Khamco
was in the death throes of ovarian cancer. Racing as quickly as he
could through the mountain passes, Ali arrived too late—he found
his mother with her head on Shainitza's lap. The life breath had
flown.

Her will, which was read aloud shortly thereafter, was crystalline: ashamed that her children had not avenged her rape at the
hands of the people of Khormovo and Gardiki, she bestowed a
curse upon their heads. Ali pledged to Shainitza that their mother's desire would be honored: a cascading tempest of violence would
visit these two towns.

To begin, Ali insinuated a peaceful visit to the Greek village
of Khormovo in Albania with "only a few hundred troops as an
escort." What could the village say? Ali Pasha entered with over
1,200 soldiers, boarding the men among the villagers. Town leaders
were invited to meet him at a local church. Promptly, Ali's soldiers
invaded the holy house, seizing the leaders and introducing them
to a host of long-standing Turkish tortures.

Enter Ali's half-brother. Born to Ali's father's black concubine,
Yusuf Arab had the moniker "The Blood Drinker." Refraining from

drinking blood on this occasion—at least by the accounts that have survived—Yusuf Arab instead impaled the captives alive, roasting them over campfires. In retrospect his cognomen could have been "The Impaler" or even more appropriately, "The Roaster." Sometimes history is cruelly inaccurate.

Every man in Khormovo was murdered and every woman and child was consigned to slavery in Constantinople. The village was burned and leveled. Salt was tilled with the soil. And then Ali waited.

Nearly twenty-three years later, in 1812, Ali Pasha would finally rid himself of his mother's curse. Now age 72, Ali Pasha invited all males over seven years old from the Albanian village of Gardiki to meet with him in the town square so he might pardon them for their prior offenses. Ali personally interviewed almost eight hundred villagers. Eighty were dismissed, since they were relative newcomers to the town.

Ali Pasha's army of three thousand descended on the courtyard. Within an hour and a half, over seven hundred men and boys were slain. Ali delivered the *coup de grace* to several with his long knife. Learning that he had three Gardikiotes in his own regiment, he disemboweled them and then dragged their bodies through the square, the men's entrails leaving dark tracings in his horses' wake.

Twelve men from Gardiki were spared and set in chains.

Bloody and incensed, his troops raped every female in the village. Afterwards the women were herded to a nearby town, where his sister Shainitza had the women's hair sheared to stuff her pillows and their skirts cut to just below the waist. She proclaimed that no village was to offer any Gardikiote woman shelter or comfort under penalty of death, and cast the captives into the wilderness.

Riding back to Ioannina, Ali had the throats of the twelve chained Gardikiote men slit over his mother's grave. When he returned to Ioannina he had another sixty-four Gardikiote hostages executed and dumped in a well. Ali said, "At last my mother is avenged! Mother, here's the blood I promised you! Ah, I feel young again." Ali would live another ten years until the Sultan of Constantinople sent his butchers to cut him down at the age of eighty-two.

༄ ༄ ༄

That this arc of revenge lasted two decades speaks to both Ali's powerful political ascension but also to his slow descent into something akin to madness (or at least a type of solipsistic rationality that was opaque enough as to be indecipherable). By 1812 Ali Pasha was considered untouchable. The Sultan in Constantinople knew Ali ruled these territories not through the mandates of the Ottoman Turks but solely through his own notions of retribution and self-preservation.*

Almost whimsically, Ali Pasha annihilated garrisons of foreign troops, annexed several of Epirus's largest towns and ports, and almost wiped out the Souliotes—an independent Greek confederacy in the mountains of Thesprotia. Yet every act of murder had a personal, vindictive flair.

Lake Pamvotis became a repository of sorts for Ali's sadism: it was in this icy body of water that he disposed of many of his victims. One story held that he impregnated the wife of one of his three sons to gain filial piety and political advantage. Shortly after the child's birth, Ali promptly drowned his deflowered daughter-in-law, her

---

* Ali Pasha obeyed the dictates of Constantinople much as Colonel Kurtz followed U.S. Army orders in *Apocalypse Now.*

   Kurtz: "Are my methods unsound?"

   Willard: "I don't see any methods at all, sir."

Indeed the atmosphere surrounding Ali Pasha during the later part of his rule suggests that he could easily have played the role of Colonel Kurtz as a demigod among the Cambodian Highlanders during the Vietnam War. Much as in the nightmarish sequence of Willard approaching Kurtz's compound, François Pouqueville—the general consul for Napoleon in Ioannina—remarked that he saw so many severed heads impaled outside of Ali's private chamber that over time he ceased to notice them.

midwife, her doctor, and a host of eunuchs and ladies-in-waiting. Those who carried out the execution—some Roma from outside of Ioannina—had their heads cut off so that they couldn't repeat the tale.

Another story tells of an insult delivered to one of Ali's wives, the Greek Vassiliki. A flock of Greek noblewomen of Ioannina wearing fancy petticoats mentioned her name followed by a wave of cackling and laughter. Vassiliki was within earshot and ran off in tears. Once Ali found out the cause, he dispatched his enforcer, Yusif Arab "The Blood Drinker," who sewed three dozen Greek women in burlap sacks and cast them in the middle of the lake.

Ali became the stuff of legend and song. Those who knew how to negotiate the turbulent waters of his wrath were primarily educated Europeans—English and French doctors and diplomats and, most famously, the poet Lord Byron. In letters home, Byron would say of Pasha, "His Highness is a remorseless tyrant, guilty of the most horrible cruelties." This understatement would stick with me throughout this and every return visit to Epirus.

I can't help but be awed by Ali. His long-term vision of vindictiveness—what I would describe as "mindful vengefulness"—was singular. Pasha's calculus of revenge reminds me of a lyric popularized on 78 disc by the Georgia Crackers in 1927.

I'm gonna start me a graveyard of my own
If these old rounders don't leave my women alone.

Contemporary Epirotes view Ali Pasha in a complex if not irrational light. Northwestern Greece would see its first glimpse of freedom from Turkish occupation while under the rule of Ali. However, the notion of an independent Greek state was very far from his mind. He essentially wanted his own state—neither Greek, nor Albanian, nor Turkish. He wanted to start a graveyard of his own.

Early aerial photograph of Ioannina with ten minarets visible.

Though he spoke Greek and used this language in his court proceedings, his wrath saw no linguistic, national, or religious barri-
ers. The results of one half-hearted head count yields slightly more
than 22,000 people that Ali killed directly, executed, or tricked others into killing, or that died in combat against him. These deaths
spanned various nationalities and creeds and included a large portion of Greeks.

Under his rule Ioannina would boast schools, men of letters,
commerce, and prestige that Athens would not see for another one
hundred and fifty years. Ali did this to secure the obedience of the
affluent and powerful. Everything was done by Ali *for* Ali. But I
would hear from contemporary villagers during later visits that Ali
was indeed a nice man, if not guiltless. A friend told me, "He only
killed people that deserved it. Those who resisted paying taxes, for
example."

Before driving north to Vitsa, among the first of the forty-six vil-
lages in Zagori, Jim and I had lunch by Lake Pamvotis with Maria,
Charmagne, and Riley. The other side of the lake held the Kastritsa
Cave, a site of human habitation during the late Paleolithic age,

roughly 26,000 to 13,000 years ago. But my mind was on the last two hundred years of skeletons scattered among the sediments of the lake: Ali Pasha's victims lay uneasy in their watery grave. While devouring a local specialty—a skillet of lamb, chicken, and pork stewed in tomatoes and mountain herbs—I imagined schools of catfish cleaning their bones.

We finished our lunch as I glanced again at the cold water. It is said that in the early twentieth century and before, Romani musicians heading north to play at *panegyria* dipped their instruments in Lake Pamvotis to imbue their playing and their songs with sadness. There is also a legend that all the tears of the world are contained within the reservoir of this lake. Both legends seemed true to me as I watched a lone white stork skim the still surface of the water.

3

"YOU KNOW, GREEKS DON'T EVEN LIKE THIS MUSIC"

Music is not noise. Music is something that has to be enjoyed in a peaceful way. But now what they've done is they have destroyed music. It's finished. Except that there are some people that hold to the old ways. Who knows . . . maybe they will go back to the natural way of playing.

—*PERICLES IN AMERICA*, A FILM BY JOHN COHEN, 1988

HOLD IN YOUR MIND FOR A MOMENT AN OLD-FASHIONED ANA-log timepiece, a gold pocket watch from the turn of the twenti-eth century. Perhaps your grandfather or your great-grandfather purchased it to complement his high-peaked, single-breasted suit, natty gray and impeccably tailored. The watch may have been given to him for his thirty years of service for the railroad or for dutiful, soul-crushing work in a state agency. More meaningfully, maybe his parents handed down this now obsolete timepiece to him as a *legacy*.

Its purpose is simple—to measure the abstract passage of time—but the internal workings are complex. Under the gleaming yel-low case etched by the all-eroding touch of Khronos, everything is tightly arranged with brass gears, steel springs, and shimmering jewels. The parts are finely handcrafted, and yet under a magnifying lens one can see the springs propelling the gears, the gears balanc-ing the wheels, and gems buffeting the metal parts. Indeed, the pul-sating tension and release of the main spring within the watch—the soft, precise *tick-tick-tick*—resembles the pumping of the heart, the transference of lifeblood, of power, to all the other parts.

The watch is a neatly compressed orb containing an interconnected environment, itself representing the eternal workings of the universe. Unlike the eternal workings of the universe, however, the watch requires human care. Its function depends upon two fundamental factors: the construction by the makers and the maintenance by the keepers. The watch's ability to measure time rests upon the builders of the timepiece and their precision in crafting the parts, and upon the current owner of the watch, who must clean and care for the object, winding it daily until this treasured tool is passed to a new generation.

Imagine this pocket watch as a metaphor for a musical biosphere—a complex organic mechanism of social and psychological exchange that has sustained song and dance unique to small geographic pockets. Now conceive a vast landscape of such musical biospheres, thousands covering the surface of the planet. Around one hundred years ago—perhaps just when your grandfather obtained this watch—this was how folk music existed.

Now, the fertile environments that once grew such timepieces— such music—are fallow and atrophied. The landscape is littered with dead mechanisms, disarticulated likenesses of music, once coursing with life. Neither cared for nor maintained, these fragile expressions became languid and frail. Most fell apart, ceasing to exist. No one took the time to "wind the watch," to maintain the continuity of the music.

Except here in Epirus, where everyone winds the watch. Every villager is part of the tension and release, the coursing of the lifeblood. The ancient Greek philosopher Pythagoras proposed that the planets made music while they passed across the sky. He believed that an attentive person could hear "the music of the heavenly spheres." Nowhere else can one hear so clearly the celestial harmonies than in the mountains of Epirus.

The humanly organized sounds of northwestern Greece are brooding because the surrounding sonic space is ponderous. The landscape sculpts the sounds—the sparse outcroppings of stunted bushes, the cauterized precipices, the copper bells of grazing goats and sheep producing a blinding spectrum of chimed rhythms. What you hear is reflected in what you see.

Music is hard here because life itself is uncertain, indifferent. Everything could disappear in a wisp and a whimper. Despite its outward obsidian nature, Epirus is fragile.

When we arrived in Vitsa, Jim introduced us to everyone who crossed our path. Watching Jim negotiate in a variety of languages, smoothly transitioning from English to Greek to French and a host of other tongues, is like observing a thoughtful, intellectual version of James Bond, using reason and nuance rather than secret weapons supplied by Q.

Making introductions in Vitsa is not a short order. There is no rush; life in the village meanders along at a calmly measured pace, much like a donkey ascending the hills via the *kalderimia*, the cobblestone roads stitching throughout the villages. Greeting a stranger in Epirus is not an empty formality. Although all Greeks esteem hospitality, among the Epirotes it is a high art. People from the Peloponnese, from Athens, and from the islands all look to Epirus as the pinnacle of traditional Greek values, of old-fashioned things.

A villager will offer a *kafe helleniko*—a Greek coffee—along with some sweets and then perhaps a *tsipouro*, Greek moonshine, normally served with a savory *meze* of cheese, pastry, or greens from the garden or meat from their stock. More than likely you will eat a combination of all that they have to offer. The *tsipouro* bottle is never empty, and, if there is a constant virtue among the few thousands that live here, the homemade spirits are of the highest quality.

In return, they ask only that you be human. Drop any pretensions. You are in their village, therefore you are one of them, if only for a brief time. This, then, is the exchange.

"Tell us why you are here."

"I'm here because I have fallen in love with your music. The old sounds that surround your village brought me here. And your *tsipouro* is especially fine!"

"Are you sure? Most people don't like this music. Especially Greeks. Please have some more *tsipouro*."

Every house we visited offered coffee, moonshine, and conversation mixed with friendly, predictable interrogation. A consensus formed in my mind—itself inhabiting a space between caffeinated clarity and inebriated bliss—that most people from "the outside" don't care for the music of Epirote clarinetists and violinists, which sounds atonal. This is what many of the people here believe.

I was, however, unable to form a clear picture of exactly *what* the villagers thought outsiders heard in their music that is so disagreeable.

Perhaps it is the various rhythmic shifts, maybe even the rhythms themselves, that do violence to an outsider's ears? For instance, a *syrtos* rhythm is tenebrous and sedate, like a bruised storm cloud approaching the Vikos Gorge where Vitsa sits. Originally a dance performed only by women, it is said to have been one of the rhythms played in Athens of the third century BC during festival events. In Epirus, it possesses a very simple three-beat measure: $1 \pm 2 \pm 3 \pm$ with the emphasis on the rest between the beats, the $\pm$. Could the languid tempo put off a potential listener?

On the other end of the rhythmic spectrum is the fast *tsamikos*, said by both old-timers and musicians to have originated in Ioannina. It is probably a relative latecomer to the repertoire, since it was intended for mixed dancing with men and women holding hands together, a sight that would have been rare elsewhere in Epirus prior to World War II. Because of its lilting tone and relatively brisk tempo, it tends to convey collective joy.* Like the *syrtos*, it contains three beats for each measure, but with a different emphasis: 1 + 2 + 3 +, stressing the first beat and the pause at the end of the measure (sometimes also grabbing the third beat for elongated solo passages on the clarinet). The rhythm is difficult to those raised on the predictable swing of Western popular music.

There is also the *kleftiko* dance, an angular, asymmetric pattern that was intended for male showmanship. *Kleftes* were outlaws but also hero archetypes in the minds of most Greeks. Like the American folk tunes "Wild Bill Jones" and "Jesse James," the *kleftiko* songs celebrated the good deeds performed by men with ambiguous moral footing. *Kleftes* controlled travel between villages—they kidnapped well-to-do travelers and collected ransom.

Contemporary Greeks portray *kleftes* as stealing from the rich only to give to the poor, as protectors of villages. Just as it is a half-truth that Ali Pasha was an ally of Greek independence, so too is the notion that the *kleftes* had only a benevolent nature. Both the *kleftes* and Ali Pasha were interested in self-preservation and their own autonomy, evidenced in part by the fact that Pasha and the *kleftes* were sometimes allied, but often at each other's throats.

The deftness of the *kleftiko* meter is hard to capture, as it depends almost exclusively on the inspiration of the lead dancer and the skill of the musicians that follow his or her movements. The rhythmic sequence varies considerably from one location to the next.

---

* Two of my favorite dance tunes, "Helios" ("Sun") and "Kalokeraki" ("Summer") are *tsamikos* pieces. As the names imply, they radiate the light and heat of August; the rare, fleeting ebullience of existence when everything is bountiful, full of hope. These are among the few tunes in Epirus that are not endued with infinite sadness and longing. Nikos Tzaras (1892–1942) along with Sideris Andrianos cut one of the most perfectly executed Greek instrumental duets of *Kalokeraki* in 1934. Tzaras was from Ioannina and was recorded by Melpo Merlier in 1930 for folkloric preservation. Sideris's tasteful accompaniment drives Tzaras's clarinet to a level of sonorous lyricism rarely heard outside of this time and place.

In the region around Ioannina, including Vitsa, the pattern is +1+2+3+4+<u>accent</u> +5 and then +1+2+3+4+. The older musicians often felt free to add extra beats to the measure if the instrumental solo elided into the next passage.

The other dances, such as the *arvanitiko* and *tsifteteli*, may be disagreeable to a non-Epirote simply because of their uninhibited nature. The *arvanitiko* is a low-down funky three-beat pattern, syncopated and hypnotic. My friend Vassilis Georganos's characterization of it as "Epirotic Delta Blues" corresponds perfectly. Originating in southern Albania, the *arvanitiko* is a feral thing.

Writing in 1812, Henry Holland, a British physician visiting Ali Pasha, described an informal music concert in Ioannina in one of Ali Pasha's chamber rooms:

> The national airs of Albania were sung by two natives, accompanied by the violin, the pipe [*tzamara* or a "shepherd's flute"], and tambourine [*defi*]; the songs, which were chiefly of a martial nature, were often delivered in a sort of alternate response by the two voices, and in a style of music bearing the mixed character of simplicity and wildness.
>
> The pipe which was extremely shrill and harsh, appeared to regulate the pauses of the voice; and upon these pauses, which were very long and accurately measured, much of the harmony seemed to depend. The cadence, too, was singularly lengthened in these airs, and its frequent occurrence at each one of the pauses gave great additional wildness to the music. An Albanese dance followed, exceeding in strange uncouthness what might be expected from a North American savage: it was performed by a single person, the pipe and tambourine accompanying his movements. He threw back his long hair in wild disorder, closed his eyes, and unceasingly for ten minutes went through all the most violent and unnatural postures; sometimes strongly contorting his body to one side, then throwing himself on his knees for a few seconds;

sometimes whirling rapidly round, at other times again casting his arms violently about his head. If at any moment his efforts appeared to languish, the increasing loudness of the pipe summoned him to fresh exertion, and he did not cease till apparently exhausted by fatigue. . . .

This national dance of the Albanians, the Albanitiko [*Arvanitiko*] as it is generally called, is very often performed by two persons; I will not pretend to say how far it resembles, or is derived from, the ancient Pyrrhic, but the suggestion of its similarity could not fail to occur, in observing the strange and outrageous contortions which form the peculiar character of entertainment.

If the *arvanitiko* evokes wildness, then the *tsifteteli* suggests licentiousness. It too has a heavy syncopated rhythm but it is spread over four beats per measure rather than three. Stereotyped as a "Turkish belly dance rhythm," it is likely similar to the rhythmic motif developed in classical antiquity for the *aulos*, the Greek pipe played during Olympic competition, as well as for the *kordax*, the phallic dance performed by followers of the Dionysian mystery cults.

I was told that the *tsifteteli* was rarely played in Epirus—perhaps because it reminded people too much of the Turkish occupation—but hearing it irresistibly conjures the carnal. The *tsifteteli* is demanding for any clarinetist. The player must master the precise syncopated stresses, and have strong and disciplined lungs for long, uninterrupted passages over four slow beats, and an innate knowledge of the *Ousak* mode, a Greek-Arab scale created possibly just for this one dance meter.

Perhaps the rhythms are not the hurdle in approaching this music. It could be the requisite tonal awareness, the species of deep listening and introspection that this music demands in order to be properly appreciated. Maybe the scales themselves—the internal sounds that constitute the melodic structure—clash violently against our ingrained Western notions of harmony, pitch, and intervals. The timbres of the instruments, too, are "shrill and harsh," as Holland says.

Demetris Halkias's violin performance of the *Selfos* or "Nightingale" exemplifies this aspect of Epirote music. Captured on shellac in Athens, January 9, 1929, the *Selfos* is a showpiece for the skilled violinist. With this melody one may demonstrate not only one's technical command of the instrument—intonation, speed, and smooth bow-work—but more importantly, one's ability to manipulate emotional tension in the listener. How does one do this?

Our typical Western diatonic scales—seven notes plus the octave of the key note—exist in two main fixed patterns of whole and half notes, the predictable major and the minor scales. However, in Greek-Arabic music theory, most scales utilize intervals not present in their Western counterparts. There may also be slightly different arrangements of notes in ascending or descending pitch.

For instance, the *Selfos* is in the *Hijaz* mode or scale. In the key of A, the pattern is A–B♭ (or B)–C♯–D–E–F♯ (or F)–G–A. The distance from the first to the second and the fifth to the sixth notes in this scale can either be a whole or half step. The variability or restlessness of B♭ and F♯ increases auditory tension: the ear expects to find some resting place, but the musician denies it.[7]

This is an emotionally calculated reading of a phrase. Could the tension and release found in these scales be a reason why Epirotic music is taxing to the outsider's ear? After all, music like this requires just as much of the listener as it does of the musician.

In the middle of my coffee-*tsipouro*-fueled musing, Demetris Dallas phoned Jim. Having taken the ferry from Corfu to Igoumenitsa and then a bus to Ioannina, he would arrive in Vitsa shortly.

Zagorian songs are just too hard, too heavy. Greeks just don't care for it. For instance, there is a *klarino*-club in Athens—a place for people to listen to clarinet playing from their home regions. Men who moved from their villages to work in Athens frequent this club in order to listen to a "little bit of home" and to have something to drink. Inevitably some old codger from Zagori will pull out his clarinet and play tunes from the home soil. He, in effect, clears out the building.

This was a speech Demetris made to Jim and me as we sat in the cooling shade of the towering plane tree in the *mesohori*, the village square in lower Vitsa. We had consumed between us many small bottles of *tsipouro*—dead soldiers crowded the margins of our table. But I still couldn't connect how the music here that had found such an abiding home in my heart could be so unpleasant to others.

What Demetris said echoes the sentiments of musicologist K. A. Romaios: "In Epirus and Roumeli they sing very slow tunes, which are incomprehensible and tiresome to outsiders, especially islanders. They are sung slowly and monotonously, like an old goat boiling quietly in the cauldron. It may be for this reason that such songs are called '*vrasta*' (boiled)."

Songs and instrumentals played in Epirus inhabit a sonic space that is difficult to parse in theoretical terms, but this space is undeniable to those born listening to it. Here the music sounds like women weeping at a grave, like birds crying as they fall from heaven, like the Earth is ending. And to some outsiders, like a goat boiling in a pot.

There are sounds here that you can't understand but that you *feel* that you should, as if you were nostalgic for an alternate self.

Ultimately it may not be the rhythms or the structure of the scales that outsiders find so disagreeable. It may be the dense embellishments of the musical phrases that sound ponderous and atonal to the unaccustomed ear. Musicians here are schooled within their Roma clan to reproduce two key motifs. These motifs form the basis of northwestern Greek musical vocabulary—the *ostinato* and the descending *glissando*.

An ostinato is a phrase, passage, or motif that is persistently repeated throughout a tune. It is used in northwestern Greece as a personal signature immediately recognized by all listeners.

"Ah, that is Thomas playing, do you hear!"

The descending glissando of this region is a sliding ornament, either subtle or hyperbolic, from a higher note in a scale (normally the tonic or a note slightly above the tonic) to a lower register note. This elision is typically languid, as if all the blood is being drained from the instrument while playing.

These two motifs are home-schooled or, even better, homemade within the Roma clans. The descriptions are imprecise approximations used to express an equally ambiguous yet recognizable melody. This is the key to Epirotic improvisation but also—possibly—to why the sounds are so alien to the casual listener.

Several years after this first visit to Vitsa, a documentarian, photographer, and musician, John Cohen, gave me a copy of his film *Pericles in America*, released in 1988, about the music of Epirus. *Pericles in America* is told through the lens of multiple persons, including a young Epirote jeweler working in New York City named George Rabos, and Pericles Halkias, a direct descendant of the Halkias musical family. The opening scene, shot in a seedy jeweler's workshop in Times Square on 45th Street in New York City, answers in part why the music of Epirus creates discomfort—ear torture—for most Westerners and Greeks alike.

We meet George Rabos, a jeweler preparing to be married back in Greece. He works steadily at setting and polishing gold rings while his boss, Jack Gold, supervises his work.

Rabos is anxious: a dark, fitful stubble defines his full cheek and jaw while he focuses on his job, scarcely looking at the camera. A small Walkman by Rabos's side blares an Epirotic song on cassette.

Jack's eyes float and fidget beyond the camera's eye, as if appraising a loss of productivity in the workplace while giving no thought to how his words would sound almost thirty years later. Staring straight into the camera, he refers—perhaps jokingly—to George as a lunatic and says of the people in George's village, "They didn't look that intelligent. She [a woman who gave Jack some eggs] looked very backwards in a sense." (Jack had visited Epirus before hiring George full time.) A short dialogue ensues:

JACK: You know, Greeks don't even like this music. Greeks despise this music. The average Greek turns his nose up to this music. It's really backward: what you would call primitive. I mean, who the hell wants to listen to quartertones all day long?* . . . We have to listen to this Epirotic noise all day long. It sounds like a film score for a Boris Karloff movie.

GEORGE: Epirotic music . . . [cut off by Jack]

JACK: Is a repertory of five pieces. Each piece has about six notes. And you know, they can never hit the note right in the middle so they keep sliding around and George thinks these—um— variations are really astonishing. These guys are half drunk so they never hit the right fret. So they go in between: a semitone too low, a semitone too high. And they never play together, right? So you think it's beautiful, right?

GEORGE: *Yes.* I tell you, I couldn't live without this music.

In this scene, the necessity of Epirotic music to George is palpable.

It's easy to understand how someone who is accustomed to clean vocal allocution and the precise intonation of notes in Western popular music would find the home-schooled music of Epirus a disorienting cacophony. Even to those attracted to primal sounds, this music is difficult to embrace.

After trading a stack of Epirote and Albanian 78s in exchange for artwork to grace the cover of one of my reissue collections, I received a letter from Robert Crumb, the 78 record collector, artist,

* I do. #quartertonesalldaylong

and writer. Having listened to these 78s from this region, he said, "This music is so amazing and other-worldly I don't even know what to say about it. I haven't a clue about where these people are coming from."

Some people—such as Jack Gold—find the apparent primitiveness in this music offensive. Other outsiders like Jim Potts and Robert Crumb are attracted to its "otherworldliness," its depth and richness. There are, of course, those from northwestern Greece who love this music because they made it themselves. And then there is my obsession with it, borne from hearing something authentic and curative.

The music of Epirus is not for everyone. In fact, considering the minute population, it is almost for no one except those who live there or return at every possible opportunity. This cultural asset—this continuity of music—is crucial to Epirote identity and part of their history.

❧❧❧

Even though our understanding of prehistoric Europe is based largely upon assumptions and bumbling guesswork, we do know that after the last Ice Age the populating of the Balkans developed along similar lines to that of western and southern Europe. Along with the "standard toolkit" for survival—spears for hunting and needles for sewing—the Paleolithic (and later, Neolithic) Balkan peoples fashioned flutes for music making. Before transitioning to a nomadic shepherding culture, the early tribes of Epirus followed the migrations of the ancient red deer and lived a seasonally governed hunter-gatherer existence. It was during this period that spans the Paleolithic to Neolithic that proto-Europeans may have first learned how to control sounds so that they could guide the movements of animals, just as they harnessed fire to produce more durable and versatile tools.

One specific tune-type, the *skaros*, also known in the mountainous parts of the lower Balkans as a *tzamara*, may have emerged from this narrative. It is an air largely improvised from a distinct scale and intended to direct the movement of a flock. In isolated areas of the Balkans one can observe old men playing a similar melody for their sheep, causing them to take shelter, take water, to move in one direction or another. It is a simple form of communication between two species sounding like a wordless lullaby.

There is an abundance of evidence suggesting that at the end of the last Ice Age, humans in Europe developed tools to express melodies and perhaps to address deeper, more mysterious concerns. Sites north of the Balkans, particularly the Geißenklösterle Cave in southern Germany, produced flutes that are upwards of 40,000 years old. From the Pyrenees in France to caves in Austria, the earth has given up flutes that date between 19,000 and 40,000 years ago. Similar instruments found in northern Greece are around 7,000 years old.

It is easy to visualize a group of hunters huddled together in a rock shelter in Klithi in Epirus, or in Franchthi in the southern Argolid in the Peloponnese, engaged in the sounds of the flute while the wind howled outside. Over tens of thousands of years, early humans may have explored the notion of sound as psychological self-medication—a precursor to the lullaby, the prayer, or any soothing introspective melody.

As the environment changed we in turn altered what confronted us. When the ice retreated from valleys and plains of Europe and transformed the Mediterranean, we took charge of our surroundings. Agriculture and herding emerged from the Fertile Crescent and spread throughout Eurasia, Africa, and the Middle East. Our notions of borders, possessions, and language spread as well. When the spoken word became the written word another ancient form of music developed.

Originating as heroic tales passed orally from one singer to the next, the Homeric epics blended story-songs with epitaphs. The former became narrative balladry as we understand it in the West.

The latter became a form of metrical poetry—*mirologia*—vocalized laments and funeral dirges. The dark keening of the *mirologi* eventually became both formulaic and innovative. As a funerary dirge, it acquired standard verses along with predictable meters and stresses. However, as a form of folk poetry it gradually encompassed all forms of loss: the loss of a great city (such as Troy), the dismal epithalamium or loss of a family member to marriage, the loss of a patriarch to a foreign land to serve as a soldier or as a breadwinner, and even the metaphysically bleak loss that all life implies.

Mirologia evolved into instrumental pieces. We do not know when this transformation took place or why. When larger communities recognized the necessity of a collective remembrance—when thoughts of loss converged and transcended the individual—perhaps it was easier to participate with instruments than with the human voice.

As villages became larger and loose confederations of towns formed, the regions with the largest populations developed into city-states. The concept of the *polis* emerged. From the Greek Neolithic Age, roughly 7000 BC to the end of the Bronze Age and the Mycenaean Era, around 1100 BC, mainland Greece and Asia Minor experienced tumultuous growth and transformation. Territories expanded and coffers grew as money from military conquests returned to the growing cities. The newfound wealth flowing into urban centers promoted literacy among the elite. The upper class, including aristocrats, government officials, and teachers, flourished.

Unified notions of philosophy—unraveling and explaining the unseen—emerged much later in classical antiquity, between 500 and 300 BC. In sixth-century BC, the Greeks—according to longstanding tradition, Pythagoras himself—explained the phenomenon of music in mathematical terms, advancing the first written theories about octaves and patterns of notes. They also attributed extramusical properties—forces inherent in organized sound that healed or calmed an individual—to specific strings of tones. Mathematical theories of music along with notions of music's psychological efficacy laid the groundwork for a systematic understanding of melody and harmony.

Most scholars of classical antiquity assert that no Western culture valued music more highly than the ancient Greeks. Practically every social event, no matter the size, was accompanied by music, both vocal and instrumental. The ability to sing, to play instruments, and to appreciate performances was regarded as essential for the virtuous development of the soul.

The *maieutic* method—the powerful form of dialectical questioning with didactic goals advanced by Socrates—prompted inquiry into the nature of the Good and the Beautiful. One branch of this study, aesthetics, focused on the first principles of artistic creation. Chief among the modes of creation was music.

Schools of thought flourishing at this time—Plato's Academy and Aristotle's Lyceum—explored music theory. More importantly, they sought to understand how music affects humans morally and emotionally. Although these schools produced vast texts (most of which are lost to the ages), they likely had little bearing on the harmonic and melodic expressions that were developing in the rural Greek countryside.[8]

Education in standard harmonics, modality, and rhythm was essentially an intellectual exercise among the urban elite, whereas music among the isolated tribes, shepherds, and fieldworkers was existential, gritty. In my mind, the musical landscape of early rural Greece was like the Mississippi Delta or southwest Louisiana at the turn of the last century. It was not fancy-pants music. Rather, as described by Aristotle in Chapter 5 of *Politics*, music was a "remedy of pain caused by toil."

Where classical Greek philosophers and the rural villagers likely agreed was this: there was a rich relationship between musical performance and the *response* induced in the audience. Both Plato and Aristotle described the result of hearing "good" music as a properly arranged or well-ordered emotional state. This internal response was called *catharsis*. Through the skilled crafting of notes, timbre, cadence, and rhythm, a musician affected a proper reorganization of emotions.

As Greek power waned and Roman influence became general, the Latins expanded their territory and controlled the hinterlands of Europe, the Balkans and Asia Minor. Pliny and Pausanias wrote very little about the music or musicians found in these frontiers. They valued almost solely the culture of urban centers like Athens and Pergamon.

It was not until Orthodox Christianity spread throughout the Greek-speaking world that another essential thread was woven into the fabric of this folk music. The Byzantine Empire pulled the intellectual and cultural life away from Athens and centralized it in Constantinople. It was here that Byzantine tonality—the undulating and precise singing heard in the Greek Orthodox Church—developed.

Ottoman rule replaced Byzantine power. Turkish administrators and soldiers imported musical style and theory from the Arabic territories in the East under Ottoman control. Some Classical and Hellenic texts on music theory and aesthetics survived through Arabic translations. These treatises and their commentaries were absorbed within Muslim musical culture.

What resulted was a synthesis of ancient Greek, Byzantine, and indigenous Arab theory. The scales or *maqams*—arrangements of notes along defined microtonal and semitonal patterns—became the dominant paradigm of tonal awareness. Greek musicians refer to these hybrids of Byzantine and Arabic scales as *dromoi*, literally melodic "roads." Musicians traveling through Constantinople spread these tonal roads throughout most of mainland Greece.

Arabic philosophers, commenting on ancient texts, determined there were extramusical properties associated with individual *maqams*. For instance, Al-Farabi of Damascus (872–951 AD) identified effects on the soul produced by certain *maqams*: the *Rast* mode gives pleasure, *Zirgule* induces relaxation, *Saba* promotes courage. Later commentators such as the fifteenth-century Surri Hassan Effendi wrote that *maqams* had tangible therapeutic values. Music was seen as having curative properties, both emotional and physical. And much of music's power depended upon the interaction between the performer and the listener.

Central to this classic Arabic theory of music performance are three interconnected notions: *tarab*, or emotional evocation, *saltanah*, or a creative musical-ecstatic state, and *sama*, the attentive and deep listening to a musical performance. When a musician develops a skillful understanding of the various modalities attached to emotional triggers and knows how to "read" the audience, he possesses *tarab* and embodies the mystical-spiritual state of *saltanah*. The reception of such musical pathos and inspiration—*sama*—has a reciprocal aspect. Properly trained and responsive listeners know when they hear inspired music and react with appropriate praise, feeding back to the artist.

One outstanding Epirote example is Kitsos Harisiadis. He demonstrated these three notions through a recording of "Dipli Gaida Epirotiko"—"Epirotic Double-Line Dance"—made in 1930. With his clarinet imploring and exploring the listener simultaneously, you can also hear words of praise in the Athens studio, driving Kitsos to even higher sonorous levels.

In Greece, the person who hosts such interactive musical events is referred to as a *glentzes,* from the Turkish *eglenti*. He is acknowledged as one who is both a deep listener of the music and one who can encourage the musicians to perform at their full potential: praising the artists but at the same time causing them to play with greater emotion. Properly arranged, the musical experience is intended to be a sublime, mutual exchange.

For about 470 years, Arabic-Greek music theory spread throughout the Greek-speaking world. With the theory came the practice—

the idea that music could move the psyche, altering physical and mental states of the listener.

The Turkish courts and the Venetian invaders introduced Western musical instruments. The Greeks, and especially the Roma, mastered these Western musical tools. Said to be originally from northern India, the Romani people settled throughout the Balkans and, in particular, in Pogoni, the extreme northern part of Epirus. This isolated area was and continues to be the source of most Epirotic musicians, much as the Mississippi Delta used to be the wellspring of esteemed country blues guitarists.

In the eighteenth century, the violin made inroads as a lead melodic instrument. Shortly afterwards, in the early nineteenth century, the clarinet became one of the primary tools of the trade due to its lower register, greater dynamic range, and versatility. By the early nineteenth century, northwestern Greek music had a core instrumental configuration: clarinet, violin, *laouto*, and *defi*. This instrumental arrangement persists to this day throughout most of Epirus.

In the nineteenth and early twentieth century *rembetiko*—a music with strong roots in Asia Minor urban performances—developed in Athens and its port, Piraeus. With the massive influx of Asia Minor refugees following the population exchange in the early 1920s, there was a corresponding demand for music with an Asia Minor character.[9]

The establishment of *laiki* or urban music such as *rembetiko* had a profound impact on Greece's self-identity and also on how Greeks would be perceived by outside cultures. *Rembetiko* in particular became the signature sound of Greece. Nearly all regional music in Greece lost some degree of vitality with the ascension of *laiki mousiki*. Several local styles disappeared, only to return recently as "art music" or revivalisms. In the words of a bagpipe player from the Aegean island of Kalymnos, "The instruments are still being played, but the social context is gone."

Except in northwestern Greece. The larger part of Epirus was not part of the Greek nation until it was liberated in 1912–13, therefore it was less affected by Asia Minor immigration. The indigenous folk music remained vital and relatively untouched. And here I was.

Vitsa is a Zagorian village perched on a precipice of the Pindus Mountains. It was large and prosperous during the Ottoman occupation. In the 1860s, there may have been close to one thousand inhabitants contributing to the coffers of the Turkish administration located in Ioannina. For hundreds of years Greek men left their homes to find work abroad, especially in Europe or America. These benefactors sent wealth back to their family and village. One can see a correlation between the best-maintained settlements and the number of esteemed entrepreneurs who had success abroad: Zagorian villages like Vitsa are better off than the settlements outside of Ioannina and within Thesprotia.

In the region of central Zagori, mountains teem with life: lush low-lying shrubs, herbs, and small plants carpet the ground below a thick matrix of no less than nine species of native *Quercus*—oak trees. Here in Epirus, oak trees are significant not only because of the Sacred Oak of Dodoni (*O Phagos* or *Iera Phigos*) but also because acorns were the nutritional foundation for people inhabiting the region before the introduction of cultivated grains—a gift from the goddesses Demeter and Persephone. Indeed, the Greek word for food, *phagito*, is etymologically linked to the word for oak, *phagos* or *phigos*. Before this gift from the gods, we foraged like beasts.

It is likely that Alexis Zoumbas played violin in Vitsa. After all, this was a wealthy village and he was one of the finest musicians nearby. Entering the village on the back of a donkey, weaving through the dark, confusing roads, Zoumbas would have known that the jumble of alleys served to confound unwelcome (and unfamiliar) visitors.

A person in the village fleeing Turkish *gendarmes* could slip unnoticed into the maze of alleys. Some of the old homes have trap doors built under the blanket closets allowing escape through the cellar. Most traditional houses are fashioned with blocks of local limestone, double-vaulted walls with barred windows, iron-ribbed doors, and impenetrable courtyards. The oldest buildings in Vitsa have slits cut in the cellar walls through which one could easily pick off hostiles with a rifle.

The founding of one village in close proximity to the next served a protective role: settlements needed a clear view of at least one other village to see if trouble was brewing. Strings of villages thread high above the valleys along the spurs of the mountains with a clear view of one's neighbors.

Most towns in Epirus have springs flowing out of a vast stone face collecting in a pool below. If Zoumbas visited Vitsa, he would have dismounted his donkey and washed his face in this pool, marveling at the expensive stonework surrounding him in the village center. Some villages have water sources near the village center where the *platanos*—the centuries-old plane tree—grows. To capture rainfall, many houses have elaborate water-collection systems flowing into cisterns.

After cleaning up and gently unpacking his violin, Zoumbas would have looked about him and seen bankers, lawyers, and merchants, all dressed in Western garments. These were the prosperous benefactors, the businessmen living abroad, returning to Vitsa to celebrate the *panegyri*. But at the turn of the last century, this year's crowd surrounding Zoumbas would have been noticeably smaller than in previous years.

After Turkish hegemony fractured in the Balkans, the villages of Zagori suffered near-cataclysmic population declines. In 1910, for example, Vitsa was reduced to less than forty percent of 1860s population. Decline continued in the second half of the twentieth century despite the introduction of nomadic families and Asia Minor refugees. In 2001 there were 137 inhabitants in a village with slightly more than one hundred homes distributed between Ano (Upper), Mesohori (Middle), and Kato (Lower) Vitsa. Nowadays, there are even fewer. Around thirty people live here during the harsh winter. And yet, those who remain yearn for—*lament*—those who have left.

The *mirologi* is intended to mourn the dead but also to address the broader human condition of *loss* or of *leaving*: leaving as death, leaving as marriage, or leaving as an immigrant to return no more, *xenitia*. The image of distant lands and the loneliness of exile is such a reality to Epirotes, such a visceral weight, that *xenitia* became a distinct song subgenre of the *mirologi*.

This notion of absence is the heart of the *panegyri*. It is palpable when you see the dispersed villagers return home. The occasion marks the opportunity for everyone to remember those who are *not* there.

This evening in Vitsa—the first night of the *panegyri*—Jim and I saw the exiled return from *xenitia*. Despite the hundreds of tables and chairs crowding the expanse of the stone courtyard, nearly everyone was standing, trading shots of *tsipouro* or sipping Western spirits, especially Bacardi mixed with just about anything. Dozens of children, including my daughter, ran across our path to the local playground while a deafening buzz lifted from the villagers.

The phenomenon of the annual *panegyri* is best understood within the larger context of all social exchange in Epirus and to a lesser extent in the rest of Greece. Even though the greatest annual holiday is *Pascha* (Easter), the *panegyri* ranks highest among all *glendia*—happy occasions in Greece. *Panegyria* share communal space with *gamoi* (marriages), *ta tsipoura* (the making of alcoholic spirits), *Christouyenna* (the Christmas feast), and other Orthodox holidays and village parties.

The common thread found in all of these occasions is spun from five local elements: food, music, dance, *tsipouro*, and people. These five threads compose the weft of social life in Epirus, with Orthodox Christianity as the warp weaving the fabric whole. And the *pan-egyri* is the most fully articulated and oldest of all annual events.

Panegyria in twenty-first-century Greece can last one to three days, depending upon the custom of the town. In the not-so-distant past, *panegyria* could have been held for a week or just a day or two, the duration being largely a function of the relative prosperity and size of the village.

Before electricity was introduced to the more remote regions in the 1960s, these feast-dances were held during the morning or afternoon when there was ample natural light. There were exceptions. The Epirote poet Kostas Krystallis penned one of the earliest recorded accounts of a *panegyri* in Epirus in 1894.[10] Held in a village outside of Ioannina during the waning years of the Turkish occupation, the nighttime celebration on September 23—the day of Saint John—was described by Krystallis in his *Panegyri of Kastritsa*:

> After dinner . . . we also went out into the courtyard. Standing upright in the middle was the iron fire-grate. Thick pine logs were burning constantly on top of it, giving out a fantastic glow all around, and a heavy scent that filled the air with clouds of thick black smoke. Groups of *panegyri*-goers—as if the innumerable ones already gathered there were not already sufficient—kept arriving, all of them well-dressed. Around midnight the dance started, a large *syrtos* dance began around the fire grate.
>
> The leaders were three Albanians—vineyard-guards—the type of men who take part in all the festivals and weddings in the villages wherever they happen to find themselves, weighed down with heavy capes, double rows of cartridges crossed over their chests like the bandits used to wear long ago, with a pair of gilded pistols in their leather weapon-belts and with new Martini-Henry rifles on their shoulders.
>
> The young men of the village—manly and ruddy-faced—followed closely behind, and sang since the Albanians didn't know

the Greek songs, but they led the dance mechanically, just as they liked. As they were going round, they were passing the wooden wine-flask filled with wine, as if it were dancing along with the *panegyri* crowd. . . .

All the songs were about their lives, their fields, their herds of sheep, their huts, their labors, love songs, and sometimes, every so often, songs about *xenitia*. . . . But even their dances were not the lively two-steps I used to see in the mountain villages. Their *syrtos* circle-dance was smooth and calm, like a group of little boats with the rowers moving their oars back and forth. . . .

There were three thousand or more participants scattered around the old foundations and buildings. One could say that the inhabitants of the great and famed Molossian civilization had risen from their graves in their full bodily forms.

Krystallis's description mirrored what Jim and I found before us in the square. Under the starry sky, sweet-smelling smoke rose from every point in the courtyard. From the eastern corner, arranged in uniformly neat rows like soldiers on parade, long steel grills with troughs full of charcoal cooked *souvlakia* and *loukanika*, local meat-on-a-stick and pork sausages. On the western side was a massive spit, turning slowly and wound tightly with sheep's intestines stuffed with herbs, garlic, and offal, *kokoretsi*. Up the alley a charcoal burner roasted corn-on-the-cob while nearly everyone held an eternally burning cigarette.

Instead of a wineskin, bottles of *tsipouro* were passed from one person to the next—to Jim and to me—and again to the next, with an involuntary, welcoming reflex. The *kefi*—the feeling of elation—was as thick and sweet as the smoke. We were part of the *panegyri*.

Linguistically, *panegyri* implies "an assembling around" or "a dancing around." Etymologically—when one refers to its usage after Greece became Orthodox—the term signifies an *ordered* assembly to celebrate and feast during an event, normally a religious one. Its meaning, like many other Greek words, has evolved since its pre-Christian and pagan usage. Before Christianity became general in Greece—roughly by the fourth century AD—a *panegyri* could mean a "festival assembly" or a "festival for a cult" and during the latter Hellenic period, a public gathering for music or speech.

Panegyri was also a communal platform for the *mirologi*: the collective mourning with physical expressions such as dance. Margaret Alexiou describes the context of vocalized mourning in antiquity:

> The archeological and literary evidence, taken together, makes it clear that lamentation involved movement as well as wailing and singing. Since each movement was determined by a pattern of ritual, frequently accompanied by the shrill music of the *aulos* (reed-pipe), the scene must have resembled a dance, sometimes slow and solemn, sometimes wild and ecstatic.

For Alexiou and other classicists, there is a social dimension where *mirologia* fit within *panegyria*. But this juxtaposition implies that *panegyria* teetered on the margin between control and frenzy. Keeping with an anecdotal meaning, some say that *panegyria* have a distinctively pagan origin: they are celebrated *in the spirit* of the ancient Greek god, Pan. In other words, there is something simultaneously sacred and profane just below the surface of these celebrations, a force that conjures the muse and triggers rapture.

No etymological connection exists between the *pan* in *panegyri* and Pan the god.* Indeed, Pan was a divinity linked to the feral and unhinged forces of nature, whereas *panegyri* implies an organized, controlled assembly. Yet the association between the wild abandon

---

* A Homeric ode to Pan from Hesiod's *Works and Days*, "Hymn to Aphrodite," suggests that some early Greek lyricists understood Pan's name as relating to *"pantes,"* or "all," since he "delighted *all* their hearts." It is no accident that the bacchic Dionysus favored Pan especially.

of the *panegyri* and the god Pan persists in the local imagination. Shepherding, pipe music, licentiousness, and uninhibited dancing were linked with the god Pan. He was *my* kind of god.

Pan was also a deity of disorder—a sanctified pied piper of chaos, *panic*—or at least of behavior that defied the laws of men. The old god Pan was problematic to the newly emerging world order of Christianity.

Devotees of Greek religion and mystery cults were just as emotionally invested in worship as the early, fervent Christians. Greek pagans, however, differed starkly from early Christians regarding the nature of divinity. The Hellenic gods were vulnerable and fragile, unlike the Christian God. Greek deities were subject to injury and death—including Pan.

According to Plutarch in his *Obsolescence of Oracles*, Pan's death was recorded between AD 35 and 37 (perhaps earlier). As the tale goes, an Egyptian pilot, Thamos, was piloting a ship from Greece to Italy when a voice called to him directly from the coast of the island of Paxos stating, "Thamos, when you approach Palodes, proclaim that the great god Pan is dead." Approaching the coastal port of Palodes—conjectured by some to be the modern Albanian port of Butrint,[11] which was originally within the region of Epirus— Thamos did as he was told by shouting across the waters, "The great god Pan is dead."

From the dark, bruised shores of Palodes an intense lamentation —a collective *mirologi*—was wailed by hundreds of unseen voices. If one stood on the eastern coast of Corfu at that time, one would have heard the devastated cries over the sea.

Tiberius Caesar summoned Thamos to recount the story to him shortly before Tiberius's own death in 37 AD, when Pontius Pilate was serving in Judaea. What is remarkable about this tale is not that Pan—an "immortal"—died. Rather, we should notice *when* he died and who also died—and was then resurrected—at roughly the same time.

Historians have long sought a causal connection between Christ's rise in fortune and Pan's decline. Everyone had a stake in interpreting Pan's last hoof-steps. Late-nineteenth-century European philhellenes and Christian theologians wrestled over the meaning of Pan's demise, concluding generally that Christianity—wrongly or rightly—triumphed over Greco-Roman paganism.

I like to imagine Pan faking his own death when he heard of the rise of this new religion. He decided to go underground, to lay low and cool his heels—or hooves—while Christianity ran its course. Maybe he thought that we would tire of complex theological notions of crucifixion, resurrection, and transubstantiation. Then we would return to a natural way of praying—when the raspy notes of a clarinet or the hypnotic song of a shepherd's flute roused him at the beginning of a *panegyri*.

Fortunately for Pan and for most of the Orthodox world, certain pagan elements were absorbed—modified or neutered— rather than removed altogether from religious celebrations. The Orthodox Church, unlike the more dogmatic, less pliable Catholic Church, practiced assimilation rather than annihilation of folk beliefs. Music, like spirituality, borrows from what grows around it.

There was a virtue if not a mandate in maintaining continuity. Life itself was short and uncertain. It could be taken away, extinguished in a wisp of smoke. The old rituals were meaningful because they provided grounding and comfort.

In Epirus, aspects of ancient beliefs coexist with the modern. The *panegyri* in Vitsa highlights the Dormition of the Theotokos—the "sleeping of the Mother of God"—on the fifteenth of August. The Orthodox believe that the Virgin Mary died and was resurrected before ascending into Heaven. The "living church"—the place of worship in Vitsa that is maintained by the town—is dedicated to this manifestation of the Virgin Mary. Every August 15, the village celebrates the Virgin's deathly slumber and resurrection. The fif-

teenth of August is also one of the most important and widely celebrated festivals of pre-Christian antiquity: the birthday of Athena,
the Greek goddess of wisdom. This is not a coincidence.

Or consider the date of the *panegyri* described by Kostas Krystallis. The name for September, the month of the celebration, is *Tri-
gitis*—the common folk word meaning both vintage or harvester
and the harvest of grapes itself. The practice of placing a festival
at the start or end of an important agricultural cycle is as ancient
as the association of the harvester with Charon, the god of the
underworld.

Panagiotis Aravantinos, folklorist and linguist, gathered
together the first "songbook" of Epirus while northwestern Greece
was still under Turkish rule. It was published in Athens in 1880,
ten years after his death. One of the first *mirologia* that he transcribed ends in this couplet:

> *Giati o kosmos ein dendri, kai meis t'oporiko tou,*
> *Ki o Charos, pou ein o trigitis mazonei ton karpon tou.*

translated as:

> *For the world is a tree, and we are its fruit,*
> *And Charos, who is the vintager, gathers its fruit.*

This verse is mirrored in a manuscript composed nearly two hundred years earlier, but the notion of cyclical harvesting with Death
as the harvester is timeless. Here is a poetic metaphor spanning
hundreds, possibly thousands of years, just like *mirologia* found
in Homer—all rooted in religious beliefs that predate the rise of
Christianity.

To be harvested by Charon was not a punishment but rather
an inevitable part of the existential cycle, our collective fate of a
"deprivation of the good things of this life." Until recently it was

common in Epirus to say of someone who had died, "Charon took him away."

Despite continuity with the pagan past, this is the twenty-first century, and Christ's dominion is nearly universal. Celebrations here are grounded in the Orthodox Church. Vitsa's neighbors in central Zagori, the villages of Monodhendri, Elaphotopos, and Aristi, all have *panegyria* on different days, with durations chosen according to the calendar of the year as well as the money on hand to host the event. Monodhendri, a short walk from Vitsa, honors the *Hagia Paraskevi* or Saint Paraskevi at the monastery next to the Vikos Gorge on July 26. Elaphotopos's living church honors the *Metamorphosis*—the Transfiguration of Christ—on August 6. Aristi has two *panegyria*. The first is connected with another manifestation of the Virgin Mary, the *Zoodochos Pigi* or "Life-giving Fount," that occurs on the Friday after Easter Sunday. The second is a smaller *panegyri* on August 29 at the *Agios Ioannis O Vaptistis*— Saint John the Baptist chapel. The date of the main celebration of the feast-dance in a given village never varies, only the duration of the event.

The feast-dance itself must be blessed by priests and sanctified by the Church. Vitsa's *panegyri* is so well attended that the celebration here starts a day earlier than the actual saint's day. The evening before, a special prayer, the *Esperinos* (Vespers), is held immediately before the icons of the Virgin are carried in a procession past the square. Then the music starts. The next morning a mass is held and the village square is sanctified, ready for music again, both for a short period in the morning and then later in the evening after siesta. Everything is punctuated with prayers up until the evening *panegyri*.

Truth is fickle, slippery here. Some villagers deny any connection between the feast-dances of today and those before Orthodoxy reigned supreme. Some say the pagan spirit lives beneath the current celebration. Indeed, for every aspect of culture here, there are as many explanations as there are villagers.

☙☙☙

That afternoon before the music started, priests exited the church holding banners high, swaying their censers. One of these brass censers bellowing smoke clashed against the gold frame of an icon carried by a young novice. The peel resonating from this accident echoed the chime produced by the sheep bells out in the countryside.

Jim and I bought two bottles of *tsipouro*. The musicians opened their cases and began tuning up.

4

THAT'S GOING TO LEAVE A MARK

"Here's what had happened to him. Going to lunch he passed an office-building that was being put up—just the skeleton. A beam or something fell eight or ten stories down and smacked the sidewalk alongside him. It brushed pretty close to him, but didn't touch him, though a piece of the sidewalk was chipped off and flew up and hit his cheek. It only took a piece of skin off, but he still had the scar when I saw him. He rubbed it with his finger—well, affectionately—when he told me about it. He was scared stiff of course, he said, but he was more shocked than really frightened. He felt like somebody had taken the lid off life and let him look at the works."

—DASHIELL HAMMETT, *THE MALTESE FALCON*

"CHRIST! THIS TASTES LIKE THE HEAVENLY FLUIDS PRODUCED BY two angels fucking."

"Yes, I know. This is no problem."

I wondered at first though if indeed this might be a problem. Maybe I shouldn't have said "fucking" in front of my new friend Georgos. At that moment—callously—I hadn't given much thought to the angels themselves. Perhaps the din of the music had obscured what I said and Georgos replied simply out of courtesy.

We had only just met the day before in the cobblestone square in the center of lower Vitsa. Over sweet, dense Greek coffee we had talked about Andrei Tarkovsky's movie *Stalker*.

Georgos is a filmmaker and photographer. His arresting eyes, his thin frame, and his scant beard cause him to resemble Anatoly Solonitsyn, the actor made famous by Tarkovsky in his roles as the spiritually tortured writer in *Stalker* and the visionary icon painter in *Andrei Rublev*. Georgos is also a full-blooded Sarakatsanos—a member of the ancient tribe of shepherds that roamed the Epirotic countryside for centuries.

Many Greeks in these parts are religious. As we drank *tsipouro* early in the morning of the first *panegyri*, I hoped that Georgos was not *that kind* of religious and that our negotiation of crude English and Greek terms would converge in a higher understanding of one another. It was not as if I was posing a theological question such as how many angels could copulate on the head of a pin or fornicate through the eye of a needle. Apostasy was the furthest thing from my mind. And it still is.

But I could not construct a more precise metaphor for what I tasted. The effect of what I was drinking was both spiritual and carnal—it tasted of the transcendent union of two incorporeal and presumably nonsexual beings. Like two angels fucking.

This statement that I uttered to Georgos was simply a declarative, descriptive phrase intended to capture a difficult concept. I'm sure Immanuel Kant had similar problems.

I hadn't really given much prior thought to the act of coitus between angels and still find it difficult to imagine them *in flagrante*. If they had such functional parts, I am unsure of how they would fit together or even if there is a divine design behind their mutual pleasure. Surely there must be one.

We rocked back and forth—subtle like—on the stone embankment. Before I started drinking *tsipouro* in earnest at the *panegyri*, my surroundings filtered through the predictable three dimensions. My sensory resolution was gradually amplified after the first few hours of the dance and the consumption of three bottles of *tsipouro*. This heightened magnification created a fourth dimension I had previously not known. That is to say, I was witnessing a distinct psychotropic property in this local liquor.

The perception-altering *tsipouro*, angular Byzantine musical scales, and all of the elements at play in the village the night before combined to work their way into my psyche. This was pure alchemy, a primal medicine show.

Relief came when Georgos said, "You know, *all of this* is pagan." He said this while I paused my breath, taking another deep drink from my bottle. When Georgos emphasized "all of this" with a broad sweep of his hand, I knew what he meant. It was as if he were a carnival barker lifting up the edge of a peep show tent, showing me the forbidden sights. His wispy, tall frame, his long arms, and his penetrating gaze over *all of this* reminded me that I was in the presence of an immediate descendant of an ancient race, one with secret knowledge: *gnosis.*

From where Georgos and I sat, we took in the whole works— the gears and the springs of the celebration: the cascading clarinets echoing from the village center like snake charmers' hypnotic flutes, the disorienting smoke rising from the *souvlaki* pits, the hundreds of people orbiting the musicians, the unhinged aura of everything.

It happened at that instant, a flash of focused insight. There is an ancient mechanism within our souls triggered only by this music. Here in the rare environment of Vitsa exists a tinderbox capable of capturing that primal spark.

Sufi mystics arrive at divine truth and commune with the Eternal through the ceremonial consumption of wine. Indians from the Sierra Madre of western Mexico have their revelations through peyote. Sacred rites with cannabis, fungi, and dozens of psychotropic plants give people an expressway to God's ear.* I had done the

---

* Admittedly, one does not need to consume mind-altering substances to speak with or hear from God. One only needs to know how. William S. Burroughs, commenting on "spiritual addiction" during an interview with Conrad Knickerbocker for the *Paris Review* in 1965, said, "Anything that can be done chemically can be done in other ways, that is, if we have sufficient knowledge of the processes involved."

same, but through the most transcendent of earthly substances available here: *tsipouro*. It loosened the hinges on the lid of life.

"You must not drink what comes out for the first half an hour or you will be poisoned, possibly blinded, my friend *[phile mou]*." This was the advice given to me by Alexandros Spyrou while I helped him and his family make two batches of homemade *tsipouro* in the courtyard of their bucolic Zagorian manor house. Alexandros— a successful lawyer in Athens, at that time the president of the Vitsa Cultural Committee, and a respected voice among the village council—also spoke impeccable English. His carefully trimmed beard, a style now fashionable among many young Greek men, and his commanding physical presence made me feel as if I were a mortal speck next to a Titan. Yet it was the combination of his gestures that gave gravity to the threat. With eyes tightly lidded, chin jutting upwards, and right thumb, index, and ring finger pinched together as he spoke, he communicated wordlessly the results of drinking "green" alcohol, the first run of *tsipouro*. I chose not to risk blindness.

A few years after attending my first *panegyri*, I visited Epirus in late November, when individual and collective *ta tsipoura*—"the making of *tsipouro*" events—take place. While *panegyria* have fixed calendrical dates, the distillation of Greek moonshine is controlled by the weather and the amount of time allocated for the fermentation of the grape "leavings" or "must." In the middle of November the weather turns cold and the grape mash has aged appropriately for three or four weeks. The fabrication of *tsipouro* is brisk business that depends largely upon ambient temperature, orchestrated group labor, and expert moonshine craftsmanship.

The origin and development of provincial distillation, like practically every other Epirote cultural phenomenon, is clouded by the unknowable and the undocumented. Creation tales abound from one village to the next, one individual to another, and very little historical literature exists to which one may anchor a reliable narrative. One has to sift through the anecdotal and apocryphal to fashion something resembling the truth.

We know that the Turkish Empire fed upon various revenues available within its vast territory. The region, the village, and the individual also owed tithes to the Orthodox Church. This biblical mandate was onerous to honor under the harsh conditions imposed by the Turks. Non-Muslim Ottoman subjects were taxed because they were nonbelievers. A *dhimmi*—a non-Muslim—owed a *jizyah*, an annual payment for protection, to Turkish officials. One must give to Caesar (or in this case, the Turkish sultan, bey, or pasha) what was his. One must also give to the Church. Therefore rural Greece—its settlements and its affluent patrons—used every possible resource to meet these worldly and spiritual obligations. Nothing went to waste.

Tsipouro loosely translates to "bottom of the barrel" or "the leavings." Originally wine was produced by the towns and given as partial tribute to both the Turkish overlords and the monasteries instead of coin. Eventually the innovative country dwellers realized that the pulp—the skin and solids left over after the initial pressing of the grape juice for wine—could be fermented and distilled to fashion an even more inebriating spirit. Though no set date is attached to this discovery, Turkish tax documents from the late eighteenth century record the conveyance of barrels of grape pulp to monasteries in Greece. Obviously such transactions occurred earlier and under clandestine circumstances. We can presume that if the monks and priests of the Orthodox Church did not invent the process of distilling Greek moonshine, they at least perfected the technique.

During the long Ottoman occupation, Turks referred to *tsipouro* as *raki,* a liquor like *tsipouro* that was once popular throughout the Arab world. The word *raki* may be derived from an Indian term for a similar drink, *arak.* Here is a possible connection, a thread that may never be adequately unraveled. Gypsy coppersmiths possibly from North India—referred to colloquially as *halkiades*—may have fashioned the earliest *kazania*, the Turkish kettles essential for distilling grapes into hard spirits. Perhaps the Roma introduced the craft of distillation to the Greeks after they settled into the territories beginning in the fifteenth century when they left Walachia in small numbers. There were then larger migrations, especially in the early nineteenth century when the enslavement of Gypsies was outlawed throughout most of Europe.

The moonshine still has two parts. The bottom is a carefully forged copper pot. The top is shaped like a medieval jousting helmet with a sharply pronounced tapering appendage. Alexandros showed me an antique *kazani* in the basement of his parent's house reposing in the dirt next to freshly packed tins of homemade feta cheese. You could see the hammer marks—still-shimmering indentations in the scant, dust-infused light—on this two-hundred-year-old moonshine still.

Variations of *tsipouro* are consumed throughout the Balkans where Greece has left its cultural stamp. In Bulgaria and Romania it is still referred to as *rakia,* and in Crete, a similar but stronger spirit is produced that is called *tsikoudia* or *raki* (but pronounced *ratchi* in the Cretan dialect). In central and southern Greece, *tsipouro* is infused with anise or other aromatic herbs. According to almost every Epirote connoisseur of *tsipouro*—which is to say almost everyone who lives here—these odiferous additions are used to mask inferior liquor.*

You make *tsipouro* by first gathering together your family and friends in the village. In this instance it was Alexandros, his parents, his sister and her husband, his uncle and aunt, Alexandros's

---

* Here in northwestern Greece *tsipouro* is pure, unadulterated essence. #straightnoanise

future bride and her parents, and slightly more than a dozen villagers including myself. Over the course of this afternoon and evening, the numbers swelled to twenty-five or thirty people. Everyone assisted. Likewise, everyone was treated as if they lived in Alexandros Spyrou's backyard, part of an extended family.

Instead of the traditional charcoal flame, we lit and placed a gas burner under the *kazani*. Alexandros and I hefted a seventy-five-pound barrel of grape mash from its subterranean chamber and hauled it over rickety boards to his family's stone courtyard. In the old days, only the pulp and Zagorian spring water was added to the still. Nowadays they use the whole grape: the juice as well as the leavings. This makes for smoother, more complex moonshine.

Once the must is stirred, we tip it gently into the kettle and seal the lid to the lower part of the still with three threaded stirrups. Quickly, the whole family strings up a thin copper tube that runs from the *kazani* to a cooling vat placed to the lower left side of the still. The copper pipe plunges vertically into the cooling chamber as a spiraling pigtail. This coil then turns a hard right angle and is connected to an open spigot for the steamed alcoholic vapors to escape.

We gingerly position the cooling copper vat and attach a garden hose, which transfers cold rainwater to the vat from a gravity-held reservoir above the house. Another garden hose is attached to the bottom of the cooling pot, which removes the water before it becomes too warm. Much fuss and attention is taken to regulate the flow of this water from the source: too much fluid and the vat overflows, too little water and the *tsipouro* is rendered at fluctuating temperatures, causing it to shed its anticipated aesthetic and spiritual properties. Order and balance is sought and maintained; with the right care, everything functions like clockwork.

Alexandros's father, Spiros, thumbed a small wad of cotton into the spigot. This filters out the occasional flotsam while the kettle incrementally drips the first run of blindness-inducing methyl distillate. This is called "the head."

DON'T DRINK THIS.

It takes about a half hour for the *kazani* to reach the target temperature of 90 degrees Celsius or 194 degrees Fahrenheit. Only then will the still initiate its steady flow of alcohol. Another half hour will pass before the *tsipouro* is safe to drink. Steam envelops the entire operation. Peering through the mist, I watch shimmering beads of condensation gently trace the contours of the copper pigtail as they glide into the cold-water vat propped below. A light drizzle had started while the temperature rose. This added to the combination of cooling factors at play in the making of the *tsipouro*. The high atmospheric vapors, the rainwater collected in cisterns, and the surrounding springs all contain pure Zagorian water.

Epirus is the second most mountainous region in Europe, and it receives on average fifty inches of rain a year. The eastern Molossian hill country acts as a topographical filter, removing impurities—pollution—from the waves of precipitation sweeping northward and eastward from the Ionian Sea. The vast peaks of the Pindus Mountains and the deep reservoir that is the Vikos Gorge function as natural sieves and water basins. You taste this sweet airiness in the water. When one purchases bottled water in Athens, it is likely sourced from Zagori.

We pass the next hour enjoying thimble glasses of last year's *tsipouro*, talking, fine-tuning the water flow for the *kazani*, and feasting upon sublime homemade *meze* brought by Alexandros's mother, Ekaterina. In most of Greece, the very social act of drinking *tsipouro* is always accompanied by the equally social consumption of small plates of food. Neighbors and family float in and out of the courtyard sampling the old *tsipouro* and having *pestrofa* (smoked river trout garnished with fresh garlic sliced razor thin, pungent and sharp to the palate), *agriogourouno-stifadho* (wild boar slow-roasted under layers of sweet onions), Metsovone hard cheese, *tzatziki*, perfectly salted grilled pork, lamb, and chicken. Of course there is also the Zagorian specialty: *tiropita*, or "cheese pie."* Throughout the evening we feasted on this homemade culinary orgy.

A little after the first hour of firing the *kazani*, Alexandros placed a clean bucket under the dripping faucet. After this, he drifted from welcoming guests to testing the proof to gauging the temperature. Like a combination of an expectant mother and a distinguished Venetian sculptor, Alexandros fretted over every permutation of outcome for this batch of homemade brandy. All variables were corrected and every aspect was adjusted.

As he poured me a glass of the newly born *tsipouro*, I asked him how he had learned to make it. He told me that his grandfather handed the skills down to him and that he in turn taught his own father, Spiros. It had skipped a generation but folded back upon itself. He added, "Traditional is now hip!" I eased the small tumbler of *tsipouro* to my lips.

The "nose" of finely produced Zagorian *tsipouro* is a subtle marriage of the local flora and the sweet grape. But neither scent is dominant; they do not combat one another but instead form a transcendent harmony. In my mind, nature itself infuses myriad elements into the pollen of this diverse biosphere. This in turn

---

* The commonly used translation of "pie" is inaccurate in my mind, since the American concept of pie implies heaviness, density. *Tiropita* inhabits the space between pie and pastry, weight and weightlessness, a light, almost ethereal delicacy. Ekaterina and Alexandros's grandmother, Elli—born in 1929 and the oldest villager in Vitsa—rolled out the dough early that morning, so thin you could read the Bible through the delicate layers. The craft of making *tiropita* in Epirus is renowned throughout the rest of Greece. Within Epirus, the provincial variations of *tiropita* depend largely upon whether one uses Zagorian, Vlachi, or Sarakatsani cheese, all of which are distinct and delectable.

enters the bloom that yields the fruit. What you drink is what surrounds you, rarefied.

When it hits the mouth it is slightly sweet, with only a modest suggestion that what you are consuming is fiercely alcoholic. Alexandros's *tsipouro* clocked in at 74 proof, but equally exceptional moonshine from the neighboring village of Elaphotopos peaked at around 120 proof.

To be clear, the skill required to make exquisite *tsipouro* requires the all-encompassing knowledge of the finest vintner. However, those who appreciate good *tsipouro* are neither oenophiles nor the privileged, educated suburbanites who laud the virtues of preposterously expensive single-malt scotch. This is honest liquor for honest people. And a surprisingly large number of villagers know how to produce it well.

But what makes for sublime *tsipouro*, this psychotropic grape distillate? At its most fundamental level, there are three things:

a) The pollen, water, and minerals that create and nurture the grapes: their unique biosphere.
b) The selection, cleaning, and controlled fermentation of the grape must.
c) The care and judgment of the moonshine craftsman at the still.

The elements necessary in crafting excellent *tsipouro* parallel those elements responsible for maintaining Epirotic music. If the environment fostering the healthy growth of grapes depends upon the *terroir* and the purity of the life source—water—then the same analogy is seen in the music and the musicians. What feeds the continuum of music must be predictable, unadulterated, and local. The sorting of grades, the careful removal of stems, and the strictly monitored fermentation of the superior grapes represent how Zagorians have chosen the best musicians *and* the best songs and tunes for them to play at *panegyria* for countless generations.

Finally, the supervision of the distillation itself—the synthesis of honed experience with an almost mystical gnosis—mirrors how the village leaders, people like Alexandros and his friends, carefully adjust aspects of the *panegyri* every year so tradition is maintained and attendees from diverse backgrounds experience the festivities at their fullest.

In other words, every aspect must be attended to fully or else it all falls apart. One could be left with a tepid *panegyri*, almost devoid of traditional sounds and contexts, just as one could be left with a tasteless *tsipouro*, empty of nuance and transcendence. Without a doubt, these states of degradation do exist in Epirus. Here, everything is fragile.

Over the last few hours of eating and communing, Alexandros played CDs of contemporary Epirotic music, mainly those by Vitsa's favorite clarinetist, Gregoris Kapsalis. He announced suddenly he wanted a change in mood, so he switched the music. Instead of the soul-caressing sounds of northwestern Greek clarinet and violin, the air was split asunder with the jagged peal of an electric guitar, cut with the nasal twang of Ronnie Van Zant. Alexandros was a "huge fan" of Southern rock, indeed of all things from the southern United States, including the TV show *The Dukes of Hazzard*.

Anthems of Lynyrd Skynyrd filled the ancient courtyard and echoed through the Pindus Mountains. My mind formed a leather bit that my teeth sank into. Relaxing my jaws, I told Alexandros that it was ironic that I had traveled thousands of miles to hear the soundtrack of my bruised youth in Virginia. From across the Atlantic, I recalled being systematically pummeled by high school rednecks resembling the original lineup of Lynyrd Skynyrd. Greasy hair, immature mustaches, and vacant gazes beat me to a pulp, but only after their heroes had crashed and died in Mississippi when I was six years old. This image of Lynyrd Skynyrd also reminded me that I should send Alexandros a Confederate flag handkerchief for a wedding present.

I learned that part of Alexandros's fascination with the American South was the stress given to notions of independence, freedom (for some), and pride in one's culture. The same concepts are valued immeasurably here in the Greek countryside. Freedom to eat *kokoretsi*, freedom to make *tsipouro*, freedom to hold a *panegyri*. All of these freedoms have been threatened in the past.

Rebel Alexandros moved rapidly to check the proof, temperature, and composition of the first batch of *tsipouro*. We were now approaching "the tail" of the distillation, when the intense pressure and temperature had evaporated almost all the drinkable alcohol. What was left was too strong: unbalanced and fierce. Also, this portion of the must would soon scorch due to the high heat and the lack of moisture, leaving a harsh, burnt aftertaste.

DON'T DRINK THIS.

As Alexandros and his father took apart the *kazani* for the next batch, another villager, Vangelis Papachristos, walked into the courtyard and embraced me, as is the custom. With wide, glassy eyes, long, slender jaws, and a thick, dark beard, his face read like a relief map of honesty and matter-of-factness. Like many of his generation in the village, he is a long-standing member of the Cultural Committee and takes the mandate to preserve Vitsa's heritage seriously. His work ethic is like that of my grandfather's generation in Virginia, still very much alive here in the mountains of Greece.

"You know, the ear is always listening, always searching, even as an infant." This Vangelis told me as we retreated next to the open fireplace in the Spyrou house. Reclining on traditional Ottoman couches—low and wide platforms or *basia* built within the living room and covered with thick Zagorian wool upholstery—we were both rather tight with *tsipouro*.

I posed five questions to Vangelis that night, the same set of questions that I presented to almost every villager and musician from Epirus that I spent time with over the course of several years:

When did you first hear the *mirologi* and how does it make you feel?

How did you learn to respond to the clarinet, the violin, and the songs?

How does one graft an emotion onto an instrument such that it conveys an emotional response in the listener?

What are your favorite songs or tunes from Epirus and why?

Do you fear a loss of this tradition and why?

Rarely would all my questions be answered clearly. Often many were left unanswered or only partially addressed, like the poetic fragments of Sappho.

Vangelis spoke with his usual precise clarity. He said that his reaction to Epirotic music was gained prenatally and only grew, "became alive after I ceased to be distracted with other things in the world." Traditional life is well supported, since grandparents and parents "take care of everything while their children go off to work." I agreed that nowhere had I seen more closely bound families. It is not uncommon to visit a home containing four generations living in comfort, supporting one another.

But Vangelis, like many others, fears a decline in traditional values, the holding together of old-fashioned things. He told me, "That is why we work so hard with the Cultural Committee to promote the village traditions, to balance out the old and the new, '*to paleo kai to neo.*'"

"What music do you prefer at the *panegyri*?"

"The Pogonisio songs. This music contains more pain; it is slower and the words are deeper."

Jim and I were sitting at the sweetest spot of the *mesohori*, the village square. Gregoris Kapsalis played the opening *mirologi*, lowering his clarinet. We were close to the dancers and the musicians. Reasonably far away sat the monstrous audio speakers perched on tripods that distorted the music. The amplification was twisting the notes. I was awash in sounds that I could not control. I wanted to hear the natural acoustics, the unmediated vibrations from the instruments. It took twenty minutes or more for my ears to compensate for the oversaturated sounds, translated as they were through four standing microphones, four internal pickups, an audio-to-digital converter, and an analog mixing board. This delay—this translation—confounded my peculiar brain.

Through time and space all things shed aspects of themselves: water, *tsipouro*, memory, music, hope. Everything—including music—rolls and tumbles along, losing parts of itself as fragments in the wake of progress, of motion downstream. Even loss loses some of itself: loss becomes indifference. These are the things left behind as time moves forward, altering all that it touches.

When the discs that I worshipped were made, whether in Athens, in New York, or in various parts of the South, the sonic vibrations were captured and translated into ridged grooves. The sounds began their static life as electrical currents transported through a cloth-covered metal cable from a carbon fiber microphone to a cutting machine in another room. Just as the distillation of *tsipouro* is an alchemy of intensification, so too is this process of harnessing live sound and etching the signals into a record.

Two or three generations later, you have to translate backwards. Sometimes you are presented with a singular disc that may have been gouged by steel needles, scarring the delicate hills and valleys of musical information layered within the groove. In my record room, a Medusa's head of wires, an intricate grid of vacuum tubes and circuits, helps me hear these sounds as if I were in the same room with the musicians, sitting in an oak school chair and smoking a cigarette in the cool shadows.

Faced with the real thing, albeit amplified and distorted, I tried to grasp the melody. In Virginia, the old discs were submerged in crackle, but at least they were intelligible. Here, the music was not echoing the sounds of the discs because of its immediacy—its nearness to me in the present.

And then I heard it.

Oh, which rich man died, my son,
Oh, and took his fortune with him?
Oh, and took his fortune with him?
Oh, he took six feet of shroud,
Oh, to dress his body, my son,
Oh, to dress his body, my son.
Black eyes, black eyes,
Big black eyes.

Here was an ancient Pogonisio song—just like those that Vangelis favored—steeped in pain. This was not sweet sentimental bubble-gum music or something *wanting to have meaning*. Instead, here was a song born from suffering hundreds of years ago, still thriving darkly in the present. It has been slowly distilling and aging in its own grief.

Lyrically it was a lament—like a *mirologi*—but contained within the languid Pogonisio meter. Jim glanced at me with his generous, knowing smile. We both watched as the dancers glided together, circling the musicians like Kostas Krystallis's "group of little boats with the rowers moving their oars back and forth." History replayed itself before us, just as it appeared to Krystallis in 1894.

What snapped me out of this inward musing on decay and translation of sound was the fact that I had a disc of this same song, "Pios Plousios Apethane"—"Which Rich Man Has Died"—

reclining on my record room shelf. My ear traced the contours of the melody, mapping them back to the recording. The record is stark, unsettling. Demetris Halkias—the uncle of one of Epirus's most celebrated clarinet players, Tasos Halkias—made this record in Athens on May 21, 1931. He sings and plays the violin while a *santouri*, a hammered dulcimer used in music throughout the Balkans, maintains a minimal pulse throughout. And, as I learned from other collectors, the copy of this disc back in Virginia, salvaged from a hunting lodge in rural Maine, was the only one known to have survived.

The lyrics of the song also drew me out. Also known as "Plousioi Kai Phtochi"—"Rich and Poor (Must Die)"—it is an example of folk poetry transcending time and geography. This statement is not hyperbole. Here are moral verses with profound consequences. The messages are just as valid now as they were two thousand years ago: we are but mortal husks, and when we die, *the rich man and the poor man are the same*. Six feet of shroud will cover the wealthy just as it will cover the destitute. This shroud is all that we take with us as we descend into the ground.

On May 9, 1928, Oscar L. Coffey, a singer and banjo player, recorded ten 78 rpm sides in Richmond, Indiana. Tony Russell, the indefatigable music researcher, suggests that Coffey hailed from Watauga County, North Carolina, based on census documents. The very last recording that Coffey made that day was entitled "Six Feet of Earth Makes Us All of One Size," written by Gulick-Stewart in 1878. Coffey's southwestern North Carolina accent is difficult to comprehend even to this lifelong Virginian. But the message is clearly the same:

I will sing you a song of this world and its ways,
Of the many strange people we meet.
From the rich man who rolls in his millions of wealth,
To the poor struggling wretch in the street,

Though a man, he is poor and in tatters and rags,
We should never reject or despise.
But think of the adage and remember my friends,
That six feet of earth will make us all of one size.

Though there is a veneer of difference—in tempo, rhythm, instrumentation, and language—it is simply that: a veneer, a superficial thinness that dissolves when anyone listens deeply. This results in the well-worn but still fresh discovery that there is profound truth in music, especially truth in honest, ageless music grown from the soil.

✺✺✺

"Be sure not to stay up too late. We have to rise early to make it to Grammeno before it gets too hot!" This was Jim's advice—in retrospect, sage council—before he headed back to his home near the Vikos Gorge. Meanwhile, I had lost track of Demetris. He had no doubt found a table of old friends with whom he would share his favorite pastime: engaging conversation.

But I couldn't fight the urge to hear more, to see more, while the dancers and hundreds of expatriated villagers circled the musicians. As Jim cut a path to the alley leading off from the square, the band began to play the "Paleo Zagorisio"—the "Old Zagorian Dance." The choreography following the offset $\frac{5}{4}$ beat drew me back to the circle.

A woman in her late twenties with dark, curly hair gingerly placed her toe and heel from her left foot in perfect step with the tapping of the *defi*. Her right foot gracefully cut curlicues with the cadence of the clarinet as if she were genetically predisposed to make such delicate, unfailing patterns. What was astonishing was that the three rings of dancers around the musicians—probably numbering close to 150 people—repeated faultlessly the same minute synchronizations. You could hear the celestial bodies as they moved across the night sky.

Gregoris Kapsalis and Thomas Haliyiannis.

In the center of the center, directly below the plane tree, was the band. Kostas Karapanos, then 38 years old, played the violin, while Fotis Papazikos, 29, strummed the *laouto*. Tasos Daflos, 49 years old, tapped the *defi,* and George Gouvas, 41, sang the ancient songs. These four men lived in Ioannina. The second clarinetist was Thomas Haliyiannis, 56, from the town of Parakalamos. When they played as a group they called themselves *Takimi,* "group of friends."

But what completed the circuit—in this case, the circle of musicians—was Gregoris Kapsalis. At 83 years of age, Kapsalis was regarded by most in this region as the elder statesman, the preeminent master of Zagorian clarinet tunes. If the guitarist and singer Charlie Patton, the almost universally recognized "King of the Delta Blues," had lived to see 83 rather than 43, he would have shared a seat next to Kapsalis.

The clarinetist has shy eyes. Everything is reserved and proper about him: his ivory suit, his thin, immaculate mustache, and his manner of greeting: a slightly lowered gaze aimed at your shoes.

Even the way he hefts the clarinet is modest, as if it's an honor for him to bring the reed to his lips. Although his solos are short nowadays—economical—you can tell that he receives a kind of dignified deference, a margin of space and respect, by the musicians and dancers that surround him. They want to hear what comes next, as if it is a secret that he has been holding back for decades.

A pause between songs. Fotis tunes his *laouto*. An acoustic creature that evolved from the Turkish *lavta*, the eight-string *laouto* may have developed from a crossbreeding or hybridization of the *oud* and other double-course fretted instruments found in ancient Egypt, Syria, and Sumeria. It is tuned in fifths, like a violin, but instead of E–A–D–G, it goes A–D–G–C. The A strings are paired in unison but the rest are pitched an octave apart, like the bass sets of a twelve-string guitar. If a violinist plays a melodic figure, the skilled *laouto* player can mirror it perfectly. Instead of a guitar pick, most *laouto* players use a long, thin shank of cow-horn to strike the strings. In the Ottoman period, the preferred plectrum was made from the thickest wing bone of an eagle. There are not so many eagles around now.

The long, narrow neck of the *laouto* has frets made of fishing line wound tightly at chromatic intervals. In the old days, catgut was used for the same purpose. The shape of the *laouto* body is like that of a pear sliced vertically. It has a curvature that suggests sensuality or fertility if one is into that kind of thing.

A *laouto* also displays ornamentation and appointments common to other Greek stringed instruments. An intricate hand-carved rosette, gilded in gold paint, covers the sound hole. The elaborate binding and purfling complement the curved mustache bridge and the pick-guard engraved with arabesques. It is the one instrument in northwestern Greece that visually reminds you that you are standing at the gateway between East and West.

In *panegyri* or wedding photos from the late nineteenth century, you can see a mix of instruments among the musicians. The

Turkish *lavta* with its sharply angled headstock is seen in the same image alongside a *laouto* with its more tapered headstock. The old *laouto* was normally crowned at the top with a small lion head made of sawdust and glue, formed in a lost wax die and then coated in gold powder. You'll see *tsamoura* and *floyera*, end-blown pipes and flutes, and a variety of clarinets, alongside standard violins and Asia Minor double-strung violins. At this time, everything was coalescing out of the flux into the standard *kompania*: the group of musicians with their tools of trade. Primal matter yielded multicell organisms millions of years ago. Iterations of obsolete instruments coalesced in the classic New Orleans jazz ensemble around one hundred years ago. And ragtag assortments of musicians produced the Epirote *kompania* in the late nineteenth century.

While Fotis carefully adjusts the strings, Tasos tunes his *defi*. Rather than finding a proper note, Fotis seeks a tonal center, something stable to anchor all the notes from the other instruments. The *defi* looks like a tambourine, but the high grade of brass chimes, the quality of the geared brackets, and the carving of the wooden frame places this instrument in a different class of percussion. Tasos plays the *defi* by cradling it upright in his left hand while tapping it with a combination of his right hand and the fingers on the left.

The *defi* player is the foundation for his group as well as for the dancers. Without the precise elocution of rhythm, the dance would fall apart. Therefore Tasos must have an encyclopedic and mathematically based knowledge of all the time signatures and meters. He must know the rhythms and ornaments not only of Epirotic music but also of tunes heard throughout mainland Greece and the islands. Indeed, his selection of drums reflects the growing diversity of sounds wanting to be heard during *panegyria*.

Next to him sit three other percussive instruments: a *daire* (a larger, older version of the *defi*), a *daouli* (a huge drum with skin on both ends, similar to the Indian *dhol*), and a *toubeleki* (a shiny metal drum with a tight, small skin on one end and a flared opening on the other). The *daire* would be used for older dances, like those from Pogoni. When someone requests a dance or song from Western Macedonia, typically the *daouli* is used. Heavy, offset rhythms—perhaps echoes of war songs—are heard in Macedonia. Tasos plays the main beat on the top of the *daouli* with a large felt-covered mallet while tapping the bottom of the drum with a thin, light stick, producing the necessary syncopation. Similarly, when an Asia Minor dance—a *syrto* or a *tsamiko* from outside of Epirus—is requested, the *toubeleki* is pulled out. Useful for a belly dance, it produces tight patterns of rapid notes.

The ability to play a variety of tunes from regions outside of Epirus is a response to the unexpected flux and dynamism of music in this region. Two crises were responsible for some alterations in the music here: the encroachment of alien instruments and the abrupt departure of several generations that nearly emptied the villages.

From the late 1960s until the 1990s traditional music was in a dire state in Greece, especially in Epirus. Amplification, even *electric guitar*, was introduced into the kompania. Christ, even electric guitar.

Before this travesty, the piano accordion was imported to replace the declining population of decent violinists. In most of Pogoni, Western Macedonia, and Konitsa the wheezing, out-of-tune accordion is now a standard instrument for *panegyria* and other festivities. My first two questions when I am fielding the possibility of attending an unfamiliar *panegyri* are: is it amplified, and do they have an accordion? If both are answered in the affirmative, then I typically decline the invitation. Though I don't attend, I realize that tradition still lives *to a degree* within these *panegyria*, despite the odds.

Around the same time that the accordion and electric guitar crept into Epirus, another crisis struck that persisted for over thirty years—the near abandonment of villages. From the time the military junta established a dictatorship in Greece in 1967 until

Greece joined the eurozone in 2001, the pattern of a male bread-winner working abroad while the family stayed behind was broken. Instead, whole generations moved elsewhere. This massive migration almost tore apart the fabric of traditional life in the rural regions of Greece, especially Epirus. It is no wonder that almost all forms of folk music have declined or disappeared.

A vacuum was created by generations of Zagorian families leaving for the cities. This depletion of population slowly reversed when new groups moved into the region, settling down and establishing roots. Villages saw families of Sarakatsani give up on their nomadic way of life and, for the first time, live in a fixed location. Though they would not abandon shepherding and other distinctive cultural practices altogether, they did refresh the villages with their vast numbers. If it were not for the Sarakatsani, the Vlach, and the smaller numbers of Asia Minor immigrants, many of the Zagorian villages would likely have collapsed.

In Zagori and other parts of Epirus there were forces that resisted change while accommodating new groups. These mechanisms turned back the course of time, at least to a degree. And one of these forces, possibly the strongest, was *nostalgia*. There was a yearning for the way that things were remembered: a recollection perhaps not as things were but as one wished them to have been. It is this nostalgia coupled with communal pride that motivates the constant preservation efforts by cultural committees and village organizations throughout Zagori. The results are mixed, yet concrete and meaningful.

9~9~9~

I watched Gregoris Kapsalis place the chrome cover on his clarinet mouthpiece. Younger musicians, his Takimi, surrounded him in the present. But the past was gathering itself around him through the recollections of the villagers congregating in the smoky courtyard. Before Kapsalis stood here, eighty-five years earlier Lazaros Rountas was the favored musician of Vitsa. One hundred years ago,

Nikola Ninos held his clarinet before the *panegyri*. Time has erased the names of the musicians before Ninos.

Kapsalis's group was dressed immaculately in pressed black pants, starched white shirts, and shining black shoes. Only Kapsalis wore a tie. They were all smoking. Sometime one musician had two cigarettes burning at the same time. Clarinet players especially like to smoke while playing, pinching the burning cigarette between their pinky and ring finger while the rest of their digits do all the work.

Fifty years ago, at this very spot in Vitsa, Kapsalis was surrounded by a different group of musicians. They too would have smoked like diesel engines and played the same repertoire. They were the group known as Takoutsia.

All but one member of Takoutsia exists in the same dimension as those who made the 78 records that I covet. Charon has swallowed them up. What remains of them—what persists through time—are some fragile reel-to-reel recordings, one old 78, and Gregoris Kapsalis. Takoutsia served as a bridge between the phonograph records made in the early to mid-twentieth century of Epirotic music and the live music of the *panegyri*. These recordings are among the mostly highly prized musical documents to aficionados of true-vine Zagorian music. They are revered in the same way that jazz collectors—self-referred "old moldy figs"—esteem the earliest recordings of King Oliver and Louis Armstrong's Hot Five.

The original group, Takoutsia—literally "the young ones of Takis"—formed around 1923. Three brothers, Yiorgos on clarinet, Kostas on violin, and Spyros Kapsalis on *laouto*, lived in Kato Pedhina, a village near Vitsa. Their uncle Polychronis Kapsalis played the clarinet, and their cousin Christodoulos (nicknamed Zioulis) sang and played the *daire*. He was said to have a very sonorous frame, like a barrel. All of these musicians were Greek Gypsies, Roma.

Everyone wanted to play with Takoutsia. Being a part of this group held the same status as serving a stint in an elite jazz band. Had

Alexis Zoumbas stayed in Epirus, he would probably have formed a group that would have been their only serious competition. Philippos Rountas of Doliana and Haralampos Bouros of Grammeno—both students of Kitsos Harisiadis (whose discs I discovered in Istanbul)—held the group's lead role on clarinet over time.

In the early 1960s, Gregoris Kapsalis from Elaphotopos—Demetris Dallas's home village near Vitsa—joined the ranks as lead clarinetist. He was a second cousin of the founding Kapsalis brothers. Gregoris was unusual in that he was only half Gypsy: his mother was "white," a Greek, and his father was "black," a Gypsy. The Gypsies themselves employed this description.[12] Gregoris's father, Alexios, was an accomplished *daire* player. Another cousin of Gregoris, Yiorgos Kapsalis, played second clarinet with the group.

Nowadays, many in this region regard Gregoris as the best performer of Zagorian clarinet. Listening to this recording made on May 8, 1965, in the basement of Manthos Manthou in Doliana (a small Zagorian village), gives the strongest evidence of continuity between the past and the present. The group is in top form, relaxed with plenty of *tsipouro*, and inspired by the shouts of enthusiasm by Manthos throughout the performance. They play a variety of dances heard only in these parts: "Frassia" and "Grava," for instance. Both tunes are intricate like needlework, Byzantine in tonality, and—like many of the pieces of the region—shift from one time signature to another as they develop three distinct melodic statements.

They also perform "Genovefa," a favorite of mine and of Demetris. Set primarily in the *Nigriz* mode—the most popular scale of Zagorian music—the tune is melancholic, like an Italian aria where everyone dies and no one finds love. Connoisseurs of northwestern Greek music speculate that this piece was based on an air brought to Epirus by traveling Italian opera groups.

The predominant scale or *maqam* of "Genovefa"—*Nigriz* in the key of G—is the same as for the *skaros*, the shepherd's song. The notes of *Nigriz*, in ascending pitch, are G–A–B♭–C♯–D–E–F♯–G (in descending, the F♯ becomes F). "Genovefa" also uses two other minor scales related to *Nigriz*: *Nevesser* (G–A–B♭–C♯–D–D♯–F♯–G) and *Niaven* (G–A–B♭–C–D–D♯–F♯–G). This development of shifting tonality within a minor scale is one of the unique features of Zagorian music.

At this *glendi* in Manthos's wooden basement Takoutsia also played the song "Samantakas." This is a chestnut of a tune recorded on 78s several times by both Epirote and southern Albanian musicians before and after World War II. In central and southern Albania (and parts of Greek Pogoni) it is called "Osman Takas." Its languid, elided passages give temporal space for improvisation by the musicians and the lead dancers. It is one of the most introspective and difficult dances of the region. Stories are swapped in Vitsa about how one's father, grandfather, or great-grandfather lined up small *tsipouro* tumblers upside down on the cobblestones and danced the "Samantakas" on these inverted glasses without shattering a single one.

In Epirus, dance is a collective act of dignity and remembrance. Embedded within the historical consciousness of the northwestern Greek people—as if it happened only last week—"Samantakas" commemorates the bravery and agility of an Albanian *kleft*: a bandit who fought against the Turks. In the 1880s, the *kleft* Osman Taka was captured by the Ottoman army and sentenced to die. Osman was given one last request before his execution. He asked to dance. His agile expressiveness, his *kefi*—elation—and his graceful movements so impressed his captors that they gave him his freedom.

Here then is another expression of Epirote freedom:

Ah, Samantaka, if I could have your valor,
If only I had your valor; hail to you, Samantaka.
You are asleep, I stay awake,

I think of you and sigh inside.
Wake up, Samantaka, put on your tsarouchia,[13]
Twist your great mustache; hail to you, Samantaka.

೨ ೨ ೨

"You should dance the 'Samantakas'!" said Evi Kita. When Jim and Demetris left me to my own devices in the village square, Evi decided to take me under her wing and teach me some of the dance steps. I regarded Evi, with her dark flowing hair, all-embracing smile, and perfect English, as a friend. Knowing that three bottles of *tsipouro* and five minutes of dance lessons would likely not result in a mastery of the "Samantakas," I still wanted to get within the dance. In this song all the unseen forces of Epirotic music come into play. With this piece, perhaps more than any other, motifs and embellishments such as downward glissando, ostinato, and the weaving of various *maqami* and rhythms are in full bloom.

Alexis Zoumbas's violin recording of "Samantakas" was the most hypnotic piece of music I'd ever heard. A sole test pressing—the only copy known—rested in my room back in Virginia. Inhabiting the same dance tune that Alexis had recorded—and perfected—might help me plumb the mysteries of his music.

To request a song in Epirus requires both that you tip the musicians and that you know how to dance that particular piece. In my altered state I thought that a causal connection *could* exist: laying thirty euros at the feet of the musicians would result in a conveyance of all necessary choreographic skills. This was not the case. But it was also not so bad. Not being synchronized with the dance made me aware of other things going on in the music.

The steps for "Samantakas" are smooth, light—within the line of dancers you simply hold hands and move like clockwork. Pivoting on your left foot, you lift your right foot to the right for two full steps. Resting on your right foot, you swing your left foot directly behind the heel of the right and then lilt the left foot in front of the right foot, your left toe pointed down. You glide to the right and repeat. All of this while holding hands at elbow level with your neighbors.

But the lead dancer—in this case, me—must conjure something akin to levitation. My comportment dissolves, as does the strict uniformity of my steps, since my whole body must express the melody. I raise my right arm and hand above the line of my shoulder while loosely matching the forward movement of my feet to the tapping of the *defi*. Occasionally I release Evi's hand so that I can spin slowly, feeling the music on my face.

I dance around the musicians with gradually increasing abandon.

And then they want to play into me. And I want to be played into.

Most Westerners are distanced from live music by a stage, a row of seats, or a phalanx of bodyguards. "Being played into" is therefore an alien concept. At least those who play acoustic instruments have a semblance, a point of reference, to the phenomenon. For instance, when playing an upright bass, it is easy to feel the vibrations pulsating from the wooden chamber through the thick neck. But "being played into" is different from physically channeling the sounds of the upright bass. Here is what happens.

The skilled clarinetist—in this case Thomas Haliyiannis—has been watching every dancer in the circle as they pass, particularly me, the lead dancer during this song. Then his eyes meet mine. He is reading me. What results is some sort of reciprocal loop, an exchange between his instrument and my psyche.

Thomas departs the circle of musicians and moves toward me with his clarinet hovering close to my head like a snake descending on its prey. A woman next to me has wrapped a cotton towel around her arm and then around my hand. I am now bound to her. The clarinet is at my ear, the bell at the end almost touching me.

There was a sonic barrier between what the musicians were play-

Yiannis Chaldoupis playing into a listener.

ing and the amplified sounds heard by everyone else. I have passed through this threshold. When Thomas plays into my ear, there is no mediation—only tone.

Because we cannot see music, we presume that it is something other than a physical force. We are not aware that sound is a collection of things negotiating with other things in the universe, brushing up against one another. The voice of the clarinet rides the minute dust particles between my ear and the end of the instrument. Sounds ride on the back of unseen things, finding a way in.

Everything unwinds itself and goes white.

I did not pass out—I felt as if I had *passed over*. The dancer behind me cradled my arm wrapped in a white towel as if it were in swaddling cloths. She prevented me from slipping to the hard cobblestones below. I walked from the circle of dancers with the sound of the *aidoni*—the nightingale—faintly echoing in my ears.

I left something behind as I walked away from the music.

Several of my newfound friends from Vitsa congratulated me,

"*Eisai mangas!*"—a warm praise of my bravado. I walked toward their table with something rare, almost fathomable. I needed a drink.

And this was my undoing.

❧❧❧

"The first one you pay for. The rest is on us!" Alexis Papachristos said to me while he vended whiskey, gin, and rum from a small stone building—the *sterna* or cistern—about fifty feet away from the plane tree. With keenly sharpened features and a clean shave, Alexis could pass for a Hollywood actor. But his honesty and unpretentiousness would probably exclude him from the profession. Like many of the people here, he seems incapable of being anything other than forthright. Alexis was also the villager who responded to Maria's inquiry on my behalf for information on Alexis Zoumbas. It turned out that Alexis's uncle, Pavlos, knew the two living nephews of Alexis Zoumbas who lived in the village of Grammeno outside of Ioannina.

And it was Alexis who sold me a large tumbler of American whiskey with the promise that it was a bottomless glass.

Much folk wisdom surrounds *tsipouro*. In Vitsa, for instance, there is a saying: "An illness that is not killed by *tsipouro* is indeed serious." More relevant to my situation, I was told never to mix *tsipouro* with any other liquor, especially whiskey. Perhaps it was the rapture of having danced the "Samantakas," or maybe it was the sum of everything cumulating in this night. Regardless, I have no idea how many times I returned to Alexis for a refill on the bottomless glass.

❧❧❧

"Christ! What did you do to yourself! Jesus!"

There was an angelic haze surrounding Charmagne's face as she looked down at me. The room was flooded in light and the expression on her face occupied that space between fleeing and caring.

She looked holy, like an icon of a patron saint for temporarily crippled Luddites or those emerging from a hyper-auditory trance.

I slowly propped myself up on a stack of pillows like a man waiting to be told a story. Looking down the bed to where Charmagne stood, I saw a crimson outline where my right arm was. Without pause, a red border traced the contours of my right side, waist, leg, and foot. I wasn't wearing my glasses, so the highlighting of my dexter flank appeared to be part of a crime scene: "What remained of the victim was outlined in red chalk before being placed in the morgue, officer."

Glancing upward, Charmagne did not appear so saintly. Perhaps she had done this to me. I dismissed this notion after exhaling. She could easily have smothered me in my infantile state. Being a crafty woman, she would have done the job correctly.

She didn't say much other than "Jesus" and "Christ." It dawned on me that there was very little left to be said. It was all here before me. Reaching for my glasses next to the bed, I found that they weren't there. I mumbled a bit and she answered that they were outside along with the rest of me.

It was still cold, early. This was good, since Jim wanted to leave to meet the Zoumbas brothers before it got too hot. I retraced my steps from the now blood-soaked bed to the latched window opening out to the upper courtyard. There, on the last step before the sill, I found my glasses. The glasses were in three distinct parts: a cracked lens, a temple snapped at the hinge, and an errant lens, uncracked. Most of the toenails from my right foot were also here. Bits of scalp with tufts of hair clung erratically to the stone steps in an ascending pattern leading up to the window sill. This was unsurprising.

Viewed in profile, most of the immediate right side of my body—just the skin really—had been left behind somewhere. I had clotted handsomely while sleeping, but I wasn't in any pain or discomfort. No hangover. I was just at a loss as to where my skin had gone. I had at least accounted for my eyeglasses and toenails. Luckily I had packed my thick black army-issue glasses as a spare.

Standing above the bed linen now with proper vision, I saw that the white sheet could easily have passed as Lazarus's shroud. We placed the sheets in the washer and I wiped up the blood trail leading from the window to the bed. Riley maintained her deep sleep through all of this. I bathed and swabbed myself with rubbing alcohol. Before dressing, I inspected the scar that ran from my right temple to my right toe. I touched it—well, affectionately.

Perhaps there will be apocryphal accounts—folk stories—told after I'm dead and gone, like those before me that danced on the tops of *tsipouro* glasses to the "Samantakas." Years later, a villager recounted how he saw me leave the village square, bouncing like a fleshy pinball along the walls leading down to the Vikos Gorge. The faceted stones along the alley sheared off most of the clothing on my body. At some point I had decided altogether not to walk but to glide like a snake on my right side along the cobblestones until I entered our bedroom window. Those who saw me leave the dance were not worried: the *panegyri* was noisy so it kept the bears away. And they did not see buzzards in the sky the next morning, so they assumed that I had arrived home safely.

5

ZOUMBAS'S LAMENT

Songs are just words. Those who are bitter sing them.
They sing them to get rid of their bitterness,
But the bitterness doesn't go away.

—TRADITIONAL *MIROLOGI* FROM POTAMIA

My grave has grown over with grass,
Come see that you tend to it.
Make sure you cry bitter tears,
And maybe that will bring me back.

—AMALIA VAKA, "TO MNEMA MOU HORTARIASE" ("MY GRAVE IS
OVERGROWN WITH GRASS")

AROUND 2,000 YEARS AGO A LADY DIED IN GREEK-SPEAKING
Asia Minor—what is now Turkey—near the city of Aydin, originally called Tralleis. Her name was Euterpe, and she was married
to Seikilos. Her husband commissioned a *stele*, a stone memorial. Etched in Greek is the following: "I am a tombstone, an
image. Seikilos placed me here as an everlasting sign of deathless
remembrance."

Countless memorials have been unearthed throughout the
ancient Greek world: rural Greece is, after all, a burying ground.
However, this tombstone—referred to as the Seikilos epitaph—
is decidedly unique.* Written on this monument is one of the

---

* Regarding the problems of its interpretation, it is far from unique: like other
artifacts from our past, it has internal aspects that we do not understand, and

world's earliest known *complete* musical compositions with notation:

> *While you live, shine*
> *Have no mourning at all*
> *Life exists a short while*
> *And Time demands its fee.*

Etched alongside the lyrics of this ancient lament is musical script indicating tones and intervals in the Ionian mode, a diatonic scale with a tonic note and a cadence. It is a *mirologi* almost identical to what is sung and played in the mountains of Epirus today.

Around five hundred years earlier on the Aegean island of Samos, Pythagoras was listening closely to the celestial bodies as they cut across the night sky. What acoustic patterns was he able to discern from these infinite points of light?

Most Greek philosophers of antiquity, including Pythagoras, understood the cosmos as a *rational* phenomenon where mathematics, astronomy, and music demonstrated the immutable Good, the coherence of it all. But from the point of view of Greek popular religion, music addresses the *irrational*, the cessation of all good things—Death—through the *mirologi*.

᳘᳘᳘

If Pythagoras could transcribe the musical score of the planets and the heavenly spheres, then what would be the note for a vast asteroid careening toward the Earth? What *is* the sound of the irratio-

---

parts of the larger context that remain unknown. A gap in the dedication line implies that the *stele* was made either for Seikilos's wife or for his mother. The choice of "wife" is more romantic, more moving to me, but this choice should be left to you, to Seikilos, and to eternity. Even though we have a complete piece of music from octave to octave, the actual scale or *dromos* is uncertain, since we cannot determine the precise placement of the middle note in the *dromos*. A half tone higher or lower would change the scalar species.

nal, the cruel, the unexpected event that ends everything? What is Death then, if not this dissonant note that carves out an abyss?

Chill of empty space.

Every death is a cosmic event to those left behind. The order of the universe is fractured. Death creates a psychological paralysis, a fragile vulnerability. How did the Hellenes regard this injury to the soul? Indeed, how should *we* treat the obliteration of life?

When confronted with the loss that death brings, we open up two fathomless emotional reservoirs. One holds the memories of what was: *recollection* of the past. The other contains an amalgamation of expectations of what could have been: *regret* for the present and future. These two wells overflow immediately after a loss. Helplessness emerges: we will never interact with that person again. There are questions never asked, experiences never shared, journeys never made. It is, in sum, the deprivation of all the good things of life.

An abundance of ancient epigrams as well as folk poetry or *mirologia* address these two ceaseless founts of misery: memory and regret. Lamentations were intended to heal the emotional wound created by loss. The singing of *mirologia* and *threnoi* daily over the grave during the protracted mourning period was one way the ancient Greeks treated this injury to the soul.

⁐⁐⁐

Slightly more than seventy years ago, underneath the celestial bodies in the town of Paramythia, Epirus, the cosmos came to an end for 49 innocent villagers. At midnight on September 29, 1943, a group of doctors, teachers, and townspeople were shot in the back of the head seconds before they fell into the collective grave that they themselves had dug. Elements of the Nazi German First Mountain Division—the notorious *Edelweiss*—along with a militia of Chams—Greek-speaking Albanians who had lived relatively peacefully among the Epirote Greeks for centuries—chose to obey the orders from Berlin, to make an example.

Paramythia was prosperous, but the town's wealth came from hard-working merchants, not nepotism, legacy, or imperial conquest. Germany and its allies desired to expand and control more territory, including all of Greece. Here, in Paramythia, the territorial imperative of the Germans became a reflex—murder. Forty-nine were selected for slaughter.

Birds of this Earth, the earth of Paramythia,
Fly high, birds, to watch, sons, old men, and children,
Girls and mothers—ay—and tell them
To come forth, son, dressed all in black,
Lament the forty-nine innocents who died blameless.
They lie at Karkamitsi—ay—the ill-fated bodies lie there,
Into the pit they dug with their own hands.
Weep, birds, weep nightingales, for their poor souls.

Recorded on January 5, 1957, this *mirologi* was sung by Stephanos Paschalis and accompanied by Demetris Batzis. Besides the melancholia expressed by Paschalis's singing, we also hear the blending of vocal and instrumental *mirologia*, a sound almost completely unique to Epirus. This is the other side of how Greeks—ancient and contemporary—treat mourning via music: the sparse, emotive use of instruments, oftentimes stripped bare of any voice, appearing as naked, pure tone.

In the second century AD, the writer Sextus Empiricus offered a tantalizing hint bridging the ancient and the modern. In his *Against the Musicians* he says that music is "also a consolation to those who are grief-stricken; for this reason, the *auloi* playing a melody for those who are mourning are the lighteners of their grief." This use of an *aulos*—the ancient Greek double flute—anticipates the instrumentals played on clarinet and violin in Epirus in the twenty-first century. Among Epirotes, the playing of a *mirologi* over the grave by a favorite clarinetist of the deceased is both acceptable and traditional. The musicians are paid *before* the individual's death, by the soon-to-be-deceased, promising to deliver this music for the departed as well as for the family during the mourning period.

Imagine a string of tones—in this case a distinct pattern of five pitches—carefully shaped and crafted to contain transformative powers or curative qualities.

This series of five pitches—the pentatonic scale that in the United States forms the basis of the blues scale—is actually not so limited. A violin, a clarinet, a guitar can express four octaves quite easily. Within these four-octave spans, there are almost endless permutations. Each one of these arrangements can contain subtle flourishes—elision, vibrato, ostinato, glissando—and each variation can express tension, release, or suspension. What appears on the outside as a limited musical vocabulary can contain within itself the infinite elements needed to tell a nuanced story.

Similarly, five words, combined with punctuation and emphasis, form the poetic power of the vocalized *mirologia*. For instance, take the following words: "oh," "where," "have," "you," "gone." Since syntax is fluid and semantic value changes with punctuation and emphasis, each variation offers different context and meaning. Think of these words arranged metrically and then improvised in song over a fresh grave:

Oh, where have you gone?
Have you gone? Oh! Where?
You have gone where? Oh!
Where, oh, have you gone?

Each verse concludes in a single melismatic plea for the dead and for the living: "I long, I remember, I regret, I must go on."

Mirologia—either as songs, as instrumentals, or as combinations of the two—placate human loss. They reorganize the psyche through some inexplicable alchemy of sound and sinew. For the individual, these pieces of music confront a basic necessity, and for humanity, they answer a fundamental need to mourn and to heal.

These laments are strong medicine. And like all purgatives, they can have unpredictable consequences and side effects.

The first time I played a recording of "Epirotiko Mirologi"— "Lament from Epirus"—by Alexis Zoumbas, a dark vastness opened. When the needle dropped into the groove, I perceived an unwinding in myself: an exploration of private, internal space. I felt as if I was witnessing an agonizing crucifixion but was unsure of the victim. Was it myself, humanity, Zoumbas? The sorrowful variations of these five notes tapped into a place within me that I did not know I had. They opened up in me longing, remembrance, and regret. It was some elevated state of *having the blues* with which I had no prior experience.

It was then that I realized that Zoumbas's *mirologi* was the sound of a looming asteroid right before it smacks into Earth, ending all life and hope. *Here* was the echoing sound of the irrational and the cruel.

Sₒ Sₒ Sₒ

On September 20, 1926, a short, doughy, and impeccably dressed Alexis Zoumbas ambled into the recording studios of Victor Records and Phonograph, located on 28 West 44th Street in New York. The director of the session—possibly the one responsible for arranging the recording—was Leroy Shield, legendary bandleader and composer of the music for all the Hal Roach shorts including the *Little Rascals* and those featuring Laurel and Hardy. Zoumbas shook his hand as he stared down at Shield's polished patent-leather two-tone wingtips.

Tucked under Alexis's left arm was a weathered yet sturdy Lifton leather case containing a violin made by the Homenick Brothers— or, in the standardized Ukrainian-to-English transliteration, Humeniuk. Zoumbas's coal-black hair was flecked white along the

R. Crumb portrait of Alexis Zoumbas.

temples. Ample jowls terminated their journey when they converged within the flat, thin recess of his lips. His mouth was fixed in such a way as to suggest that there was nothing meaningful upon which to comment.

If we could read faces as we read maps, we might see in the portrait of Alexis Zoumbas the topographical expression on his visage as an overlay, a shared border with two distinct regions: an uncompromising confidence in his own skills and a calm, assured disdain for the efforts of others. As Robert Crumb told me in a letter upon finishing the portrait, made from the only known photograph, "In the process of drawing him and having to look closely at the photo for several hours, I have changed my mind about Mr. Zoumbas. Close scrutiny of his face gradually revealed a sinister, dark side of his character, capable, perhaps, of *ANYTHING*."

Zoumbas was, at the very least, a man incapable of questioning his own expressive power. I like to think that he assured himself that he was the best, therefore he deserved the best: the best clothing, the best violin, possibly the best women. Yet he had to acknowledge that the finest suits that he could scarcely afford would not hide his walnut-brown skin—the skin of a Roma— and the finest violin would not cover up his thick northwestern Greek accent when he spoke. A careful look at his face disclosed that he knew one axiomatic truth: self-doubt was the real killer. With this notion constantly in his mind, he brushed all secondary thoughts aside.

Alexis also had a slightly drifting and dropsied right eye, an anomaly common with the Roma of Epirus. This marked him as spiritual kin with the poor blind black musicians of the American South. Until World War II, the most popular of rural Negro music makers came ready-made with a prefixed moniker indicating loss of the visual dimension: Blind Joe Reynolds, Blind Blake, Blind Lemon Jefferson, Blind Willie McTell—"blind" *ad nauseam.*

Being blind and black in the American South and poor and Roma in northwestern Greece during the early part of the twentieth century opened very few doors. Both groups sought one of the more lucrative occupations open to them: that of professional musician.

Perhaps this is one reason why their recorded legacy is so exceptional. Given few choices in life, they chose to perfect their craft such that they were indispensable to the community. They did not half-ass anything.

In return for their efforts, musicians such as these would be subject to an almost mystical reverence and zeal by those who listened to them. They would also receive compensation as long as they could play: healthy tips, food, lodging, and possibly train fare to etch their recordings onto disc. And—this is cold comfort—they would be immortalized, remembered forever by those who coveted their records and lauded their performances.

Alexis was led to a small room trimmed in oak. Thick brown tapestries were angled in the corners so that in every direction Zoumbas saw draped envelopes of wool. He stepped forward onto a richly piled rug that ran from edge to edge of the room. Soft right angles formed where the rug met the wooden wainscoting. To his right was a vintage *santouri*—a hammered chordophone popular in the hash dens and cafes of Athens and Piraeus but rare in Epirus. An oak school chair was placed behind it. To the left was a stool that leveraged the heft of a gigantic bowed contrabass, another instrument that would have been alien to the music in northwestern Greece. Between these two elements, suspended from the ceiling, was a shimmering chrome case: an early prototype of the first RCA electric microphone. A thin, fragile metallic ribbon encased within the porous chrome box was itself suspended—caught—in the center of a metal circle by eight long, taut springs. The device appeared to be trapped in a futuristic spider web, one that could not decide if it was in the style of *art deco* or *art nouveau*.

I imagined Mr. Shield clapping his hands together, producing a sharp crack with no lingering echo. "Perfect acoustics, just as I said. The best!" Whatever mechanism existing within Zoumbas that registered courtesy responded with a drifting nod of approval to Shield's shoes. He knew that if he had stayed behind in Greece, the studios in Athens would have been inferior, unworthy of his skill.

An hour after walking into this room with Shield, Zoumbas recorded the first three of four traditional instrumentals from Epirus. "Alimbeis" ("Chief Ali"), "Tsamiko Makedonias" ("Macedonian Tsamiko"), and "Liaskovitikos" ("Dance from Liaskovo") were dances lightly accompanied by *santouri* and contrabass. After finishing these three pieces, the *santouri* player—an undocumented phantom—left the studio.

When the light flashed green three times, the first four notes of

"Epirotiko Mirologi" vibrated from Zoumbas's violin. For exactly four minutes and sixteen seconds, Alexis played an ancient instrumental lament in the key of D, primarily in the major pentatonic scale but with three passages in the minor pentatonic on a keynote lasting no more than ten seconds per section. It was only during these three brief phrases that the bowed contrabass—the musician unlisted within the Victor ledger sheet from that day—played the low D note, eliding to the low G note, creating the eternal tension and internal magic heard in Epirotic music. He never lifted the bow from the strings. As his violin fluttered, wept, ascended, levitated, and cried like a wounded bird, the constantly droning D acted as a dark tonal anchor. There was no beat, no rhythm, no time signature. Everything was holding together and falling apart at every instant.

A discerning listener from Epirus who heard this record would likely mention that the profound sadness of this piece has no *closure*, no resolution, quite different from what one would hear at a *panegyri*.* It sounds dismal, aching, and wounded precisely because it was being played thousands of miles away from Epirus, a place that—in 1926—Zoumbas did not know he would ever see again. *Xenitia*—the longing for one's home soil and the reciprocal yearning of the people of the village for the exiled person to come home—infuses this piece of music like no other.

Alexis's recording of "Epirotiko Mirologi," although thoroughly traditional, had transcended whatever restraints had been imposed on the form for thousands of years. The distinct species of anguish—of *xenitia*—translated into this performance by Zoumbas made it *sui generis*: an apogee of expression, peerless.

---

* The listener might also mention that besides the presence of contrabass (which would never have been heard at a *panegyri*), there is something "off" with the tone. This would be correct. Zoumbas chose to play in the key of D when most *mirologia* are played in the key of G on the violin. He must have had his reasons, lost as they are to us today.

And this music was sourced from the deepest spiritual place. Every person that I've ever played this 78 for has acknowledged this. From the moment I heard the record until the moment that I write these words, I've wondered what turmoil Zoumbas was experiencing; what was he thinking and feeling as he played? What was the emotional landscape that surrounded and created this particular *mirologi*?

Milan Kundera offers the closest approximation to an answer. A word exists singularly in the Czech language: he was in the depths of *litost*. "As for the meaning of the word, I have looked in vain in other languages for an equivalent, though I find it difficult to imagine how anyone can understand the human soul without it." The closest definition offered by Kundera is "a state of agony and torment created by the sudden realization of one's own misery."

Zoumbas was not alone in this visceral reflection of his own misery and torment. He was not alone in the blues.

> ᕼᕼᕼ

On December 3, 1927, less than one year after Alexis recorded for Victor, Willie Johnson was led into a similar—albeit more improvised—studio in Dallas, Texas. Blind Willie Johnson was a different kind of a man: younger and leaner but just as spiritually expressive as Zoumbas. Just as Zoumbas had the skin of a Roma, Johnson had the skin of a Negro, the child of the first generation of freed slaves. Born in Pendleton, Texas in January of 1897, he was raised within the confines of a region struggling with the devastation of the recent Civil War. In this period, parts of the southern United States were not unlike the environment of Epirus that emerged after World War II and the Greek Civil War. Oppression and violence against the marginalized—sometimes out of sheer spite and jealousy—were cruel, everyday occurrences, part of the life cycle.

Zoumbas had been born with a slight compromise to his vision. According to Johnson's widow, Willie's stepmother blinded him when she threw acid in his face after his own mother had died. Little reason was given except that it was done out of spite and jealousy.

When Frank Walker, the executive who supervised regional recordings for Columbia Records, met the blind musician at the makeshift studio in Dallas's North Lamar Street, he had no idea that this session with Willie Johnson would produce one of the most profound pieces of American folk music ever captured. Likewise, Walker would have been stunned to learn that a recording made by Blind Willie Johnson that day was the spiritual twin of the recording made a year earlier in New York by Zoumbas, itself a lament developed thousands of miles across the Atlantic, countless millennia in our past.

Like Zoumbas, Johnson waited till almost the end of his session to play his masterpiece. With his guitar tuned carefully to open D (D–A–D–F♯–A–D), Johnson began sliding a glass bottleneck across the strings, playing a piece he called "Dark Was the Night, Cold Was the Ground." Although the title is based on the first line of a Wesleyan hymn, "Gethsemane," penned by Thomas Haweis in the nineteenth century, there is very little melodic similarity with the English religious song. Indeed, what Johnson played for exactly three minutes and thirty seconds was a lament barely of this Earth.

Played in the key of D, this piece follows the major pentatonic scale yet moves into the minor pentatonic in the same key. An open note—the low bass D—acts as a dark, tonal center. It floats freely with no beat, no rhythm, no meter. Everything is holding together and falling apart at every instant. Occasional phrases in G pull the scale gently from the major to the minor pentatonic. There are moans and sighs that parallel the guitar phrases, caressing the notes, but there are no coherent vocal phrases: only suggestions of wordless agony.

As the bottleneck wisps along the strings, repeated patterns and motifs, like the sounds of weeping and mourning, emerge from his guitar. A languid vibrato punctuates almost every phrase and the passages themselves are repeated insistently. There is a transcendent economy to the recording. Every note and every space without a note is intentional: nothing is wasted. When the red light flashed three times to signal the approach of the dead wax—the end of the groove—someone, likely Walker himself, tapped Blind Willie Johnson softly on the shoulder to conclude his playing.

Those who hear this recording have a predictably visceral reaction. Most will identify the music as "the blues," but question the significance of the title, *Dark Was the Night, Cold Was the Ground*. Undoubtedly, it is *the blues*, insofar as the modal pentatonic structure has defined the genre. But it is also a species of music that came *before* the blues. This type of modal music was a transition, a liminal stage of development before the blues became a predictable trope of commercial success rather than the earlier form of profound expression. It, like the *mirologi*, is ageless, eternal.

Skip James, a Mississippi musician recorded in 1930, could have spoken to the depth of these two pieces of music by Johnson and Zoumbas. His dark misanthropic musings, a stark view of humanity, were brilliantly captured by Stephen Calt in his book, *I'd Rather Be the Devil*. Though James was a *bluesman*, he regarded his own music as something different—*higher*—than the music of those other musicians esteemed as his peers by collectors and scholars. His music was meant to "deaden the mind," to move the thoughts, to bring the listeners into another place.

James's songs, according to Calt, had an ability to "assault the senses. He [James] conceived of blues as having the mesmeric effect of spirituals. Instead of uplifting listeners, it would stun them."

If Johnson and Zoumbas's pieces were played to James, he would likely agree that their music was like his: transfixing, arresting the thoughts of the listener. This deadening, this stunning of the mind is the commonality between the *mirologi* and the blues. Or, as Jim Potts puts it best, Epirotic music is "deeper than the deepest blues." And you can't get much deeper than these two recordings.

The title Johnson chose is itself poetically suggestive. Perhaps what moved Johnson to craft this piece of music was the underlying theme of the hymn itself: suffering, longing, and a *return to home*:

> *Dark was the night, and cold the ground*
> *On which the Lord was laid;*
> *His sweat like drops of blood, ran down;*
> *In agony He prayed:*
> *Father, remove this bitter cup,*
> *If such Thy sacred will;*
> *If not, content to drink it up,*
> *Thy pleasure I fulfill.*

"Gethsemane," the original title of the hymn, refers to the garden where Jesus and his disciples slept before his crucifixion. This was where He agonized, remembered, and mourned. Death was waiting the next day. Although Christ wished to stay with His disciples, he also longed to return to His Father, leaving behind this cruel physical world. And His Father longed for him to return home.

Xenitia.

※ ※ ※

Gazing up at the Indian summer sky when I was fifteen, all I could see was the thick pillar of black smoke curling from the sharecropper shack that my grandfather had minutes earlier lit with a match. The crackle of flames was deafening. If the hundreds of hornets dying at that second produced a sound, it was obscured by the incineration of their home. It was as if an asteroid had wiped out their planet.

Next to me on the ground was the box of 78s that I had saved. Contained within—likely not played since the early 1930s—was a copy of *Dark Was the Night, Cold Was the Ground*. With hindsight, the contents in this box had an unfathomable aura and power: a musical aperture to the past teeming with dark energy.

In 1986, while the smoke rose from this insignificant farm in the Highlands of Virginia—less than a speck on the planet—Voyager 1 was traveling toward the edge of our galaxy. Just as I was clueless what was contained in this box at my feet, I also was ignorant of what was within this space probe launched in 1977. Conceived as a device to explore the realm of the celestial bodies, it was also designed as a cultural offering, a time capsule of sorts. Voyager 1 was blasted into outer space as a "calling card" for any intelligent life that might exist outside of the Earth. In retrospect, the information contained on the probe could be imagined as a pathetic profile page for intergalactic social media:

> *Here are some things about us.*
> *We number in the billions (and growing!).*
> *Some of us are single . . . :)*
> *We use language, art, and music to express ourselves.*
> *We teach. We listen. Sometimes we put out records.*

What I imagined as an introduction from Earth to unknown intelligent life was engraved on a gold-plated disc. Housed within the interstellar explorer, this Golden Disc contains a variety of languages, images, and music created on Earth. The purpose of the disc is to convey to alien beings that there is a diversity of culture and landscape here. Carl Sagan and his group of scholars were tasked with selecting the contents. They believed, rightly, that an essential part of our collective psyche was our ability to articulate feelings through music. A combination of emotional and psychological states—longing, remembrance, and regret—appeared to them to be contained within one song: "Dark Was the Night, Cold Was the Ground." Therefore this recording from 1927 is among those pieces of music meant to communicate something vital about humanity to beings that may exist outside of our solar system.

With synchronicities and commonalities so perfectly mappable and mirrored between Blind Willie Johnson's masterpiece and Zoumbas's *mirologi*, one could easily replace one recording with the other.

In 2012 it was thought that Voyager 1 left our solar system and was now entering interstellar space. It will be another 40,000 years before the probe approaches a star within another solar system. During that time, perhaps a cold, angular rock will careen into our planet and tear everything asunder.

There would then be an unintended consequence of the space probe and those who forethought its purpose. It would not contain evidence of biodiversity and culture on Earth but rather the sad trappings of what once was. It would contain *recollection*: an everlasting sign of deathless remembrance.

Maybe the aliens who retrieve the probe will be able to comprehend the larger context of the device—its internal workings as well as its source and larger purpose—and eventually play back the Golden Disc. Then they could ask what the function was for this piece of music, what was being expressed by "Dark Was the Night, Cold Was the Ground," and if this now extinct form of life had produced anything else like it.

But all artifacts left on the broken husk of Earth—including the monoliths and the curious black discs of Alexis Zoumbas and Blind Willie Johnson—would be rendered useless. Without a listener, what would be the function?

Chill of empty space.

"Vaka! Vaka! That *turkala** woman did it!"

An informal accusation of murder is how I remembered my first meeting with the Zoumbas brothers at Grammeno. In this village, music intersected with death, the two phenomena forming a crossroads.

Maria Potts invested much time and hassle on the phone, first with Maria Zoumbas—the wife of one of Alexis's nephews, Michalis, and then with the Zoumbas brothers themselves. During the conversation a goat broke into Napoleon's grape arbors and the call had to be aborted. Eventually Maria made arrangements for us to meet the brothers at the main *taverna* in Grammeno.

To the west of Ioannina and south of Vitsa, the village of Grammeno appeared on the edge of extinction, despondent, as if it were waiting for a call from the doctor with some *very* bad news. I watched for tumbleweeds to drift across the path of Jim's car. Along the approach to the village center, weather had eroded the facades of buildings to crumbling veneers. Everything was surrendering to the black soil.

After parking the car, Jim, Charmagne, Riley, and I tried to distinguish what was the main *taverna*. It was Charmagne who saw a tall wisp of man from across the desolate expanse. Although my scars had healed miraculously, the August heat at midday was now attempting to kill me. There is, after all, a good reason for the traditional *siesta* in the Mediterranean: it is to prevent Neanderthals like myself from perishing.

---

* In contemporary usage, *turkala* implies either a Turkish woman or—more broadly—a woman who may have converted to Islam. But in the memory of the oldest villagers, who live in Zoumbas's time, *turkala* carries with it the negative connotation of otherness, the status of an outsider: the subtle distinction of being among Greeks but excluded from their approval or acceptance. This term is in the same historical family as *tourkopouli*, the word used for the white stork that used to thrive around Lake Ioannina.

Under the shade of an awning stood Michalis Zoumbas alongside an equally tall and wizened villager. Forgetting my manners, I quickly rushed inside to purchase several bottles of water. Greedily guzzling one as I exited, I saw that Jim was already conversing with Michalis.

After Jim introduced us, I asked him if he could translate some questions. The combination of dehydration and the early stages of brain fever drove my curiosity. Before I expired, I wanted to know what had happened to Alexis. Did they know? Jim posed the question.

That was when the wizened villager next to Michalis started stabbing at the air in front of him, gesturing with his hand the universal "pistol finger" and exclaiming that a woman, Vaka, had done this, had done him in. A pantomimed offing of a musician of northwestern Greece by a *femme fatale*. It suggested to me the tales of black songsters of the American South murdered by angry women.

My eyes drifted left to Napoleon Zoumbas as he slowly appeared from the shadows. Shorter than Michalis, he had an instant smile that exposed a single gleaming gold tooth nestled among the pearly whites. Michalis wore cat eyeglasses above a neatly trimmed mustache. They were both thin and taut, like a violin bow at peak tension. Although they were in their eighties, they showed a vitality often lacking in men half their age. Perhaps their lifelong engagement with music from this region explained their health and longevity? Napoleon was a celebrated *klarino* in Ioannina, and Michalis was a gifted *laouto* player who had resided for a brief period in Cleveland, Ohio, a place he admitted was abysmal and not suitable for living.

Before we walked to Michalis's home, the Zoumbas brothers insisted on paying for a round of Greek coffees, a stimulant that I sorely needed. They shared American cigarettes with us and gave Riley a deck of cards.

After a deep drag from a smoke, I casually asked Michalis and

Napoleon if they had heard that Alexis was involved in a murder. They looked at me and then at each other with a mirrored expression of vacant puzzlement. The brothers could have been twin heads strung from the same bobbin. Simultaneously they said, "That was a very long time ago."

During this exchange, the wizened villager that had greeted us with Michalis disappeared. He remains unknown, lost to the ages. Despite yearly visits to the brothers and several inquiries, the name and very existence of the man so familiar with Alexis's fate is a mystery.

⁂

The two houses where Michalis and Napoleon live sit on the same plot of land where Alexis was born. All that remains of Alexis's home is part of a foundation jutting up from the dry soil that separates the two patios where tomatoes grow beneath the grape arbors. Michalis's house was spotlessness. Maria, Michalis's wife, had been ruthlessly cleaning the house for decades prior to our visit: a home must always be clean, as guests may arrive unannounced. Maria brought *glyko*—spoon sweets made of fruit such as quince, boiled and preserved in sugar water—to the living room. There I set up my recording equipment and, through Jim's expert Greek, asked questions about their uncle, their family, and their village life.

To be clear, neither Michalis nor Napoleon had ever met Alexis. They would have been infants when he last set foot in Epirus. Photos and letters from Alexis were stolen along with the family *laouto* when Michalis lived overseas in Cleveland. Christ, they had even grabbed his new black-and-white television.

There are two stories—two lives—Zoumbas lived. One is largely mythological, a folk perspective. The other is less romantic, a narrative based on documents such as ship manifests, draft cards, census, naturalization, and death certificates. But they inform one another, converging and folding into something that is an approximation of truth.

〜〜〜

The first story—the folk perspective—is slim, suggestive, and loosely stitched together from discographies, oral anecdotes, and a curious biographical sketch contained in a provincial memoir from Grammeno. Alexis Michalis Zoumbas, familiarly referred to as Letsios, came into the world in 1880 and took up the violin in his youth. In 1913, when Ioannina was liberated from general Turkish rule, he and another villager from Grammeno bound rocks to the side of their porcine *turko** landlord, Yoakoub, and threw him down a chasm to his death.

Murder owns an exclusive spectrum, from grim to horrific. This act by a young Letsios was horrific but, within the context of the time, somewhat patriotic. Even the *New York Times* echoed the nationalistic fervor of the time:

> Athens—March 6, 1913—The happy issue of the campaign in Epirus by the capture of Janina [Ioannina] has caused immense enthusiasm in Athens. In military circles the fall of Janina is considered as much more important than the campaign in Macedonia, for Janina is a fortified city in which the main body of the Turkish army was concentrated behind formidable fortifications. From a political point of view, the taking of the city is looked upon as an event that will carry the greatest weight in upholding Greece's claim to Epirus. Athens today [March 6th] is bedecked in bunting and crowds are parading in the streets.

According to this story, the next year, 1914, Alexis fled Ioannina to America, where he recorded and lived in symbiosis—a beautiful word if there ever was one—with his music. Here the biographical sketch ends abruptly, as if Zoumbas were swallowed up by the same dark passage into which he threw his landlord.

---

* The male equivalent of *turkala*.

While living in New York—it is said—he had taken up with a young *tourkala* singer named Amalia Vaka,* also from Ioannina, who performed and recorded Turkish and Greek pieces and with whom he sired two daughters. As these stories go, at the end of the Second Great War Zoumbas wanted to return to Greece. Vaka prevented his departure by shooting him twice, hastening his visit from Charon.

Those who have studied obsessively the confessions of prewar musicians from the Delta, or the third-person narratives thereof, can admit in hindsight that almost everything gleaned from these accounts of their lives seems fabricated, contrived, or embellished to such a degree that while it should be believed, indeed could be believed, it is ultimately far from the truth.

A litany of examples exist on my record shelf. Charlie Patton—according to one apocryphal tale—met his end at the hand of his knife-wielding common-law wife. Son House, Skip James, and the southern banjoist Dock Boggs created rows of corpses, stacked like phantom cordwood. These musicians recounted how they killed out of vengeance, self-defense, or cool indifference. But most of these stories are fabrications created by the musicians or by others to fill the space they left behind. These larger-than-life artists were replaced with a mere literary device when the majesty of their recordings should have been enough. The mythology of musicians from the hill country of Mississippi mirrors that of the musicians living on the outskirts of Ioannina.

🙵 🙵 🙵

But here is what happened to Alexis, according to the paper trail. Born on September 29, 1883, in Grammeno, Alexis had two brothers, Kostas and Stephanos, and three sisters, Theodora, Vasiliki, and Harikleia. Though all of the brothers played music well, Alexis

---

* Although her anglicized name on record labels and catalogs appears as *Bakas*, the Greek spelling of her name, Βάκα, is pronounced "Vaka."

showed a particular fixation and drive to play the violin, traveling by foot north to Gjirokastër and Pogoni (a historic region of
Epirus that now stretches on either side of the Greek-Albanian
border). This was where Alexis's father was born and where he
fled after a predictable blood feud erupted. Kostas and Stephanos
became a coppersmith and a cobbler, respectively, but Alexis only
wanted to fiddle.

At the turn of the twentieth century, Alexis had established himself as one of the leading violinists in Ioannina, and also as a *ban-
tidhos*, a poor young man with no visible source of income but with
money to spend at the drop of a hat. His main source of pay came
from playing *panegyria*, weddings, and other social events. This
was hardly enough money to sustain him, his wife Marina, and
their two infant daughters, Christina and Anna. Early one morning in 1910, Alexis boarded a ship to the nearest island, Kerkyra,
playing violin with the local band. He had left his family, and his
home, sailing to America.

A naturalized U.S. citizen by the end of 1910, Alexis played in
the Greek and "Oriental" clubs and restaurants of Manhattan,
sending his money home and longing for fine homemade *tsipouro*.
During this time his life became intertwined with three influential
women, Marika Papagika, Coula Antonopoulos, and Amalia Vaka,
all of whom were singers of Greek *rembetic* and *demotic* songs and
Turkish and Asia Minor folk melodies.

Zoumbas initially recorded in New York for Antonopoulos's
label, Panhellenion, the first independent American label to specialize in Greek music. He also played violin on dozens of performances with Papagika, and accompany Vaka on perhaps sixteen
sides. Coula herself would record for Columbia some time in 1916
or 1917 before starting her own label in 1919. Papagika would etch
her voice on shellac in 1918, and Vaka in 1923. Vaka had immigrated
two years after Alexis, in 1912. Worthy of note: wherever Zoumbas
moved, Vaka would soon be found.

It is doubtful that Zoumbas recorded elsewhere before his four traditional violin pieces were issued by Coula's Panhellenion label in the early 1920s. Acoustically captured and poorly pressed, these four sides do not convey the full command that Alexis would display on his solo recordings later in 1926. In my mind, perhaps even at forty years of age Zoumbas's playing had not matured fully. He had not moved beyond the limitations imposed by the social aspect of his traditional repertoire. The introspective alchemy—his vulnerability and sensitivity combined with the curative qualities of Epirotic music—would emerge in 1926. His bow would transcend, but only after he experienced the anguish of *xenitia*.

By the mid-1920s, Zoumbas might have realized that he would never return to his home soil and so his bow took on that expression of fate, that pathos of longing. Perhaps he even foresaw what sadness was contained within this acceptance. Although his musical skills would have impressed classically trained violinists of Europe, his technique by 1926 was not cerebral, but almost wholly visceral.

From September 1926 to August 1927, Alexis recorded only eight solo sides, including "Epirotiko Mirologi." During this time he also accompanied Papagika and Vaka on several performances. However, in the span of a month, from January to February of 1928, he recorded no fewer than sixteen intense violin pieces, and added his violin to another sixteen sides cut for Papagika and Vaka. This increased recording activity may have served to provide an adequate dowry for his daughter, Christina. Dowries at this time were expected, if not required, particularly for a man like Alexis who had made a name for himself in America. On the streets of Ioannina and Athens, his 78 rpm discs were displayed and quickly bought.

After these February sessions, Alexis did what few poor Greek immigrants would do before World War II: he traveled back to Greece for a visit. There he attended the wedding of his daughter Christina to Tasos Halkias, the prolific Epirote clarinetist, a friend from an early age with Stephanos Zoumbas, Alexis's brother. Like Stephanos, Tasos was a cobbler and musician in an area called Aghios Spyridon, on the poorer outskirts of Ioannina. Like the Zoumbas brothers, Tasos was a Roma. One of Tasos's sisters would later marry Spyros Zoumbas, Alexis's nephew.

Alexis returned to New York City in July of 1928. It was not until 1930, though, that he recorded four more sides, his next to last session, for another Greek-owned label, Greek National. By the early to mid-1930s a combination of the Great Depression, creeping urban blandness, and the imperative of cultural assimilation had largely killed rural ethnic music in the United States, and the outbreak of World War II stopped most studio recording altogether.

In the early spring of 1941 the European Axis powers invaded Greece. Alexis's son-in-law, Tasos, joined the Greek army and was wounded in battle. He was at the General Hospital of Ioannina when the aerial assault of the town took place. Christina would have heard the terrifying shrieks of the dive-bombers seconds before the explosions killed her and her two sons, Alexis's grandchildren. Marina, Alexis's wife, had been killed earlier in an air raid. The fate of Anna, Zoumbas's other daughter, is unknown. News would have arrived in nondescript Red Cross letters addressed to the apartment in New York that he shared with three other Greek men.

Alexis moved to Chicago to play violin at Peter Houseas's Oriental Cafe on Halsted Street by the end of 1941. At fifty-eight years of age he had been issued a draft card in case the fascists decided to invade the already rusting Midwest and occupy Cook County.

Amalia Vaka and her daughter had moved to Chicago in 1940 to play the Pantheon, a nightclub near Halsted Street. Following the "Feta Circuit," Vaka and Zoumbas appeared in Philadelphia, Detroit, and Gary, Indiana.

By 1943, Zoumbas had settled in the absolutely cheapest flophouse in Detroit. As I would find out some time after my first meeting with the Zoumbas brothers, this same year Alexis cut one last record. He likely never held it in his hands, since shellac was rationed until late 1945, after the war was over.

Alexis, listed as a "musician" on his draft card at this time, reacted much as I would have if sentenced to live in the suburban Midwest. Late in January of 1946 Zoumbas fell ill. He died on February 7, 1946, from a respiratory infection. He was sixty-three years of age.

Zoumbas passed, not swallowed up by the Void along with Yoakoub, nor felled by a series of bullets from his *tourkala* common-law wife, but rather cut down by the pedestrian machinations of viral pneumonia.

He is buried in a potter's grave abutting Van Dyke Avenue in a crumbling part of Detroit. Referred to as "Section 31," this plot of land is reserved for those who could not afford to be properly interred: the indigent and the unknown. This section of the graveyard is strictly delineated from the area holding the "paying customers." Here, six feet of earth does *not* make us all of one size.

The marker for his grave, #396, is underneath three inches of sod and weeds. A white spruce grows from his grave, the same species of spruce that would have been used to fashion the top of his violin. His grave is grown over with grass. No one sang bitter tears here.

⌒⌒⌒

Napoleon's and Michalis's faces radiated a timeless bliss when I asked them what they thought of their uncle and of the music of their region. Though Zoumbas's name would scarcely elicit a raised eyebrow in America, the musicians in Epirus esteem him as highly as blues guitarists in the United States regard Robert Johnson or Charlie Patton. They were proud of their uncle and equally proud of the music produced by their family.

When reconstructing a life story, sometimes it is not the depth or width that matters—it is the distance, seeing some speck over the horizon and connecting it with points fixed in the present. I couldn't see clearly at first, blinded as I was by the contrast between the vastness of Epirus where Zoumbas had once lived with the banality of the American Midwest where he died. Because I had no perspective, I saw only the dead, Alexis, and not the living, those he left behind—the Zoumbas brothers.

When I thoughtlessly concluded my interview and turned off my recorder, Michalis and Napoleon asked simply, "Are you done? What about us?" In my nearsighted haste, I had forgotten that they were not merely family, informants, but musicians who sustained the continuity of tradition here. Their lives, their pain, their music was just as valid as that of Alexis.

Embarrassed, as if I had just been smacked red-assed by some omnipresent Being, I quickly turned the recording equipment back on. For a half hour we relaxed as they recounted *their* past, *their* opinions on the music, *their* concerns. They were not specters of my imagination like Alexis. Every time I see Michalis and Napoleon— every visit to Epirus—our conversations move farther from Alexis and more toward them, their memory. We travel closer to the present and further from the phantoms I carry with me.

Before we left from this first visit, Michalis and Maria insisted upon pouring us a cool, thin ribbon of *tsipouro* and serving us a *meze* of fresh goat cheese with tomatoes fetched from the garden fifteen seconds earlier. It was difficult to leave. When I shook their arms, I knew that they had the vitality and creativity, the lifeblood of Epirus, coursing through their veins. The Zoumbas brothers were not merely larger than life: they were life itself.

❧❧❧

Riley skipped and sang along the slick cobblestones that formed the alleys meandering through the old Jewish neighborhood outside the castle walls of Ioannina. Her voice and footsteps echoed off the muted yellow and orange walls of the houses that tightly abutted the narrow passages. The scent of freshly planted basil— refreshed by the sudden rainburst moments ago—mingled with the smoke from the restaurant grills along Lake Pamvotida. Verdant ivy climbed the walls of the houses and the cold ironwork encasing each window at eye level. Jim suggested that we walk through this neighborhood on our way to eat some lunch after we left Grammeno.

This area of Ioannina could have been contained in Bruno Schulz's impressionistic short story "Street of Crocodiles." The ardent, dreamlike scenes that Schulz drew of his small Polish (now Ukraine) town of Drohobycz mirrored the neighborhood where we now strolled, except that Schulz's neighbors were Polish Roman Catholic and Vaka's were Greek Orthodox. Like Bruno Schulz, Amalia Vaka—Alexis Zoumbas's love interest—was a Jew. Vaka would have skipped and sung along these wet cobblestones smelling of basil one hundred years ago. Now, the Jewish populations of Drohobycz and Ioannina are miniscule.

Schulz and Vaka were different types of Jews. Schulz was, like most European Jews, Ashkenazi. The Ashkenazim were part of the exodus from the Middle East that migrated north, living variously in Germanic lands, Russia, Poland, and other areas, moving in response to oppressive conditions. When not speaking German, Polish, Russian, or some other language of their surroundings, the Ashkenazim spoke Yiddish, a German dialect. Another Jewish lineage, Sephardim, are Jews who were expelled from Spain after 1492. The tongue they shared among themselves was Ladino, a derivative of Spanish. Many Sephardic Jews settled in Thessaloniki—the largest port city in northeastern Greece—making it the "Jerusalem of the Balkans."

Vaka belonged to a third branch, a distinct and ancient community of Jews. She was a Hellenized Jew, a Greek-speaking Romaniote. And the robust center of Romaniote culture was Ioannina.

Hellenized Jews traversed mainland Greece nearly three hundred years before Christian converts landed on its shore. They were probably the first monotheists that pagan Epirotes encountered. Alexander the Great likely had Hellenized Jews among his train of soldiers and craftsmen as he advanced the Greek Empire.

Apocryphally, the Romaniotes of Ioannina are said to have been slaves on galleys that ran ashore along the Ionian beaches of Epirus. Released and granted freedom, they moved inland to Ioannina. When Byzantine rule filled the vacuum created by Rome's decline, most slaves experienced a change in status. Among these would have been the Greek-speaking Jews.

During the Ottoman domination of Greece, particularly under Ali Pasha, the Romaniotes prospered as merchants and craftsmen. Many Jews were part of the same working class that included most Christian Greeks. But Muslim Turks gave preferential treatment to their Jewish subjects. Christians and Jews both paid the *jizya*—the tax on the household of a non-Muslim—as well as assorted tariffs that Muslims avoided. Cultural, legal, and societal burdens were imposed on Jews and Christians alike. But the Ottomans allowed the Romaniotes to build a synagogue within the *kastro*'s walls, and they established picturesque neighborhoods for their Jewish subjects both inside and outside the walled fortress of Ioannina.

From the exterior, there is little to distinguish a Romaniote from a Greek Christian. Artemis Miron, one of the last surviving Jews born in Ioannina, said in an interview with Marcia Haddad Ikonomopoulos:

> I want to tell you that outside of our homes there were no differences between the non-Jews and us. We studied together in the same schools with the non-Jews, we spoke Greek like them, and we dressed like them. Outside our homes there was no difference between Jews and non-Jews pertaining to business, to neighborliness, to education—but in our homes, we strictly observed our Judaism.

The Romaniotes sing liturgical poems in mixed Greek and Hebrew. The chanting and the organization of the Sabbath rituals are different from those of both the Ashkenazim and the Sephardim. The Romaniotes are *both* Greek and Jewish, assimilating into the Greek life cycle in Ioannina yet retaining their own religious identity.

What happened to the Jews of Ioannina is not unlike what happened to the rural Orthodox Christians of Epirus: mass murder. One form of execution was systematic—distanced and cold—and the other was retaliatory and vengeful. But ultimately both types of murder were unfathomably cruel, motivated by a combination of territorial envy, spite, and a hatred of the other.

❧❧❧

The Axis Powers declared war on Greece after it refused to surrender to Italian fascists on October 28, 1940. On April 6, 1941 Germany came to Mussolini's aid. In less than two months, all of mainland Greece was under Axis occupation. Following the victor's logic, Greece was compartmentalized and divided into regions under Bulgarian, German, and Italian control. Until June of 1943 the Italians administered Ioannina in Epirus.

Except for the Greek partisans (both Christian and Jew) leaving Ioannina to fight in the resistance in the mountains—just as the *klefts* did hundreds of years earlier—the cycle of daily life changed little. That is, until the hard-core Nazi Mountain divisions, including the infantry of the *Edelweiss*, descended in the summer of 1943. German intelligence had learned recently what the Allied powers had known for some time: Italians excelled at fabricating pasta but lacked ruthlessness in warfare.

Napoleon Zoumbas told me that during the Italian period of the Occupation, *panegyria*, weddings, and social events went on as before, except that Italian soldiers would flirt with the women while trading cigarettes for contraband. When the *Edelweiss* appeared, there was no flirting. Social gatherings of all types were *streng verboten.* When Mussolini capitulated, the occupying German forces executed over 5,000 Italian troops stationed in Greece just to drive home the point.

Jews living in Greece—Ashkenazim, Sephardim, and Romaniotes—were not accustomed to the intense pogroms, blood libels, and surges of genocide that had been visited on their Ashkenazi cousins to the north every hundred years or so. The Jews of Ioannina were integrated with their Greek Christian neighbors.

But these were different circumstances now. Forces outside of Greece were imposing their designs at the end of a gun barrel. Those in control knew exactly how to manipulate the results. Naïvety, guilelessness, and perhaps wishful thinking contributed to the outcome. Jealousy and spite served as a tinderbox. In the words of Agnieszka Holland, the Polish filmmaker interviewed by Arthur Allen after the release of *In Darkness*, "People live together for centuries, nothing major is wrong. Suddenly one little match and everything is on fire."

The Germans and their collaborators systematically calculated and contained all Romaniote assets—material and human—on a freezing morning on March 25, 1944. Troops and irregulars herded 1,725 Romaniote Jews into trucks bound for the railroad. Auschwitz was their final destination. After the end of the war, 48 survived.

Chill of empty space.

The *Edelweiss* issued a general order to several Greek citizens immediately after the deportation that morning. One reached Anastasios Vlachopoulos, the president of the Chamber of Commerce for Ioannina. It stated that all goods left by the Jews should be redistributed and that Greeks could now occupy the vacant Jewish stores and homes.

The guilt for the actual murders—for the organized collection and eradication of all European Jews—clearly belongs to the Nazis, to the Germans and to those who conceived, assisted, and executed the Final Solution. But what of the environment itself? Considering greed and fear of the other, guilt is distributed widely. There are as many perceptions as there are victims.

Esther Cohen, like Artemis Miron a Romaniote survivor, had a different view sourced from a different experience:

> When they were pulling us out of our homes and dragging us through the streets so they could send us to Germany, not a single neighbor even peeked through the curtains to see what was going on.

When she returned from Auschwitz to Ioannina, to her home,

> I knocked on the door and a stranger opened it. He asked me what I wanted and I told him that it was my house. "Do you remember whether there was an oven here?" he asked me. "Why yes, of course, we used to bake bread and beautiful pies," I replied. "Well, get out of here then. You may have got away from the ovens in Germany, but I'll cook you right here in your own home." I was horrified.

In truth, many Jews in Greece escaped the Nazis and survived because of their Greek Orthodox Christian neighbors. Many fled to Athens, where they hid amid the urban landscape, passing for Christians, or they retreated to the mountains of northern Greece to aid the resistance. But the Germans took advantage of one perception among certain Greek Christians: that the Romaniotes lived together in *Ta Evraika*, "the Jewish neighborhoods," laid out and ceded to the Jews by the Turks during yet another earlier and brutal occupation. This impression of separateness—this ploy— was used to manipulate the jealousy and spite that we all contain within ourselves.

But the description of Amalia Vaka as a *turkala*—as an "outsider"

—likely had nothing to do with her being a Romaniote. The label had more to do with what the oldest generation knew or thought they knew: that she spoke and sang Turkish, that she shot and killed Alexis, and that she ran away with his millions of dollars. These thoughts were exaggerations and falsehoods. Alexis did die penniless, but of pneumonia, in 1946. And he likely would have spoken Turkish, if only so he could play music in the "Oriental" cafes of New York City.

❧❧❧

Overlooking Lake Pamvotis, north of Ioannina, sits another "everlasting sign of deathless remembrance." Here, though, the sign is neither an epitaph on a tombstone nor a disc containing the cultural relics of a dead world. Rather, here is a remembrance of the second kind of murder: the retaliatory, the vengeful.

I had come to Epirus in November to drink *tsipouro* with my friends and to experience the change in seasons. In the words of my friend Vassilis Georganos, "The weather in November is when everything comes together. The atmosphere is like the music." The dark skies at this time reflect the heavy sonorous qualities of the songs.

Picking me up at King Pyrrhus Airport in Ioannina was my friend Alexis Papachristos—the man who helped me acquire the indelible mark from my first experience at a *panegyri*—and his cousin Aphrodite Psina. Aphrodite is an English instructor originally from Vitsa who had attempted on several occasions to teach me the proper footwork for the Zagorian dances. Aphrodite's father Pavlos was ultimately the man responsible for connecting me with the Zoumbas brothers. He had given his nephew Alexis Papachristos the address and phone number for Napoleon to hand to me in Vitsa.

After lunch, we drove up to the village of Lyngiades. Brooding clouds holding cold rain swept north above this small village, perched high above Ioannina. Here, on October 3, 1943, a massacre took place.

In September a dispatch had been issued to all troops in north-western Greece that "There must be no hesitation, even toward families . . . suspects must be executed on the spot. Weakness would cost German blood." Lyngiades did not contain suspects. Rather, on October 1 General Hubert Lanz released a general command for "ruthless retaliatory action" for a twelve-mile radius around an area where a German officer had been killed by partisans. Here was vengeance, a blind lashing out.

The *Edelweiss* waited until the late afternoon when the shepherds and farmers had returned from the fields. Vehicles surrounded the small settlement. All ninety-six villagers were herded together. A variety of machine guns were leveled at the Greek peasants and fired for about fifteen minutes. Before leaving, the Germans burned most of the town. The only four survivors were those who fell underneath the ninety-two that had been murdered.

A stone memorial containing the names and ages of the slaughtered is positioned in the village center. When I returned to the United States a few weeks later, I rendered the names and ages from Lyngiades on my typewriter. Numbers—figures—have some value. In Epirus 7,936 civilians were executed by Germans and 12,978 houses were burned during their brief visit. Having your feet on the ground gives you a greater appreciation of the suffering experienced on that darkened soil. Having actual names, families, and ages gives you a deeper understanding of what was lost.

As we returned to Alexis's car, an old shepherd was standing above an emaciated stray dog, whose rib cage pulsated in intervals between gasps for air. Aphrodite approached the man as the northern gale blew across Lyngiades. They talked briefly, hushed, Aphrodite's hands gesturing curiosity and then resignation. All that I could make out was the phrase at the end, *ti krima*, "what a pity."

When she returned to the car I asked her what was going on. She explained, "The shepherd wouldn't feed the dog. He said it was a lost cause. I answered back, '*ti krima*,' what a pity."

Victims Of Lyngiades Massacre - October 3, 1943
***

Eleni Avyeri	42	Yiannoula Maraphas	42
Eleftherios Yerakos	30	Marina Maraphas	58
Aristoula Yerakos	28	Vasiliki Mastoras	45
Yeorgios Yerakos	6	Vasileios Pagidas	65
Maria Yerakos	4	Yeorgitsa Pagidas	58
Christos Yerakos	2	Konstantinos Pagidas	15
Christos Yerakos	78	Konstantinos Pappas	67
Evangelia Yerakos	74	Paraskevi Pappas	9
Eleni Yerakos	35	Xanthi Pappas	7
Christos Yerakos	11	Sevasti Pappas	5
Olga Yerakos	6	Nikolaos Pappas	3
Stavros Zotos	56	Nikolaos Petrou	68
Maria Zotos	54	Anna Petrou	60
Photeini Zotos	6	Christodoulos Petrou	48
Xanthi Zotos	4	Zoitsa Petrou	38
Vasiliki Katsaros	40	Yeorgios Petrou	13
Ekaterini Katsaros	18	Dimitrios Rouskas	61
Eleni Lappas	60	Olga Rouskas	2
Marina Lappas	28	Nikitas Siaphakas	3
Stathis Lappas	8	Panagio Toli	60
Ekaterini Lappas	6	Vasiliki Tserikis	18
Paraskevi Lappas	7	Ioannis Tserikis	36
Lambrini Liouris	57	Angeliki Tserikis	35
Achilles Liouris	1	Photeini Tserikis	9
Eleftheria Liouris	30	Christos Tserikis	7
Ekaterini Liouris	11	Evangelia Tserikis	5
Angeliki Lolis	63	Maria Tserikis	3
Theodoros Lolis	90	Aphrodite Tsoukas	7
Ekaterini Lolis	68	Angeliki Phoukas	65
Vasileios Lolis	30	Paraskevi Phoukas	4
Tarsitsa Lolis	30	Vasilios Phoukas	5
Panagio Lolis	18	Eleftheria Phoukas	1
Paraskevi Lolis	7	Maria Phoukas	60
Leonidas Lolis	5	Christos Phoukas	63
Yeorgios Lolis	5	Dimitrios Holevas	66
Avaptisto Lolis	4 months*	Lamprini Holevas	38
Eleni Batetsis	36	Georgitsa Holevas	9
Theophanis Batetsis	5	Nikolaos Holevas	7
Evdoxia Batetsis	3	Alexios Holevas	4
Paraskevi Manthos	34	***	
Marina Balaskas	42	On the same day at the nearby	
Dimitra Balaskas	6	village of Amphithea, these	
Eleni Bambouskas	30	were executed:	
Ioannis Bambouskas	5	Maria Kolokas	27
*Avaptisto was not baptised		Eleni Kolokas	7
		Vasileios Kolokas	5

Victims of Ligiades Massacre—October 3, 1943.

The expressions that Aphrodite conveyed with her face and hands while talking with the shepherd—a vulnerable curiosity followed by a fragile resignation—were the same gestures that I imagined the ninety-six villagers of Ligiades made on the afternoon of October 3, 1943 in front of the Germans as they were collected, encircled.

Ti poli krima. What a *great* pity.

6

KITSOS'S SHEPHERD SONG

PO: Close your eyes. What do you hear?

CAINE: I hear the water, I hear the birds.

PO: Do you hear your own heartbeat?

CAINE: No.

PO: Do you hear the grasshopper which is at your feet?

CAINE: Old man, how is it that you hear these things?

PO: Young man, how is it that you do not?

—*KUNG FU* (PILOT EPISODE OF TELEVISION SHOW, 1972)

WHERE THE JAGGED EDGE OF THE HILLS ENCOMPASSING THE village of Klimatia merged with the sky, a muted spectrum—crimson wine and the golden pulp of summer—saturated the landscape. Outcroppings of brick red soil flowed forward and streams of pink and yellow minerals undulated out from below towers of raw marble. These formations magnified the larger flora—all untamed—of the cherry, the pomegranate, and the quince tree. Each gave willingly their tones to the sun and to the refracted halo ribbon before me. Grass and shrub spread from the fissures below this tinted panorama.

Every wavering step that we took downhill released a fume of wild oregano. The smell was neither sweet nor savory but something in between—something earthly and affirming—exuding growth and decay equally. Here was an alien soil: a landscape where you would stumble over an unexpected expression of nature, pass it by, and discover yet another unlikely fecund phenomenon three steps beyond.

Sheep and goats had recently grazed through this patch of land skirting the northern boundary of Klimatia, a village west of Ioannina and south of Vitsa. It was near the town of Zitsa, a spiritual center for the club-footed poet Lord Byron when he visited this region. During Byron's time this village was known as Veltsista. Perhaps he hobbled down this same path, reflecting on the ancestors of these animals as they gathered in the shade.

I could smell the wildness of the flock in the dark recesses. A cluster of thrushes exploded into the air as I crept downhill.

The ravine below, just beyond sight on the right, was where Kitsos Harisiadis communicated musical skills to his students. This rocky cleft in the Earth—a primordial riverbed—was perfectly situated between east and west. In this natural amphitheater below, countless generations of musicians—possibly Alexis Zoumbas himself—from the villages around the Zagori region, Zitsa, Ioannina, and Grammeno visited this place to develop their ears. The ghosts who etched their playing on the discs that I coveted learned to speak through the language of music here.

There were four of us. Leading the way to this hidden antechamber of sound was the ex-mayor of Klimatia, Michalis Katsanos, and a village woman, Glykeria Phili. The third—moving like an eager specter—was sweet, young Vassilis Georganos. He would be three steps behind me and then, in an instant, two steps before me. As we entered the ravine, he cautioned me not to get entwined in the browned barbed wire that lay over a pile of rocks forming a gateway to this mystical place. We were walking into the low sun.

Swinging north—to the right—into a corridor, I was arrested by an intensity of sensation. The lush cacophony of birdsong became intelligible as a melody. The wind sweeping the field became a discernible rhythm. Insects harmonized as nature transformed into song. Even the light appeared as a dark tonal register. As the sun faded, a profound melancholy shaped the landscape.

Across the ravine from us to the west was a mass of stones. This arrangement was a bench made of local marble perched above the vastness of the ravine. Behind me to the east was another platform, almost identical in construction. A thicket of fig trees and brambles shaded both areas and a rocky embankment ran parallel to the platform across from us. The span between the two stone benches—some sixty feet between—suggested that you could see and hear someone across the ravine, although the distance would obscure the fine details of a person's movements.

The closer I moved to the rock bench behind me to the east, the more conscious I became of the sounds magnifying in the ravine.

Here was the organically formed music sanctuary of Klimatia— a holy place in the middle of Epirus where master and disciple faced one another with a ravine of experience separating them. This was where the alchemy of music took place.

Instinctively I felt like clapping my hands to produce a sharp crack with no lingering echo. Just as I imagined Leroy Shield did for Alexis Zoumbas ninety years ago: "Perfect acoustics, just as I said. The best!"

Unlike the dead space in New York City where Zoumbas recorded, this miniature valley concentrated and distilled nature into melody. Here, the musicians made their instruments mimic the feral, elemental sounds.

From the platform behind me young students took their lessons from Kitsos. With the master sitting on the other side of the ravine, the understudies could only hear the melody and the rhythm. They could not see the technique. The fledgling musicians had to grasp the phrasing and the meaning on their own.

Kitsos did not teach them. Rather, he helped them train their ears so they could hear the subtleties of *dromoi*, musical roads, and how these patterns of notes related to the external world of nature and to the internal landscape of the listeners.

When students practiced the phrases that they heard across the ravine, the rock wall that ran parallel to them would reflect back

Natural musical sanctuary of Klimatia: A is the seat of the docent, B is the seat of the Master, C is the line of rocks echoing the sound back to the student.

and amplify their sounds so that they could hear themselves and their mistakes. Through this process the young learned from the old. Kitsos Harisiadis was neither the first nor the last clarinetist to teach in this way. He was simply the greatest of the gnostic instructors of music from this region to record 78s.

For a music that demands as much of the listener as it does of the performer, it seems that technique should be central to a musical education. But in Epirus, only the melody is eternal. The skill to craft such music is idiosyncratic, drawing from the inner muse. Technique must, in some ineffable way, be sourced from oneself.

I imagined the spirit of Kitsos Harisiadis sitting on this stone bench across the ravine intoning the saddest note: the low-register A on the clarinet. His understudy could not see him. He could only focus on that desperate tone and imagine sounds voicing darkness.

Here the student was blind, like a child learning a language without seeing his parent's lips move. The ear of the understudy became tonally aware with Kitsos as his guide.

A year earlier—almost to the day—I asked Napoleon Zoumbas in the parched, windswept village of Grammeno how he expressed

Napoleon Zoumbas demonstrating how musicians must be blind to convey feeling.

feeling through music. I wondered how he could graft an emotion onto an instrument such that he could convey that emotion to a listener.

He looked at me as if we were speaking the same language. "You must play as if you are blind, as if you are a child," he said.

"What do you see inside?"

"I see many things. Many curious things."

We could have been Howard Carter and George Herbert, Fifth Earl of Carnarvon, peering into King Tut's tomb in 1922. Instead, it was Vassilis Georganos and me, eight months before we walked down to Harisiadis's teaching area in Klimatia. We were now in Limni, a village rumored to have been Kitsos's birthplace, stretching our arms through a window grate in an abandoned house. Just as Carter and Herbert had gazed at funerary artifacts from over three thousand years ago, we thought that our flashlights were illuminating a time capsule of Harisiadis's life from the earlier part of the twentieth century.

Faded photos were suspended on a wall. One was a family portrait with a man on the right, slight of build and densely mustached, resembling the only image we have of Kitsos. Boxes scattered on the floor perhaps held unissued test pressings of Harisiadis. Discs of unheard music—notes frozen in amber—sat unplayed for over eighty years.

But like Zoumbas, Kitsos's phantom was fickle. The documented lives of both men were obscured by their folk aura, a mythological dimension forming a thin surface around them. Discovery only came when you pierced through the aura. We were skimming the outer edge of Kitsos's life, looking for some way in.

This small settlement of Limni was our starting point. Limni means "lake" in Greek. Such a body of water figures prominently in Kitsos's apocrypha. Some have said that he was born in an ancient settlement called Zaravina in Pogoni. Later in life he relocated to become a coppersmith and to perfect his clarinet skills. When he left, the wells and springs of his village overflowed with water like the uncontrollable tears of a mother at the last glimpse of her child. The weeping produced a deep body of water named Lake Zaravina.

Nearly forty-five years later—it is said—Nazis were retreating from Ioannina into Albania, past Lake Zaravina. The Germans were struggling to reach safety north of Pogoni. To rid themselves of unnecessary burdens, the troops loaded barges with their dead, their dying, and their useless armored vehicles. These were then sunk in the middle of the icy lake.

I had stood by Zaravina's waters with Jim Potts during my first visit to Epirus. In my mind, a languid aquatic ballet took place just below the surface. A pale blue choreography of Nazi skeletons wrapped in rusted iron cables tethered to tanks and other machines of war undulated slowly above wellsprings still weeping for Kitsos Harisiadis.

Limni lay less than two miles from Lake Zaravina. Vassilis and I walked along the village's cobblestone paths seeking signs of human life. In mid-November, we saw ripe fruits scattered among the snow. Walls along the road had crumbled and in between these fractures grew wild cherry trees—*kerasies*; pomegranates—*rodies*; and yellow plum trees—*damascenies*. Dead foliage encased in opaque ice cradled bright sugary colors.

Sweet young Vassilis ran ahead of me, calling out for anyone who might be present. I'm certain that he was irked by my conjoined appellation of "sweet" and "young." But it rang true. He was half my age: "young." And despite being, like myself, an obsessive collector of 78 rpm discs—a tortured, self-inflicted state of solitude, guilt, and longing where the main conflict is between one's misanthropic tendencies and the acknowledgment that one *must* interact with others to acquire more records—he was kind, thoughtful, and deferential. In a word: sweet.

Which is not to say that he wasn't bitter and disenchanted in other ways. Like other Epirotes, Vassilis loved the old music—the "natural" way of playing, as Pericles Halkias put it—and detested the modern manifestation of the *panegyri*. He hated commercialization, homogenization, amplification, and the loss of meaning. In Vassilis's words:

> Many people have told me that they don't want to listen to this old music because it reminds them of the hard times they had in the past: the poverty, the hunger, and the everyday difficulties. But I wonder, isn't that a function of this music, to remember? So, I don't attend the *panegyri* now and prefer to play my 78s. They help me preserve an illusion of the old-time *panegyria*.

I could hear—or *believe* that I could hear—in the live music of Epirus the things that Vassilis perceived as dead or altered beyond recognition. As an outsider, was I sensitive to things that had vanished to many of the natives? Or was I imagining sensations that could not exist, like the phantom twinges that an amputee feels in the extremities that are no longer present?

These were my thoughts as I watched Vassilis go from door to door asking if anyone was home, if anyone knew of Kitsos Harisiadis, dead for almost fifty years.

Finally an old man emerged from a doorway, pointing us in the direction of a house that belonged to the Harisiadis family. It was here that we picked through the underbrush and peered through the barred windows.

But this place was a dead end, a tease. Limni was known as Zaravina in an earlier age, but Kitsos only came to visit his uncle Mitro-Tsitos. The house Vassilis and I found was built on the land belonging to Kitsos's father, and Mitro-Tsitos and his daughter Efthalia lived there.

At the time of our visit, we did not know that Limni was a false start. Only after months of research by Vassilis would Kitsos's life become illuminated. But in his own words, as he recalled the rush of finding this abandoned house, Vassilis felt "awakened," as if he had brushed against the Eternal.

 ᕦᕦᕦ

Why this obsession with one clarinet player who last walked the earth nearly fifty years ago? What makes him singular when so many Epirote clarinetists made 78 recordings? There are a plethora of reasons, some of which are subtle and others that are as obvious as the blinding midday sun over the mountains of Pogoni.

The primary reason is this: Harisiadis is regarded by many as the true vine, an embodiment of both the music of the region and the spirit of those who never left Epirus. In the former respect, his playing contains the definitive reading of tunes and clarinet styles, the songbook of northwestern Greece. In the later respect, his life echoes the story of generations of villagers who held to the traditional ways.

Kitsos Harisiadis was born poor and remained so until Charon visited him almost eighty years later. He left little material wealth behind. His was a humble life with an existence confined to a small geographic footprint in Epirus of less than forty miles in diameter.

That he was a musician of modest means rooted in his home soil may seem like a minor point. But this is essential to appreciating his esteemed status among his peers, his students, and the village folk. An artist like Kitsos could have relocated to Athens and become a studio clarinetist. This happened to one of his students, Haralambos Bourbos from Grammeno, who married one of his daughters. Kitsos could have amassed wealth and fame like other musicians from the region. Travel abroad or even moving to America would have been easy for a man of his skills.

One of his best students, Phillipos Rountas of Doliana, near Kalpaki, did just that. He traveled to America in 1962 to play for well-off expatriate Epirotes. As Rountas lay dying of cancer sixteen years later, a friend who had collected his tips presented Rountas with over one hundred thousand dollars so that he could die in comfort, knowing he was a wealthy man. But Kitsos needed neither fame nor wealth.

From those interviewed we learned Harisiadis had only one desire: to heal people through his music. He knew the rhythms of most of the villages, the secret voices and special dances that people wanted to hear.

Kitsos was known above all for his humility. The deference he received from his listeners and students was much like that given to religious saints and ascetics. Harisiadis rests in my mind as a kind of Greek-Shaolin monk: a modest, spiritual man who was one with himself.

Musical expression to him was the ability to play curative music and to midwife that skill in others.

His life story is unremarkable, unlike that of Alexis Zoumbas: there is no darkness, no hints of murder or infidelity, no despair for a lost home. If both men represent the apex of their craft—technically they were equals—then the values used to plot the range of their mastery lies beyond musical skill. Their greatness derives from how they navigated their spiritual worlds: the unseen things that sustain musical inspiration. The contrast in their playing inhabits the region where darkness and light separate: the psyche. How did they respond to the universe around them, and how did they translate that response into music?

Alexis and Kitsos chose—or were fated with—different primal emotions to channel through their instruments. From Zoumbas I hear expressions shaped by alienation, inner anguish, and longing: his music *hurts*. From Harisiadis, I perceive tones informed by familiarity, tranquility, and belonging: his music *heals*. Alexis wept for his home soil. Kitsos never left it.

Harisiadis's eyes would have surveyed the cruel, waning days of Ottoman rule, the bloodletting that transitioned into the Balkan conflicts, both world wars, and the Greek Civil War. But there is lightness in his playing. His existence on Earth almost precisely matched the period during which Epirus was unified with Greece. The narrative of his life is a reflection of the collective memory of Epirus and his music is the soundscape of the region.

Kitsos was neither the first musician from northwestern Greece to record nor the most prolific. These honorary titles are meaningless categories perpetuating falsehoods about the nature of musical influence. Being the first or the most prolific does not insure that a musician's style has any lasting effect on a repertoire, particularly a body of music that is stubbornly rural. Robert Johnson was neither the first nor the most prolific bluesman from the Mississippi Delta. Yet his legacy persists in the song body defined as Delta blues.

The first musicians from Greece to etch Epirotic repertoire onto shellac were Alexis Zoumbas, Athanasios Makedonas (another violinist), and possibly Takis Zakas, a clarinetist. All three of these men recorded for the Greek-owned Panhellenion label in New York

City between 1919 and 1921. But folk musicians learn from their peers within the context of a live, interactive setting—a *panegyri* for instance—and only rarely from recordings alone. These pioneering artists rarely visited Greece, and so their influence was slight.

Tasos Halkias—the clarinetist wounded during World War II and married to Alexis Zoumbas's daughter—recorded more 78s than Kitsos. Though Tasos played throughout Greece with other musicians, his strength was with Pogonian pentatonic tunes. But the complex rhythms and scalar structure of Zagorian pieces was just outside the scope of his playing. Halkias influenced those performing the repertoire near the Albanian border and the popular tunes of Ioannina. You see this stylistic limitation even today, among younger musicians who express themselves perfectly in the Pogonian style yet struggle to master the Zagorian tunes.

R. Crumb portrait of Kitsos Harisiadis.

Over several tumblers of *tsipouro* in an *ouzeri* in Vitsa under constant sheets of November rain, Demetris Dallas and I concluded that the depth of Kitsos Harisiadis's influence on the music of Epirus was due simply to his greatness; his ability to translate emotions through perfect phrasing, rhythm, and touch. He was a singular transcendent stylist. He captivated three generations of dancers and instructed three generations of musicians. The living masters—Gregoris Kapsalis, who plays every year in Vitsa, and Napoleon Zoumbas, Alexis's nephew—absorbed some of his style. Like any master, whether artistic or spiritual, he had legions of students to insure his influence.

A holy man's material existence scarcely equates with his spiritual legacy: the acts of healing and divination or the homilies and confessions he leaves behind. In Harisiadis's case, the dozen or so double-sided discs of his music are the physical vessels of sound proving his sainthood. His discs are holy relics. And every time a needle drops into the groove of one of these 78s, a miracle is performed.

Kitsos was born Christodoulos Harisiadis, in Vissani, Pogoni, on October 15, 1889. This village is a few miles north of Limni and Lake Zaravina. His father Yiannis was a day laborer, and his mother Diochno tended the five children: Vangelis, Kitsos, Manolis, Thanasis, and Martha. At the age of ten Kitsos moved to the town of Zitsa to learn the traditional Roma occupations of coppersmith and musician. While in Zitsa, Kitsos was apprenticed to Thanasis Yiannopoulos (born 1857), a respected musician who played *laouto*, clarinet, and *floyera*—the shepherd's flute.*

Kitsos married Lemonia Efthymiou on August 25, 1910, and they moved to her village of Klimatia. They had four children that would survive to adulthood: Sophia, Yiannis, Ourania, and Lambrini. Two

---

* At the turn of the twentieth century when Kitsos was learning, the clarinet had only been in Epirus for roughly seventy years.

other children—Vangelis and Diochno—would die in infancy. Yiannis, his only son, became a clarinet player but died young. For roughly fifty-five years, Kitsos lived in Klimatia and performed for countless *panegyria*, weddings, and *glendia*. Between the years 1929 and 1931 he traveled to Athens to record twenty-four sides* for three different record labels. He died in Klimatia, Zitsochoria, on January 8, 1968.

This is Kitsos's paper trail. It's a thin obituary. The deeper narrative comes from those who are still living.

We discovered two people who knew him well: Elli Kavvakou, his niece, and Michalis Katsanos, the former mayor of Klimatia.

During one visit in August, Elli allowed us, two rabid record collectors, into her modest courtyard in the sleepy village of Vissani. She was born in 1928 to Thanasis, Kitsos's older brother, and like her father, she spent most of her life in this village. During our conversation she giggled, her sweet bright eyes recollecting Kitsos.

Her father, Thanasis, learned clarinet from Kitsos. Thanasis was the village cobbler and the town's favorite clarinetist. Elli told us a story of Kitsos and Thanasis, and how their playing was regarded by the villagers of Vissani:

> During our *panegyri* on the fifteenth of August, our village chose to have Kitsos play. Every year until then my father played. By that time [in the mid-1930s], Kitsos was famous, since he had made records in Athens. But when he started to play, no one wanted to dance, since he didn't know the dancers in our village and what they wanted to hear. The villagers sent someone to our house to fetch my father to play. When he returned from playing that night, he kept repeating *"Ti krima, ti krima."* "What a pity, what a pity."

---

* Two of these twenty-four sides have never been found by collectors and remain unheard. The lost record is HMV-AO-1000.

It was not that Kitsos played poorly: that would have been impossible. Rather, he had no experience with the special rhythms of this village—his birthplace that he left at the age of ten. He couldn't interact musically with the dancers. Following the embarrassment of this *panegyri*, he stayed at his brother's house whenever he could so that he could learn the sounds of his home village.

Everything in these dwindling villages is local: gossip, food, and music. Elli's favorite song is, appropriately enough, a very old one that would rarely be heard outside of this small settlement. Kitsos used to play this for her. It is simply called "Vissaniotissa" ("Young Lemon Tree"). She sang it for us:

> *Young little lemon tree*
> *Of many lemons, Vissaniote maiden.*
> *As I kissed you I took lovesick.*
> *Young one, how did you rise so tall?*
> *Your branches have grown, Vissaniote maiden,*
> *As I kissed you I took lovesick,*
> *But I didn't ask for a doctor.*
> *Let down your branches now*
> *That I may touch a lemon.*
> *As I kissed you I took lovesick.*

At 89, the memory fades. But Elli recalled vividly that her uncle was small, dark, and quick to learn. He also loved to play the *skaros* and the *mirologi* for her.

I asked her before leaving, "How do you feel when you hear the *mirologi*?"

"I weep."

"Why do you weep when you hear it?"

"I weep because it is a *mirologi*."

❧❧❧

Vassilis and I visited Klimatia the day after we sat in Elli's somnolent courtyard. The village was preparing for their *panegyri*. Those not helping with the event filled the dark, cool spaces between buildings, drinking and obsessing over a soccer match between an Athenian team and the PAS Ioannina team. A frenetic energy pulsed throughout as mopeds charted hazardous courses through the maze of cobblestone streets.

We were hungry. There was a *kafeneio*—a local restaurant—that crested the village center smelling sweetly of *tsipouro*. Plates of fried cheese and roast pork were on their way when three men from a nearby table drew us into their conversation. A stranger, even a Greek from Epirus like Vassilis, attracts attention. An *americanos* adds a wild card. "News from the outside," everyone thinks. Within fifteen minutes the patio of the *kafeneio* was filled with two dozen ears forming a loose circle around our pork-scented table, cell phones making urgent calls. "We all knew him. Why, we talked about Kitsos last night even though he died almost fifty years ago," one man said to us.

After my third *tsipouro* the former mayor, Michalis Katsanos, arrived by car. This was the man who would lead Vassilis and me down to Kitsos's musical sanctuary later that afternoon. Almost everyone on the patio stood at attention as he approached. Katsanos didn't carry himself like an ex-mayor as much as a barrel-framed, decorated general: George C. Patton before addressing his troops.

After introducing himself, Katsanos sat at our table. Older villagers slid their chairs closer. He had been waiting decades to tell outsiders about Kitsos and his village of Klimatia. After ordering a round of *tsipouro*, he explained that he was twenty-five years old when Harisiadis died. During his youth, he would drink coffee with Kitsos, passing the time until the musician would teach students or go down to the marble mills to play clarinet.

Both activities, said Katsanos, proved Kitsos's kindness and humility.

Kitsos rarely accepted money for instruction. Instead, he received foodstuffs, homemade goods, or raw materials from his students. Money was not the point. The burden was squarely on the young musicians to develop their ear and to source their own technique.

In the village's heyday, the cutting and milling of marble enriched Klimatia's economy. By the river below, Albanians and Greeks from Pogoni worked in the mills to slice and polish blocks of marble for export. The Arab states especially prized the pinkish hue and durability of this metamorphic stone for their palatial estates. Kitsos played almost every day—for free—the slow Pogonian-style music for these laboring men.

The languid "Stroto Pogonisio"—"Smooth Pogonian Dance"— would have cut through the dull noise as they hefted a rough ten-ton plinth of stone through the blades of the mill. The workers' sweat would bead, fall onto the marble, and quickly evaporate in the heat of the day. But instead of the three-minute-and-six-second disc that Harisiadis recorded in 1930, these men would have heard a piece lasting well over half an hour.

"Stroto Ponisio" is smooth, as the title implies, but the sedate melody is punctuated with unexpected angular phrases, like utterances from a startled crow. When Kitsos reinstates the theme, the tranquility suggests gentle ocean tides. To this very day this pentatonic tune has the ability to put me under. I have no doubt that it did the same for the mill workers.

While telling this story Katsanos beckoned an older man sitting a table away to approach. Katsanos said, "This man here has some of Kitsos's old records!" Some Pavlovian—or more accurately, reptilian—arousal reared within Vassilis and me. An army of corpuscles rallied under our skin, spreading across the backs of our necks and arms: a biological response to a speculative reward. This translated into larger patterns of anxiety across our faces. Synchronized, we asked, "Can we see them please?" The elderly villager ambled across the street to fetch them.

We both knew that one disc by Harisiadis has never been found. These two sides amount to less than seven minutes of music: infinite hours of ecstasy for us. Just as battered 78s of Charlie Patton were squirreled away by poor black folk throughout the Mississippi Delta, so too might copies of Harisiadis's discs lay hidden in Klimatia.

The old man was hauling a grossly overloaded plastic bag with one quivering hand as he returned. It looked like he was carrying a bowling ball suspended in tissue paper. The sack was so thin you could see the stonework of buildings, parked cars, and oblivious faces through the gathered translucent top as he ascended the road to the *kafeneio*.

Within a blink, the plastic bag could split, sending the discs crashing on the hard cobblestone: seven minutes of unheard music divided by a thousand broken pieces. I ran to grab the fragile membrane of the satchel: gaping holes had already formed where he had held it with his fingers. Gingerly lifting each disc out of the bag as if they were infants, I scanned the labels. There were about two dozen discs, mostly Epirotic music recorded before World War II. But no records by Kitsos. I checked twice.

Vassilis's breathing was animalistic. He stared over my shoulder.

"No, there are no discs by Harisiadis here," I said. The old man shrugged indifferently, "I didn't want to sell them anyway."

"May I see, please?" The question came from behind me, focused and desperate. Something had come loose in Vassilis's voice.

At that instant I saw in Vassilis an axiomatic truth about the collector's deplorable nature. His eyebrows—thick black smudges—were normally at ease below his closely cropped dark hair, reclining emotionless on his forehead. But when I passed him this stack of discs, these brows began to fidget, arching with expression. First they signified curiosity. When met by the old man's entrenched reluctance, his repeated refusal to sell—"No, I could never give these up"—his brows took on a sinister, resourceful urgency.

Vassilis saw a record as I flipped through them: HMV-AO-1085 by the *Pente Gliniotes* (*Five Men from Glina*). This is a disc with a distinctive type of polyphonic singing unique to the Pogoni region (Glina is a place now inside of Albania) recorded in 1936. It was impossibly rare. Likewise, he was impossibly fixated. I had a mint copy but knew of no other until now.

But the machinations of Vassilis's dark smudges had no effect on the old man. Clutching his deteriorating bag of records, the owner retreated from this spectacle.

That night after we left Klimatia, Vassilis vowed a return. His black eyebrows formed an ominous cloud: "I will get that record. I *need* it. He *will* sell it to me."*

❧ ❧ ❧

"Life was difficult here, sometimes dangerous. Not like it is today," Katsanos explained over another round of *tsipouro*. When he said this, I wondered to myself if Harisiadis—as a Roma—would have felt the danger here. For several hundred years a hierarchy thrived in Epirus: Ottoman Turks and their Muslim Albanian administrators ruled the nest, Greek landowners and officials occupied the next lower position, poorer working Greeks lay just below, and the Greek Roma held the lowest stratum. Hardship was at the bottom of this social ladder.

---

* Truth be told, he does *need* it. But what is this Great Whatsit, this thing that Vassilis needs? What emptiness does it fill? Collectors like Vassilis and myself are maligned for our fixation on objects. Those on the outside—noncollectors— perceive our obsession, turning away in disgust or offering a diagnosis. Rarely do they see how the collector transcends the yearning for a thing. Many systematic hoarders obtain fullness by grasping the unifying elements that thread through these obscure objects of desire.

When Turkish rule of Epirus ended in 1913, a vacuum was created but an instinctual urge to enforce preexisting social positions prevailed. Since the Roma were the lowest in the pecking order, discrimination and violence against them went largely unpunished. The effects of this quasi-medieval notion can be discerned to this day.

There were two deeply ingrained social factors in most Epirotes of the time guiding the day-to-day behavior and long-term choices of most Roma—including Harisiadis—in Epirus: the Romani were *vulnerable* and the Romani were *necessary*. Kitsos would have been acutely aware of his status as a Roma despite the deference given to him as the leading *klarino* of Epirus.

Their vulnerability was obvious. Romani were poor and uneducated. Many Gypsies lived in impoverished areas, such as the outskirts of Ioannina and the margins of villages. Not only did they live physically apart, they maintained a cultural distance as well, speaking a distinctive language among themselves and bearing antipathy toward assimilation.* Living on the fringes of acceptable society, the Roma suffered from an ever-looming threat of violence.[14] Things have changed in the modern world for most Greek Gypsies, yet there is still a haze of inequality. Horrible things could happen.

---

* Many Greek folk beliefs documented in the nineteenth and early twentieth century cast the Gypsies in a disparaging light. From the explanation of their cursed social position—that they had forged the nails used to affix Christ to the Cross—to the belief that they possessed supernatural powers—that Gypsy sorcerers could cure the evil eye and other spells when Orthodox priests failed—the Roma played a negative role in rural Greek thought. The perception of the Gypsies bordered on blood libel. In many ways, the Roma were viewed as metaphorical lice hosting societal vices—larceny, vagrancy, and indolence to name a few—yet they were presumed to have extraordinary powers. A Greek variation on a familiar trope emerged: Gypsies were untrustworthy, dangerous, and—above all—magical.

❧❧❧

Remember earlier when I had received the indelible scar from drinking *tsipouro* the first night of the *panegyri* in Vitsa? This happened before Jim and I visited Yiannis Chaldoupis, Jim's favorite Romani *klarino*, outside the town of Parakalamos. Most of this village is Greek Romani, and many here make a living playing music.

Parakalamos skirts the edge of lawlessness. It has a feeling of barely contained anarchy. The town is run down, haggard. Cars and mopeds are scattered along the road like a jumble of playing cards. Windows are boarded up or covered in black paint.

Yiannis Chaldoupis lives on the margin of town. In his early fifties, he shares his farmstead with his wife Nellie, a variety of livestock, and some unexpected fauna.

His skin is walnut brown and his coal-black hair is speckled gray, spiked in a manner that was fashionable twenty years ago in the United States. A black tee shirt with metallic gold dragon patterns running the hem of the sleeves, black jeans, and black biker boots complete his *mangas*—badass—wardrobe. A single curved bear claw dangles on a leather lanyard around his neck, reminding me of the toenails that I no longer had on my right foot.

Jim and I were late due to my *panegyri*-related scarification two days earlier. Chaldoupis gave my wound a circumspect look after Jim nodded toward me saying "*tsipouro*." Chaldoupis had to leave soon to play for a *panegyri* in the nearby village of Sitaria, but we were welcome to attend. Before we left, we talked a little.

I ask Yiannis how he grafts an emotion onto an instrument such that he conveys that emotion to a listener. He looks at me as if he's been waiting decades to answer this question. He says:

> When I play in a village I feel more like a psychiatrist or a doctor than a musician. I look around to see what the people need, what they need to hear for their souls. I look around to see what their

pain is, what hurts them. Every village is different and they have different spiritual and emotional needs.

Yiannis follows with a caveat. He whispers furtively, "We Gypsies have it very bad. We are treated less than dogs. They only want us for our music."

Chaldoupis looks at his cell phone, "We must go, now!" At that moment a dark Gypsy emerges from underneath the shrubbery next to our table. Leaves stick out at angles from his hair as he clutches a guitar case. "We played a *panegyri* late last night and he just fell asleep in the yard," Yiannis says as they sprint to their minivan. I glance back to see if any other *Homo sapiens* fauna will spring from the yard.

Jim and I follow their van to Sitaria. Rows of wooden benches spread underneath the ubiquitous plane tree in front of a church. The sun breaks dappled through the leaves as a few dozen villagers mill about waiting for *souvlakia* and the musicians. I spy a dark, wrinkled Gypsy holding an accordion, gray duct tape forming large Xs patching holes in the leaky bellows.

At the enormous *souvlaki* pit, several young men, husky high school–age guys, turn the spits. Yiannis and his wild bunch of musicians crest the hill behind us, carrying their instruments. There is shouting from behind the smoke. One of the young men yells at the Gypsy who emerged earlier from the bush—leaves still sticking to his hair and guitar in his hand. The young villager pushes the Gypsy hard in the chest, pointing down the road with his other hand: there is menace in his voice. He grabs the guitar from him.

"The young man is telling the Roma that he must go back and get his *laouto*. They've never had a guitar in the village for a *panegyri*. This appears to be pretty serious," Jim says. The *laouto* was the only instrument traditionally accepted here. Quickly, the Roma musician drives home and fetches his *laouto*.

In an earlier, more lawless time this confrontation could have escalated into a bloody confrontation, broken teeth, or worse. Musicians like Kitsos Harisiadis would have been mindful of such reactions, particularly eighty or ninety years ago. A grievance— real or imagined—against a Gypsy was an everyday reality in Harisiadis's time.

❧ ❧ ❧

Michalis Katsanos, sharing another round of *tsipouro*, spoke of this darker time. He told us of the Retzos brothers, two infamous gangsters who operated near Klimatia. They were professional thieves with patriotic and governmental aspirations. Nowadays we could simply call them politicians. These Greek mobsters often threw *glendia* and invited Kitsos to play. Kitsos knew firsthand that they were "wanted men" whose parties were prone to violence. Often he would disappear for several days when a gangster *glendi* was announced so that he could avoid danger.

Katsanos told a story. In 1922, Harisiadis and his band of musicians had just played a wedding at a village outside of Ioannina. On their way back to Klimatia, one member of the band, Tsourlis Phakos, was murdered in the village of Arachovitsa (now called Lefkothea). A drunken villager stabbed Tsourlis for refusing to play a song. Kitsos comforted Tsourlis during his agonizing last hours on Earth.

I had heard the name "Tsourlis" at the very end of a 78-disc recording of "Pios Plousios Apethane" ("Which Rich Man Has Died") by Demetris Halkias. This is the same song that I had heard on my first night of the *panegyri* in Vitsa. At the end of this recording made in 1931, Halkias sang a lyrical remembrance:

Oh the misfortune that we have suffered, my son,
Oh we poor Gypsy [black] musicians,
Oh we poor Gypsy [black] musicians,
Oh they killed our Tsourlis.

A memorialization grafted onto the end of a song is not rare. Folk melodies often acquire such subtexts as they meander from region to region, as in the case of the Scots-Irish murder ballad "Pretty Polly." With this song Halkias devoted the last whole stanza to a Gypsy violinist, Tsourlis.

Halkias was not with the band of Gypsies when Tsourlis was murdered. But he created a musical time capsule about a violinist who he both knew and admired.

We only know a few things about Tsourlis, many of them apocryphal. He may have played the violin or the *laouto* or both. His music caused songbirds to fall from the trees. From Michalis Katsanos we learned how he was murdered and that Tsourlis Phakos was one of Kitsos Harisiadis's favorite musicians. These things are revealed only because Tsourlis's name, etched in a curious black disc, emerged from Katsanos's memory of this doomed violinist.

Oh they killed our Tsourlis.

☙☙☙

Michalis Katsanos was quick to amend these stories: "No one would harm a hair on the head of Kitsos. He was *our* clarinet player!" Katsanos then went on and on about how Kitsos, although a Gypsy, was a different *kind* of Gypsy, not a Roma but rather a Spanish Gypsy. Although Kitsos was certainly a different kind of *man*, he was not a different kind of Roma. He was neither Spanish nor an Eastern European "traveler." He came from a long line of Greek Roma who had settled throughout Epirus.

Katsanos was trying to say that Kitsos was exceptional, not a run-of-the-mill Roma. In Katsanos's mind, Kitsos was more exotic and powerful than a typical Greek Gypsy.

Kitsos's singularity was bound up with the notion that he was Klimatia's musician. He was special to the village, since he knew what the dancers needed. Similarly, Gregoris Kapsalis is valued in Vitsa as well as in his home village of Elaphotopos. Both men's clarinets tapped into the villages' collective psyche. This speaks to the other notion Kitsos and other Roma musicians embraced: they were *necessary*.

Musicians are essential to the social fabric of rural Greece because of the primacy of music here. Those who engage in the craft of making music have a singular goal: to get the village off. Wherever and whenever they play—a *panegyri*, *glendi*, or wedding—the musicians are expected to interact with the dancers so that the audience is emotionally transformed, taken to a higher place, psychologically healed.

The importance of these social events with music cannot be overstated, particularly when a small isolated village may have only one or two celebrations a year. People in these places are starving for curative music. The population anticipates ecstasy, transcendence and catharsis, which can be delivered only by extraordinary musicians.

At some point, amorphous in time and lacking documentation, the occupation of making music in Epirus was entrusted to the Gypsies. It could be that early Romani tribes that settled in Greece demonstrated exceptional skills at performing on traditional instruments, singing dirges, breaking and mending hearts. Or perhaps the perception of native Greeks that the Roma possessed magical, spiritual, or unseen powers was conjoined with the notion that music *itself* functioned on a magical, spiritual, or unseen level. A shaman performing his ritual healing through music would be the perfect metaphor, except that the ethnic group of this conjurer of sounds was kept at a distance.

Romani were marginalized from the wider spectrum of Greek society by the middle of the fifteenth century and continuing well into the early 1960s, when Westerners visited the hinterlands in search of pre-Christian folklore. Richard and Eva Blum—a sociologist and anthropologist couple—lived in Epirus from 1957 to 1962. They observed in their book *The Dangerous Hour*: "The peasants are suspicious and fearful of the gypsies, who are reputed to have particularly efficacious—and sometimes noxious—magical powers." At this time, the Roma lived outside of many settlements; they could only visit the interior to ply their trades.

Traditionally, there were few acceptable professions for these dark-skinned outliers. The male breadwinner could be a smithy, a cobbler, a basket weaver, or a musician. Refuse collection and rag picking could also be practiced by the infirm or handicapped.

Metalworking, particularly the crafting of copper, was a Roma occupation linking the Gypsies with the surrounding shepherding culture. To this day, coppersmiths specialize in sheep and goat bells, *koudounia*.[15] In Ioannina, bronze, first forged from copper and tin, is hammered, then finely ground on a carbon wheel, kicking up a haze of fine dust smelling like gunpowder and giving the craftsman a resemblance to wizened Hephaestus. A head shepherd, a *tselingas,* is the primary customer for *koudounia.*

But the Roma inhabited the lowest position in the pecking order of the Greek population. Their social mobility, both horizontal and vertical, was severely limited. Apprenticeship was the traditional mode of learning a skill, yet there were few guilds that accepted Roma. A musician could make more money than a metalworker. During the halcyon days before electricity and wide-scale migration, there were hundreds of Gypsy musicians in Epirus.[16]

In this earlier, more isolated time, people wanted to be penetrated by music—taken apart and made whole again by the musicians. Dancers in these remote places desired to hear the local nuances, the subtle musical lace that distinguished their dances and songs from those of the neighboring villages. They wanted to experience the crooked notes and angular phrases of their youth, the songs of their great-grandparents.

A long-dead villager could say to a long-dead musician, "Create for us a nostalgic landscape of music, something that we can inhabit and lose ourselves in. And make it *intense.*" If a musician could deliver these goods then he would be paid well, tipped even better, and given a promise to play at the next celebration. He might be invited to other villages—even strings of settlements and towns. And here is where the dynamic between necessity, vulnerability, and virtuosity plays out.

If a musician wants to be paid well, to be necessary to a village, and to be less vulnerable, then he must excel at his craft of playing an instrument. As a virtuoso—peerless and versatile—he must craft music that the villagers need. Within this context, the Roma can capitalize on the otherworldly powers that they are presumed to possess. If the Greeks from the countryside see someone as a reservoir of supernatural potency, then why not give them a taste of their magic?

The major hurdle facing an aspiring artist during this golden age of Epirotic music making was that there were hundreds of other musicians competing for the same compensation and security. How does the artist rise above the fray? To capture attention and drachmas of a village, he had to hone his skills, learn hundreds of tunes, scalar patterns, and rhythms (along with local variations), develop stamina and technique, and perfect his ability to read the dancers. If he half-assed the work, he would sink back to the bottom of the enormous pool of potential music makers.

The most resourceful musicians excelled at their craft through constant practice, obsessive listening, and a naïve, childlike curiosity with the phenomenon of sound—and this is still the case. Thomas Haliyiannis and Kostas Karapanos, the clarinet and violin players in Gregoris Kapsalis's group, are perfect examples. Thomas is a Roma from Parakalamos and Kostas is a Greek from Megalo Peristeri in Metsovo. Both men sleep with their instruments. They play incessantly. The only evidence that they have a life outside of music is the presence of their many children at *panegyria*. Sometimes, they do not sleep only with their instruments.

When these two musicians do not have gigs—which is rare—

they teach or make music for themselves. Thomas and Kostas sometimes play music for eight hours with little or no break. Most of the time they play for much longer, ten or twelve hours. The audience scrutinizes every minute.

Thomas and Kostas know the nuances of tunes associated with each village, even with each dancer. When a person leading a circle of dancers agilely steps around the band, Thomas's and Kostas's eyes never leave them. They are musician-hunters stalking their dancer-prey. Every note from the musicians matches every step of the lead villager. The inner workings of an Epirotic dance ought to be as flawless as the gears within an analog timepiece.

An elderly woman with raspberry-dyed hair and a subtle south-paw limp requires an extra quarter-note pause between beats so that her left foot lifts behind her right foot during the "Paleo Zagorisio."* *But* only on the first and third beats, since the other beats rely more heavily on the right foot. Thomas and Kostas fixate on her tiny steps. The musicians elongate the melody slightly. The percussion of the *defi* is fixed, and every dancer—there are around one hundred and twenty—becomes synchronized with this slight variation in the "Paleo Zagorisio."

This is not a smoke-and-mirrors act. An obsessive immersion in the musical life of this region results in this ability to read a dancer's movements and tailor the song. Though many see these Gypsies as exotic—as conjurors of sound—they are simply people that are driven to perform in extraordinary ways.

The effects of the music *are* magical. But those who deliver this

---

* She wears red shoes that are too small and heels that are too high, and she is a superb dancer. A little over a year before she danced at this *panegyri* I attended, she fell and injured her left foot. The musicians now compensate for her movements because a good dancer expresses *kefi* or enthusiasm while leading a circle of villagers. A deep symbiosis between music and dance—the interaction between sound and movement—implies that one expression cannot exist without the other.

potent balm are musicians existing within a special context. And nowadays these craftsmen of sound know how to work a once-oppressive system to their advantage. Many of them realize a fundamental truth: the exotic is exotic because it is inaccessible. Shrouded in the unknowable, it is a mystery to their audience.

During my fourth visit to Epirus I asked a teenage *klarino*—one who did not know me or my prior experiences here—how "you heal a person through playing your clarinet." His face was without expression, a lake of still waters, and his response suggested no follow-up. This boy who was just learning how to shave, mend souls, and read the dancers said, "To do this, you must know how."

> I am a simple artist. When I play, I feel like a child of nine or ten writing a paragraph, a story. I tell a story like a child. If I must play a mournful piece, I must first make myself sad.

These are the words spoken to me by Napoleon Zoumbas during my third conversation with him. Demetris Dallas accompanied me to Grammeno, this time as a translator, a year before I visited Klimatia. When we are conversing with musicians, Demetris's questions and explanations are rendered like Zen koan phrases. Napoleon spoke freely during this last visit. It could have been the presence of Demetris, who as a poet understands cadence and rhythm. It may also have been because I had become a familiar face, an annual visitor. During this third conversation Napoleon disclosed that he was Roma. Among the oldest generation, being a Roma is a shameful thing, a truth that one avoids acknowledging.

Napoleon is not unique in this respect. Gregoris Kapsalis will avoid admitting his Roma ancestry—he is half Roma on his father's side. Most Epirotic musicians over the age of sixty circumambulate the issue of ethnicity. Alexis Zoumbas probably relished the notion that he could walk the streets of New York City as a *Greek immigrant* without adding the qualifier of *Roma*. Now that Gypsies have settled in towns and cities, where they can disappear into the crowds, why should they admit the suffering of discrimination?

This modern age carries with it paradoxes of identity. Napoleon's children, now middle-age adults, did not want to be defined as another generation of Gypsy musicians. Because they could pass as assimilated Greeks, they chose more lucrative professions. But among the younger generation of Roma, what was once a cultural liability is now a cultural asset. "Traditional is now hip!" Alexandros Spyrou stated about the popularity of handmade *tsipouro*. What is true about *tsipouro*-making is also true about music making in certain parts of Epirus and many other places in Europe.

Younger musicians such as Yiannis Chaldoupis easily admit their Gypsy heritage, capitalizing on their ethnicity. His choice of wardrobe may be contemporary—a mixture of Hellenized Goth and late-period Elvis—but he is quick to stress that he is a traditional Roma. He is mindful of the long-standing belief that Gypsies are vessels of potent tones, the best artists for delivering medicinal sounds to the Greek villages. There is unassailable value now in being perceived this way.

Exoticism in this economy only works in one direction. A Romani musician may pass as being an assimilated Greek, but it is nearly impossible for an assimilated Greek to pass as a Romani musician. There's too much cultural baggage—subtle ways of interacting, of speaking, of being—for a non-Roma musician to appear as a Roma.

In the last thirty to forty years many non-Roma Greeks have become outstanding—at least in a formal sense—Epirotic musicians. Motivated by a nostalgia for the sounds that existed in their childhood, many of these Greek musicians have studied under and played with Roma musicians.

Ultimately I can hear a subtle disconnection—something missing or contrived—in the way many of these modern musicians play. Most have mastered the technique, but there is thinness in the emotional depth. This thinness, this missing thing, is best conveyed in "The Mirologi of the Gypsy," a short story written by an Epirote, Phrixos Tziovas. Tziovas was born in 1919 in Asprangeloi, a village close to Vitsa. The story has a loose, ambiguous feel. Jim Potts and Phillip Sougles summarized passages that I've rendered as a parable:

> A young Gypsy boy aspired to be a great clarinetist. His family saw him as shiftless, yet he would take his grandfather's instrument down by the River Kalamas and practice. He tried to mimic the sounds of human anguish and the sounds of nature. But he did not know how to translate these sounds into music.
>
> After the war broke out, he joined the army in 1940. On the front line he heard a dying Italian soldier play the fading strains of "O sole mio" on a harmonica. The young man was constantly surrounded by death. Suffering and misery informed his emotional landscape. In the village of Vitsa, in front of a church, the Gypsy boy stopped to talk with an old man, Manousis, who was the best *defi* player in Zagori. The military unit did not notice the low-flying airplane until it was too late. A bomb exploded nearby. When the smoke rose, the young man saw Manousis's headless body lying on the church's steps as if he was begging for forgiveness.
>
> Something became loosened within the Gypsy boy. He reached inside of his jacket and pieced his clarinet together. After wiping tears and the blood from his face, he put the instrument to his lips. The first few notes found the path that he had been seeking all of those years. The knots loosened inside him as he lamented the dead Italian soldier and poor old Manousis who would never tap the *defi* again. Like the flood from a burst dam, the sounds of the clarinet inundated the countryside. Through the *mirologi*, humanity—in the form of this young Gypsy boy—lamented the evil that it had encountered. All of humankind then wept dark tears.

Nearly seventy years later when the teenage Gypsy clarinetist told me "To do *this*, you must know *how*," I knew that the "*this*" was to play Epirotic music effectively. I now know that the "*how*" is parsed into two skills: an ability to develop a personal technique and an ability to tap into some individual and collective pathos.

A Harisiadis or a Kapsalis can midwife virtuosity. The solitary musical sanctuary of Klimatia is the perfect environment for such a process. But one's technique must be personal. On this, Napoleon Zoumbas said,

> There cannot be authentic Epirotic music without individual style. Before the introduction of [mass media] every musician was unique. Afterwards idiosyncratic style collapsed.

However, tapping into pathos is different from harnessing the expressive powers of an instrument. You may master an instrument, but pathos masters you. Then the instrument plays you.

In Sitaria, I asked Yiannis Chaldoupis to demonstrate his ability to channel emotion through his clarinet. He replied sharply, "I'm a man, not a machine!" He needed time to conjure pathos before he could play a deep *mirologi*: he was not in control of this emotional reservoir; rather, it controlled him. Similarly, Napoleon Zoumbas told Demetris and me that "When I play a good *mirologi*, tears would stream down from both of my eyes. I have to allow the emotions to take over me. And then the audience would be crying as well."

This is why some of the youngest generation of musicians tend to ring hollow when it comes to this skill. Perhaps they've yet to be overcome by emotion. To source your own technique, you can seek the assistance of a master. To source your own pathos, you are on your own.

When I think of Kitsos Harisiadis I don't visualize his face. Instead, I hear the opening notes of the *skaros* that he recorded in 1930. Kitsos and the *skaros* are one and the same: two expressions spiritually interchangeable.

The word *skaros* possesses two distinct yet related meanings: a cultural-linguistic definition and a musical definition. In the cultural context, *skaros* is understood as the time of "midnight grazing" when a shepherd gathers his flock together to eat, to take water, and to take shelter. At this time, the temperature is cooler and the animals have a better appetite. But this midnight grazing implies risks: predators or storms could scatter the herd. Here is a situation—a dangerous hour—that tests the shepherd's skills at calming and collecting his flock.

In the musical context of *skaros*, it is the artist playing for his village. But the intention of the tune is largely the same.

The *skaros* is an instrumental with complex improvised passages. During the performance of the *skaros*, the clarinet and the violin exchange solos. A musical conversation emerges. Phrases imitate sounds found in nature: the singing of a nightingale, the babbling of a brook, the baying and barking of animals, and the surge of a storm. This piece, like the *mirologi*, is not meant for dancing but intended for deep listening. Villagers who are attentive to the *skaros* are drawn into a calm, trance-like state. A well-crafted *skaros* induces introspection in the listener.

In my record room in Virginia, the mechanism in Harisiadis's *skaros* from the 78 disc works the same magic as the *skaros* played in Vitsa by Kostas Karapanos on violin during the *panegyri*. The first few notes ask a simple question: "What troubles you?" The soothing response formed in interlaced variations is an untying from anxiety: "You are at peace, safe."

During *panegyria* the *mirologi* bookends the celebration: it is the alpha and the omega. But the *skaros* is played in the middle of the night, not at midnight but around two or three o'clock in the morning, a spiritually appropriate hour when you look up at the celestial bodies. When your ear is drawn to the *skaros* you are part of the village, part of the flock.

Think of the *skaros* as a soothing proto-lullaby, an ancient melody without words. As a social animal we often seek to comfort or to care for those around us. If we are a gregarious musical species, then our impulse to mourn through song such as the *mirologi* may be just as powerful as our instinct to pacify through music like a lullaby or the *skaros*.

Remembrance and regret, sympathy and compassion: these are undeniable aspects of the human experience. We often remember the first funeral we attended, the first person we lost. But can we recall the first or the last time that our parents sang a lullaby to us? This musical activity predates our memory, yet it informs everything good within us. Just as certain musical expressions predate human recollection, so too do our fundamental emotional responses.

Imagine Kitsos seated on his stone bench in the musical sanctuary of Klimatia. His understudy's ear waits for the first few notes of the *skaros* to travel across the ravine. Birds, insects, and wind inundate the landscape. Everything is peaceful—at one with itself—in this organic temple of sound. Could the young student, even for a moment, imagine that the sounds about to enter his ears form a thread reaching back thousands of years when music was a tool for survival and as necessary as the air that the student now breathed?

7

SATYR DANCE

Our civilization goes in the wrong direction. Our spiritual development drags so far behind technical progress that we are in a constant spiritual crisis. The conflict between material and spiritual is the fact and our marrow just reacts, looks for a solution in such situations.

—ANDREI TARKOVSKY, INTERVIEWED BY VADIM MOROZ

With the gods overthrown like that, nobody knew which way to turn. . . . The cunning ones adjusted quickly. . . . They changed the names of streets and temples: improvised substitutions. Zeus and Dione gave way to Jesus and the Virgin. Theodosius added the finishing touches. . . .

—YANNIS RITSOS, *THE END OF DODONA II*, TRANSLATED BY EDMUND KEELEY

ON THE SECOND NIGHT OF A *PANEGYRI* IN THE VILLAGE OF Xxxxx,* I passed into the liminal stage of musical possession. It was early morning before dawn crested the peaks of the Pindus. My hands were secured within both of my neighbors' hands. I was part of a single circle composed of several dozen villagers orbiting rhythmically around the musicians. Our bodies were gliding, feet skimming above the cobblestones. We were matching our movements with the asymmetric beat of the *arvanitiko* dance. A crooked

---

* I've redacted the name of this village in northwestern Greece out of paranoia that hedonist libertines and priapic voyeurs would descend on this largely unspoiled place.

tune presumably of southern Albanian provenance, the *arvanitiko*'s languid tempo dissolves thoughts, collapses time.

Strings of naked light bulbs suspended around the vine-entangled courtyard cast shadows on every face. Evolving from dancer to dancer, the darkness seeped upwards and the light faded downwards. Within this palette of sepia and shadows, each face contained an expression of abandon. The walls encompassing the courtyard where we danced reflected every undulating note.

Across from me in this circle of dancers was a respected elderly caretaker of the village. He was a man tasked with overseeing the preservation of tradition. His peppered hair was well manicured—feathered and neat—and only slightly offset by a loose blue windbreaker and wrinkled trousers. Leading the dance, he was as agile as a young buck. His eighty-year-old frame moved gracefully, like a stork hovering above the surface of Lake Pamvotis.

As the dancers stepped forward, every soul holding hands recollected that which had been lost the year before, the decade prior, centuries past. As the clarinet played its lowest, most desperate note, my eyes drifted toward the elderly caretaker's face.

Everything went tilt.

Temporal and spatial anchors were pulled, surrendering their immutable roles. Circuits were flipped and completed. The atmosphere instantly rarefied, like the subtle vacuum formed when a lightning bolt touches the ground nearby: an airless heat flash. The dance shifted from the dark, languid *arvanitiko* to the searing, high-voltage "Hasaposerviko," a Slavic melody that skirts the edge of control. Despondence became exuberance, despair became ecstasy.

My eyes formed a freeze-frame capture of the old man while mid-stride in this dance, precisely where the starkness of death and the richness of life intersect. Tears intensified the eroded crevices bordering his eyes. Mingling with the sweat coating his cheeks—emotions rendered as fluids—the wetness accented his stubble, amplifying the gray margins of his sideburns.

Satyr and shepherd.

Contained within his body were these contrasts: a face creased with painful memory and a lower torso proudly displaying an enormous erection, a tumescent phallus celebrating life and everything that thrived outside of his charcoal gray trousers. Despite the confines of his pants, his fleshy chronometer unfailingly kept time with the change in dance meter.

He was unashamed, and justly so. None of the dancers or musicians saw any discordance with this musically induced display of vitality.* Hell, it happens to me when I listen to a 78 of the "Arvanitiko" in my record room.

This was a timeless ceremonial transformation: a dance in the twenty-first century rooted in the *kordax*, an orgiastic Dionysian ritual performed before the birth of Christ. Ancient poets sang of satyrs and cohorts dancing to the cascading flute notes of Pan, circling fires, organs of reproduction held attentive and majestic.

I was part of this *choreia*, an ancient Greek term used by Aristotle that encompassed choreography, song, and physical movements. This term implies a harmonious sequence—a circle or many

* Similar responses to this music have been observed in women.

Panegyri in Monodendri, early twentieth century.

circles—such as a circular line dance or an intricate transversal of heavenly bodies, the former being the mortal yearning to mimic the latter. Over two thousand years ago, rings of dancers and singers filled the threshing floors of villages throughout Greece, engaged in ceremonies and poetic storytelling like the Homeric ode "To Pan":

> *The god glides in and out of the dance, on this side and that,*
> *Now prancing on nimble feet in the very midst of the chorus,*
> *Wearing the tawny pelt of a lynx on his shoulders,*
> *His heart exalting in music's shrill sweetness . . .*

During a dance in Epirus now, everyone's arms are bent gracefully at the elbow so the hands are slightly below the shoulder line, a gesture of pride as well as of unity. Photographs of *panegyria* from the early twentieth century show men and women dancing separately, men with their arms up, hand in hand, women with their arms firmly at their sides, stern. By the middle of the last century, conflicts here saw women fighting and dying alongside men. Women had proved their mettle in battle, and had thereby gained equality. Now in most villages everyone dances together.* But this adaptation is just a modification in lace, a variation of trim that does not compromise the musical biosphere.

The cultural context—the function of music and the deep medicine of dance—has scarcely changed over the ages. Before Greek Orthodoxy there were mystery cults and polytheism. Before these religious manifestations was the unknowable—possibly a time when art, spirituality, and expression were so tightly bound together as to be indistinguishable. But braiding its way from the distant past to the present is this undeniable need for palliative, cathartic music.

Observing the rhythmic play between light and darkness, sound and responsive movement, I imagined the dancers before me as rupestrian motifs found on cave walls throughout Europe. Shamans or artists grafted the horns of a red deer or the lower extremities of a wild goat onto the torso of a man.† Some of these images would become pagan deities like the god Pan and his satyrs in a few thousand years. The dim lights above this village courtyard cast the same shadows as rushlight torches did in these caves. A clarinet mimics the feral sounds contained within the vast mountains just as the archaic flute echoed the pacifying song of the nightingale eons ago.

Of course there are no flesh-and-blood satyrs in Epirus. I never stumbled across a half-naked pagan, nor did I witness an actual *kordax*. Rather, my mind grasped elements at play during this ancient religious ceremony. The primordial spirit of the *panegyri* allows us to see the continuity in culture.

John Cuthbert Lawson, an English scholar writing in 1900 after having spent two years in rural Greece, had this to say:

---

* In the traditional and isolated Vlach villages women and men dance separately.

† One example among many is the rendering of the "Sorcerer" in the Cave of Les Trois Frères, in the Volp Caverns.

No foreigner, even though he were totally ignorant of the modern language, could chance upon one of the many festivals of
the country without remarking that there, in humbler form, are
reenacted many of the scenes of ancient days. The πανηγύρια [*panegyria*] as they call these festivals . . . present the same medley of
religion, art, trading, athletics, and amusement, which consti-
tuted the Olympian games.

Epirotic music is, in essence, an out-of-place artifact in Western
society. With most of Europe hell-bent on globalization, the tide of
culture in certain parts of northwestern Greece runs contrary to
the outside world.* Between these two poles of modernization and
tradition, persistent elements from antiquity linger, connecting us
with the pre-Christian beliefs of the region.

Think of these elements as the fossilized remains of culture.
Some fossils are ghostly impressions of organisms, a mirrored
stamp left by a skeleton or leafstalk. Delicate tendrils once coursing with life withered millions of years ago, leaving only a void for
us to study. Other fossils are copies of whole anatomical systems,
the organic matter replaced with stone. There are also living fossils, ancient things thought to be extinct yet surviving through
slight adaptation. Finally, there are fragmented remains, fossils so
broken that we cannot even conjecture their structure, let alone
their function. Epirus may be said to contain cultural remains of
each of these types, especially living fossils.

The things that connect the ancient past of northwestern
Greece with the present are found in communal spaces and physical locations, in beliefs and behaviors, and in certain groups of

---

* In 2014, writer and friend Amanda Petrusich visited Epirus with me to
research the phenomenon of *panegyria* for the *New York Times Magazine*. In the
tiny village of Sitaria a man asked her why she was there. After an exchange of
pleasantries, I overheard him say to Amanda, "Globalism is nice and all, but it's
not for us."

people. These elements have a spiritual dimension best understood through the process of syncretism, the notion that institutionalized theology absorbs religious ideas and practices from native culture. In Greece, ancient pre-Christian beliefs blended with Orthodox monotheism. Syncretism was, and still is, a controversial notion.[17] Lawson described the receptive environment created by the nascent Church that preserved these artifacts from antiquity.

> In effect, paganism was not uprooted to make room for the planting of Christianity, but served rather as an old stock on which a new and vigorous branch, capable indeed of fairer fruit but owning its very vitality to alien sap, might be engrafted.

In Greece, an impulse to reconcile the old with the new blended these religious beliefs and behaviors. Possibly the theology of the developing Orthodox Church satisfied the mind but left the heart yearning for aspects of the past.

One of the most tangible (and obvious) ways of supplanting paganism with Christianity was to construct churches on top of ancient temples. The holy place was retained while the spiritual purpose was modified, re-tasked. On this, Lawson reasons:

> It was politic no doubt to encourage the weaker brethren by building churches on sites where they had long been wont to worship: it was politic to smooth the path of the common-folk by substituting for the god whom they had worshipped a patron-saint of like name or attributes. . . . She [The Church] drove out the old gods from their temples made with hands, but did not ensure the obliteration of them from men's hearts. . . . The adoption of the old places of worship made it inevitable that the old associations of the pagan cults should survive and blend themselves with the new ideas, and that the churches should more often acquire pres-

tige from their heathen sites than themselves shed a new luster of sanctity upon them.

Not only were churches built on the sites where earlier pagans worshipped, but in many cases the older temple stones were recycled in the construction of new foundations and walls. Up until 1801, an ancient statue of the Greek goddess Demeter was venerated as Saint Demetra by villagers in the town of Eleusis in West Attica. This area was the original home of Demeter worship. Sacred objects were assimilated, and theology—particularly for the "weaker brethren"—allowed room for older beliefs.

Several years ago, on a visit to Ano Pedina, a village near Vitsa, Demetris Dallas, Jim Potts, and I surveyed one such theological accommodation in the nave of a chapel. The iconography above our heads featured Christ as the center of all truth. Radiating from Christ were vines that connected Him with New Testament saints and disciples. But on the outer tendrils of the True Vine— connected tenuously—were Plato and a variety of Greek philosophers and historians.

Groves and mountains sacred to mystery cults and polytheistic worshippers became locations for monasteries and churches. Even the ancient threshing floor or *aloni* found in practically every village shifted in function. This communal area witnessed the processing of grains and the performing of pre-Christian religious activities as well as theater and poetic performances. Gradually threshing floors became a space for *panegyria* to commemorate the Orthodox saints.

The Church fidgeted nervously over what some priests and patriarchs called "quasi-pagan" displays of faith. Some religious leaders feared European travelers would perceive the Greeks as backwards. Christian officials even wrote formal letters to village elders, requesting that they refrain from engaging in ceremonies containing "religious errors." One such ritual is the *Anastenaria*—

still practiced in some villages of Western Macedonia, not far from Epirus. During this event, bonfires are lit in the village while lyres and drums produce pulsating, hypnotic tunes. Villagers sway forward and backward while carrying sacred icons. Hot coals are raked across the courtyard. Pious icon handlers remove their shoes and walk or dance across the coals without injury. Whether the *Anastenaria* is a relic of Dionysian worship or a ritual of some other origin, the ritual has continued into the twenty-first century.[18]

Various practices were preserved in Greece because the Ottoman occupiers saw parallels between their version of Islam and the ceremonies in these isolated places. One such display of faith in the countryside is the *Kourbania*. Like the *Anastenaria*, it probably originated in Asia Minor, not mainland Greece. Both are variations of the *panegyria*. Neither ceremony occurs in Epirus.

Before the *Kourbania* is held, a cow is selected and treated as if it is an extended member of the village. For a year the cow is fed by hand and allowed to run loose in the dusty streets. Before the *panegyri*, a garland is woven around the bovine's head. The cow is then ritually slaughtered on the steps of the church. The whole village partakes of the animal. Turks permitted this ceremony, since it closely resembled their own concept of sacrifice, *bayram.**

Some people are reticent to acknowledge the pagan past of northwestern Greece. Others embrace this heritage. One man who delights in pointing out these primeval connections is my friend Costas Zissis from Zagori. With his long heather ringlets of hair, owl eyes, and lithe body, Costas looks as if he could be some ancient Greek poet-athlete leaping from an amphora, lyre in hand. His roots in Zagori are unquestionable: his father ate from the same bowl as clarinetist Gregoris Kapsalis during the German occupation. He is also a professional photographer who knows the moun-

---

* The name of the ritual itself, *Kourbania*, is likely derived from the Turkish word for victim, *kurban*.

tain passes and discreet splendors of Epirus. One picturesque place he described to me was a chapel next to the springs of the Voidomatis River in Zagori:

> The place is called *I Angastromeni* or The Pregnant Lady. Years ago, I visited the spot with an Australian archaeologist. He saw the huge hemisphere-shaped rock next to Voidomatis' springs and told me that if this formation were located in Australia it would definitely be an aboriginal place of worship. There, just next to it, lays the chapel dedicated to the *Panagia*, The Holy Mother of Jesus. The locals refer to the place mostly as *Angastromeni* and not so much as *Panagia*. The relation between the pregnant lady's belly shaped rock and the Virgin Mary's chapel reminds us of the countless scenarios where an ancient female deity's place of worship (Athena, Demetra, Artemis) became a holy place (church or monastery) for the Virgin Mary throughout all of the Greek territories.

There are songs amplifying the pagan dimension of places and structures. Arta, located in southern Epirus and hometown of young 78 collector Vassilis Georganos, possesses a gently curved Ottoman-era bridge with four inverted serpentine arches spanning the Arachthos River. The bridge's foundations are from the Roman era before Christianity reached Greece.

In Epirus and throughout the Balkans there are ballads narrating the sacrifice of a human in order to successfully build a structure. "Tis Artas To Gefiri" ("The Bridge of Arta") is the best known:

> *Forty-five master builders and sixty young apprentices,*
> *All day long were building, building the bridge at Arta.*
> *All day long were building it but at night it tumbled down.*
> *The master builders mourn their work; the apprentices all weep.*
> *A bird appeared and sat itself, at the midmost of the arches.*
> *It wasn't singing like a bird, nor as a nightingale does sing.*

But it was singing and spoke out, like a human being.
"Don't go on with the work, oh builders, and waste your weary
    efforts.
Unless you haunt a human soul, the bridge will not be stable.
Don't go and take an orphan's soul, a stranger's or a traveler's.
The first master builder's pretty wife, her soul built in the bridge."

There are variations to these folk poems—lustration ballads, or songs of ritual sacrifice—as they migrate from one region to another. But the core meaning persists: appeasing the unseen forces that govern the physical world requires the sacrifice of a living being. In this case it is the beloved wife of the master builder.

I hear this song at *panegyria* and the text is remarkably consistent. A bird with a human voice summons the master builder's wife to the bridge. She is told that her husband's wedding ring fell to the bottom of the arches. As the wife is small and nimble, she is asked to fetch his jewelry. As she nears the bottom of the foundation, the master builder—reluctantly in most versions of the song—casts a large stone that immobilizes her. As she lies dying, she bemoans her fate and that of her two sisters. The first sister was sacrificed to build a bridge over the Danube and the second for a bridge over the Euphrates. She utters a curse over any traveler that crosses this structure. Before her last gasp of air, her husband implores her to withdraw this curse.

The song ends suddenly, without resolution.

Sacrifice was fundamental to ancient Greek religion. "The Bridge of Arta" expresses a notion of sacrifice as appeasement and purification. But the offering of life to unseen forces also served to insure good fortune or to protect against and prevent harm.

Driving through waves of icy rain, chasing Kitsos Harisiadis's ghost to Delvinaki in November of 2015, Vassilis Georganos told me, "You know, my grandfather slaughtered a rooster and put the head of the chicken under the foundation of his new house in the

1950s." Even in the late 1960s, chickens were routinely sacrificed to fortify recently built homes in the villages of Epirus. This was done to bring prosperity and luck to the new households. Although Orthodox priests blessed the structure, sanctifying the poultricide, this act remains pagan. The skeletons of gamecocks, yard birds, and small mammals—often missing their heads or, conversely, the rest of their bodies—are found underneath many ancient dwellings in the Greek-speaking world.

Throughout Greece and Asia Minor, villages and small towns practiced another type of ritual sacrifice and immurement. This ceremony continued well after Christianity had spread into Epirus. Two oxen or cows would be yoked and made to draw a plow around the circumference of a settlement. Then the animals would be killed and buried near the town. Sometimes the plow would be buried with the cattle, but often it was hung in a secret location. This elaborate ceremony was thought to keep disease, invasions, and droughts out of the village.

And it did.

Costas Zissis told me this story:

> My grandmother Kassoula kept cows and goats. She always had delicious milk products for us relatives as well as anyone visiting her home in the village of Aristi. On April 27, 1986, the foreign affairs minister and future president of Greece, Carolos Papoulias, visited Zagori. This was the day after the Chernobyl meltdown and only high-ranking officials knew of the environmental dangers. Papoulias came to my father's restaurant. My father asked me to fetch from my grandmother some sour milk for him. I did so and the minister had his milk and enjoyed it. The next day the general population was informed. The authorities warned the citizens of Epirus not to consume milk products. I went to my grandmother with this news.

She said there was no need to worry, since our village was pro-
tected from any illnesses and other bad things because we had
two calves sacrificed and buried, together with a golden plow, in
the crossroad at the village entrance when the plague-epidemic
was approaching the area centuries ago. She also noted, sadly, that
the people of the next village, Agios Menas, decided not to do this
[the ceremony]. Many of these neighboring villagers died from a
plague-epidemic centuries ago and the survivors have spots and
freckles on their faces, even to this day.[19]

The concept of protection does not require a thousand pounds of
bovine flesh and a plow of precious metal. Nikos Petsios, an Epirote
friend who runs the finest luxury hotel in Vitsa, related this story
of talismanic belief:

> When I was born, my mother sewed a small triangle pouch of
> cloth to my undergarments. She did this not out of any religious
> belief but rather out of the insistence of my grandmother. We
> don't know what was inside this bag of cloth—it was a secret—
> but we do know that it was a charm meant to protect me as a
> young child.

Contained within the amulet—a *phylakto*—was some corporeal
aspect of Nikos himself: it was likely his hair, toenail trimmings,
or a piece of his umbilical cord. Although a priest had blessed the
amulet, ancient Greeks, Persians, and Egyptians would have worn
an object of this nature as well.

The *phylakto* has a cognate in English: "prophylactic." In rural
Greece a *phylakto* is a physical object imbued with a spiritual power
that protects an individual from unseen dangers. The evil eye—
that motif so overused as a metaphor in the West—was, and still is,
a real threat to many who live here. The simple psychology behind
the casting of the evil eye—that jealousy and spite, either explicit

or unintended, can cause damage to another—is just as valid now as it was when the concept emerged thousands of years ago.

Amulets and ceremonies are not the only ways of protecting the individual or the village from malevolent forces. A belief in unseen forces beyond perception in the physical world and social cohesion—the bonds reinforced by communal love and common decency—guard against harm. These two ideas are necessary to village life. Beliefs such as these are a condition of being a reflective, gregarious species.

Orthodox Christianity and earlier Greek popular religion shared two fundamental values: there was value in sacrifice and value in communion. Before Christianity spread throughout Greece, the "simple brethren" offered sacrifices to unseen powers. The Orthodox message, that God, who was also a man, sacrificed himself so that others may live, would not be alien to a Greek peasant who regularly gave their first fruits of harvest to the gods. Likewise, sharing food and resources is an act of love and communion. Such sharing would have been common before Christianity replaced polytheism. After Orthodoxy became widespread, often-repeated ceremonies—such as the Eucharist—provided visceral reinforcement of a preexisting concept.

When you experience the *panegyri* in the village, these notions of sacrifice and communion transcend the façade, the artifice of religion. You realize that the music, the food, and the love that is shared during the dance is not only a mechanism for survival, it is a way of reaffirming our humanity. *Panegyria* have persisted through wars, through *to kako tis Tourkokratias*—the evils of Turkish rule—and, currently, through the cancer of globalism. It should be no surprise, then, that the core elements of music and culture in northwestern Greece weathered the passage of time and the changing of religion.

The transition of spirituality from paganism to Orthodoxy may have been less contentious because the simple brethren were not that simple. They saw the commonalities and embraced them. They also saw the pragmatic—what worked or seemed to work in the older religions—and kept those elements as well. Those things that could not fit neatly within the beliefs of the Church just went underground along with Pan, or took to the mountains with the satyrs.

ୄ ୄ ୄ

"What is your ancestry? What tribe do you come from?"

I couldn't think of the Greek phrase for "white trash," the concept best capturing my inferior bloodline. Possibly there is none. I replied with the closest approximation.

"Scots-Irish" I said.

The family was immensely pleased. "You are one of us," Stratos Harisis said.

In his mind, the Celts of Scotland and Ireland share a common ancestry with his shepherding tribe, the Sarakatsani of Epirus. These proud pastoralists are among the oldest continuous inhabitants of northwestern Greece.

The Harisis clan has a home in Ano Vitsa, Upper Vitsa, among a cluster of houses perched at one of the highest points of the village. The family—Stratos, his wife Evdoxia, two of their children, Vassilis and Kiki, and Stratos's niece Ioanna—invited my friend Takis Kefalas* and me for some conversation. And conversation implies traditional Greek hospitality.

Takis and I climbed the steep serpentine acclivity from Lower Vitsa to the Harisis's house around eight o'clock in the evening. Our visit had been postponed for a few hours when Takis received a call earlier. "They are not ready," Takis said. Coexisting with hos-

---

* Or, as I know him, Takis "The Fixer." He is one of the few young men who live full-time in the isolated villages. The mode of survival in such an isolated place implies a rare breed. I gave him the title of "The Fixer" since there was no situation, resource, or opportunity that Takis could not fix. At the time of this reading, Takis will have received a full set of false teeth, carved and blessed by one of the local Orthodox priests.

pitality is the imperative for household cleanliness and order—everything must be spotless for guests.

Icy November rain cut horizontally across our bodies, rendering our umbrellas useless and our clothing accelerants for hypothermia. But inside the Harisis house was a raging fireplace. Steam rolled off us as we walked in. Low couches flanked the hearth, thick furs and woolly hides covered the floor, and a long table was set with roasted lamb, savory cheeses, wine, and—yes—*tsipouro*. Everything before us came from the Harisis's skillfully tended stock of animals, vegetables, and fruits.

Diadems of geometric patterns pulsated from the handmade embroidered blankets folded across the ottomans. Warm and welcoming, the atmosphere in front of that fire reflected the material and spiritual legacy of the nomadic lifestyle that the Sarakatsani had stubbornly maintained for thousands of years. This living room was a snapshot of the interior of a Sarakatanos hut.

After Stratos had confirmed that we were kindred tribesmen, he asked me, "Do you know where we Sarakatsani come from? I don't know myself."

And this is true. No one knows.

Some speculate that the Sarakatsani descended from villagers forced out of their settlements by invaders from the Slavic north in the fourth century AD. Other researchers suggest that they were pastoralists driven to the highlands of Zagori by more resourceful and powerful tribes. Anthropologist Euripides Makris argues that the Sarakatsani descended from Neolithic tribes of Greece. John Campbell, a British ethnographer, wrote that they were a people who had simply existed apart from society for a very long time. None of these explanations are exhaustive or conclusive, but the last two are complementary.

"Your people have lived here forever. The Sarakatsani speak the purest Greek. And your *tsipouro* is especially good."

These three statements from me were, in fact, also true. The

Sarakatsani—unlike myself—were scions of an old noble lineage. And Stratos produced some of the finest *tsipouro* I've ever had.

Arthur Foss, a soldier stationed in Epirus during World War II, wrote that through all the political upheavals experienced in the region of Epirus from Hellenistic, Roman, Byzantine, and Turkish rule, "Only the transhumant life of the shepherds continued as it had done since time immemorial."

There is evidence suggesting that the Sarakatsani, or their immediate ancestors, lived as tightly organized nomadic groups for thousands of years in Epirus, between the highlands of Zagori and the low coastal plains around Igoumenitsa where we first started our journey into northwestern Greece.

Sarakatsani life played out for millennia. Thick matrixes of charcoal and refuse form deep strata where temporary Sarakatsani settlements decayed each year only to be rebuilt the next. Herding trails run like arteries throughout the valleys. Sheep and goat hooves, wagon wheels and shepherds' boots created this rutted topography.

The migratory trails favored by the Sarakatsani and other shepherds contain the heaped bones of Paleolithic-era ibex, chamois, and red deer slaughtered by ancient hunters of Epirus. Quite possibly nomadic shepherds descended from these earlier foraging tribes.

Classical literature offers very little concerning the Sarakatsani. One gets the impression that they have always been a reticent tribe, peaceful and reserved. Their livelihood—trading among themselves and exchanging with others—has always pivoted on the production of milk, cheese, and wool. Although the Sarakatsani were necessary to village life, they could also vanish into the mountains when trouble approached.

Most Sarakatsani ceased their nomadic ways during the latter half of the twentieth century. After World War II and the Civil War, many houses in Zagorian villages were abandoned. Land was cheap. Electricity—that indispensable convenience of the modern world—was slowly creeping into the region. Imagine how the luxuries of permanent housing, heat, and light appeared to the nomads.

By the late 1960s most Sarakatsani, including the Harisis family, had one home in Zagori and another in Igoumenitsa. Underneath some of the Sarakatsani homes in Ano Vitsa lay a sacrificial lamb, a variation on the traditional chicken offering for good luck and prosperity. By keeping two homes, the Sarakatsani could continue their migrations along with shepherding, cheese making, and wool shearing but end every night sleeping in a warm bed.

Those who were fortunate enough to live among and study the Sarakatsani in the nineteenth and twentieth centuries discovered that the Greek language they spoke was not the modern tongue but rather was derived from the Greek dialect of the Dorians, a group that swept into northwestern Greece around 1150 BC. Doric Greek fell out of common use around the sixth century AD. Campbell, having lived with the Sarakatsani in 1954 and 1955, found their language anachronistic and their strict concepts of honor, morality, and familial bonds an atavism to a much earlier age.

The Sarakatsani stood apart as staunch traditionalists even within the very conservative social fabric of Epirus. For instance, largely before the 1950s in most of rural Greece, marriages were a business transaction between families. Nuptial arrangements considered class, status, and dowries. But the opinion of the potential bride and groom were considered before a deal was struck. In the Zagorian villages such as Vitsa, a large screen, a *kafassoto*, was placed between an unmarried daughter and a potential husband so that the young ladies could, at the very least, examine the physical traits and demeanor of the men without themselves being seen. This was not the case among the Sarakatsani.

The fathers of these shepherding families determined the coupling of their offspring and that was that. Since the Sarakatsani owned no land, the dowries included herds of sheep and goats, textiles and fineries, and—most importantly—status. Dowries ceded along such lines echoed practices of Athens of the third century BC. Married Sarakatsani women spent the rest of their lives spinning the distaff like one of the Fates, carrying water and building their temporary thatch-roofed huts. Studying photographs from before the 1960s, the Sarakatsani camps resembled wigwams of the Algonquian tribes or archaeological reconstructions of Paleolithic settlements in southern Europe.

European scholars traveling through northwestern Greece tended to conflate the Sarakatsani with other shepherding tribes in Epirus. In particular these writers often regarded the Vlachs and the Sarakatsani as one group when in reality they were quite distinct. It wasn't until 1914 that A. J. B. Wace and M. S. Thompson set the matter straight. The Vlachs, though Greek, spoke their own language, a Latin one and a dialect of Romanian. Vlach culture, although traditional in its own right, differed from that of the Sarakatsani in ornamentation, textile crafts, and music. The Sarakatsani have a favorite song, "Milo Mou Chryso Mou Milo"—"My Apple, My Golden Apple"; the Vlachs love a very different song, "Kontoula Vlacha Sta Vouna"—"Pretty Shepherdess in the Mountains."

It's fair to say too that the Vlachs assimilated earlier and more profitably than the Sarakatsani. The Vlachs developed permanent villages, something the Sarakatsani never did. Vlach men were known as skillful merchants, establishing robust businesses throughout Europe. Next time you walk through an airport or a swank part of town and pass a BVLGARI store or hotel, you are observing the successful legacy of Sotirio Voulgaris (Vulgari, the trademark rendered in classical Latin script as BVLGARI), a Greek Vlach. The Vlach villages—like those of the Zagorians—reflect the largesse of their benefactors.

The legacy of the Sarakatsani is not found in commercial ventures or in immaculate stone villages. What they left behind is incorporeal if not spiritual. Their legacy is in the simpler things: shepherding, Christian devotion, and flute playing.

❧❧❧

"We Sarakatsani are a *very* religious people," Stratos said with modest certainty under his trimmed, graying mustache. His family, handsome and approving, sat around him. Though his statement drove a wedge further between my godless, mongrel ancestry and that of the virtuous Sarakatsani, his statement was undeniable. These shepherds take the Christian mandate seriously.

There are close bonds between Jesus and the Sarakatsani. It was a shepherd—one of their own—who first saw the star rise over Bethlehem, announcing Jesus's birth. Christ is seen as a shepherd of men, much as the Sarakatsani are the caretakers of their flocks. And as Christ was a healer of the sick and lame, so too have the Sarakatsani tapped into the secrets of medicinal plants and botanical treatments only now being studied seriously by scientists.

Also, the Sarakatsani believe that Christ fashioned the first shepherd's flute.

The Sarakatsani love the music of Epirus to the point of rabid obsession. In this respect, perhaps I *am* from the same tribe. While bringing out bottles of homemade wine and fixing a mountain of pillows behind my back, the Harisis family opened a cabinet and produced stacks of audio and videotape documenting over twenty-five years of *panegyria*, weddings, and Sarakatsani festivals.

"This wine, this is the same wine that was made for Christ." Stratos poured me a small glass of red *krasi* and I tasted it, wondering what Christ would have thought of me drinking His wine. It was mild and warm, with a sweetness devoid of bitter tannin. The aftertaste suggested innocence.

A shepherd's flute hung in another cabinet. Stratos took it out and began to blow softly on it. He had learned as a boy while herding for his family. Unlike most Sarakatsani, Stratos also plays the clarinet, favoring the *skaros* and similar tunes.

In his book *Roumeli: Travels in Northern Greece*, Patrick Leigh Fermor described the flute playing of a young Sarakatsanos shepherd:

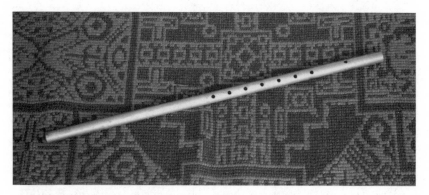

Sarakatsanos shepherd's flute on traditional woven rug.

The music that began to hover through the hut was moving and breathless. It started with long and deep notes separated by pauses; then it shot aloft in patterns of great complexity. Repeated and accelerating trills led to sustained high notes which left the tune quivering in mid-air before plummeting an octave to those low and long-drawn initial semibreves. Notes of an icy clarity alternated with notes of a stirring, reedy, and at moments almost rasping hoarseness. After a long breath, they sailed again into limpid and piercing airs of a most touching softness; the same minor phrase recurred again and again with diminishing volume, until the final high flourishes presaged the protracted bass notes once more, each of them preceded and followed by a lengthening hiatus of silence. One can think of no apter or more accurate reflection in sound of the mountains and woods and flocks and the nomad's life.

This too is what I heard while sitting with the Harisis family in a moment of shared tribal communion over our glasses of Christ's wine.

༺ ༻

How the Sarakatsani and other shepherds learned to play the flute that Jesus fashioned we'll likely never know. Undoubtedly, the flute music of the shepherds—the *skaros*, the *tzamara*, and other instrumental airs of the Balkan highlands—informed the style and repertoire of Epirotic music. The *skaros* uses the *Nigriz* scale, the same scale found in contemporary Epirotic music, particularly the instrumentals of Zagori.

In its contemporary manifestation, the *skaros* contains two *dromoi* or melodic roads—the dominant *Nigriz* and *Kartsgiar*, the lesser strain. Recall that *Nigriz* in G is G–A–B♭–C♯–D–E–F/F♯–G, (in descending, the F♯ becomes F). *Kartsgiar* in G is similar, but lowers the fourth note and keeps the F constant: G–A–B♭–C–D–E–F–G. To the tonally aware listener, this lowered fourth antici-pates a pattern where the ear relaxes on the C♯, where tension finds release. Since the potency of the *skaros* pivots on this fourth note, the intonation is critical.*

The *Nigriz dromos* was first mentioned in the thirteenth century (as *Niyriz*). But it is certainly a much older scale. *Nigriz* was popu-lar along the trade routes stitching across Asia Minor. Its scalar structure was absorbed into Sephardic, Armenian, and Romanian music. Referred to colloquially by Roma musicians as the "shep-herd's scale," *Nigriz* could have originated in Mesopotamia, spread-ing throughout the Balkans as transhumant herders likewise traveled with their flutes.

There are two narratives of the flute's origin and development in Greece. The more definitive account—which is also more recent—comes from literature and mythology. The more speculative chro-nology comes from archaeology.

---

* One afternoon in August I practiced the *skaros* on violin for a herd of sheep grazing just below Vitsa. My intonation was off because of jetlag—the notes—especially the C—were coming out flat. Playing for a little over five minutes, I realized that my *skaros* was not affecting the sheep. Rather, a dozen or more spur-thighed tortoises (*Testudo graeca*) had gathered at my feet, initiating a reptilian orgy. Some of the less fortunate males were simply acting as assists for their luckier counterparts. The low (slightly flattened) C note on my violin echoed their collective mating groans.

Starting with the literary account, early Greeks believed the shepherd's flute originated in Egypt. In the classical mind this implies that the flute was truly ancient. According to the Greek writer Athenaeus of Naucratis in his *Deipnosophists,* "Juba [Juba II, King of Numidia and Mauretania] . . . says that the Egyptians call the flute an invention of Osiris."

Gaius Julius Hyginus (64 BC–AD 17) gives us the mythological creation story. The Roman Minerva—Greek Athena—fashioned the first pipes from deer bones. She performed in front of the Gods, many of whom mocked her facial contortions while blowing. Minerva cast the pipes away, cursing anyone who would attempt to play them. Marsyas, the son of a Satyr, found the pipes and practiced relentlessly. He then challenged Apollo, master of the lyre, to a musical contest. The Muses were judges. Apollo won the competition. To make a point, Apollo hung young Marsyas from a tree, where a Scythian killed him. The blood that flowed from Marsyas's body formed the river bearing his name.

There is some confusion in early literature with the names for these end-blown instruments. In antiquity, the *monoaulos,* or single flute, was simultaneously referred to as a *titurinos,* a *kalaminos,* or a *kalamaulis.* The *aulos* was often played in pairs—two flutes played simultaneously by the same musician. Although they are commonly referred to as flutes, they are actually reed instruments. The shepherd's flute, commonly called a *floyera* and, in northwestern Greece, a *tzamara* (a slightly longer flute), has no reed and thus fits the modern definition of a flute. In ancient Egypt, around AD 200, Athenaeus of Naucratis wrote that "many people, without having been taught, can play on the flute and pipe, as for instance, shepherds."

Phoenicians are said to have fashioned their flutes from the bones of geese, birds sacred to the cults of Adonis and Aphrodite. Other tribes made them from the leg bones of mute swans. The tones of such instruments are described as "plaintive and melancholic." Julius Pollux, a Greek philosopher from the second century

AD, wrote that Scythian tribesmen played exceptional flutes made from the bones of eagles and vultures.

Just as suggestive as the instrument itself are the descriptions of the shepherds playing their instruments. Edward Daniel Clarke, an English lecturer of natural history, traveled widely throughout Europe, Asia Minor, Egypt, and Greece from 1799 to 1803. While in Epirus he wrote:

> We saw nothing worth noting except for an Arcadian pipe, upon which a shepherd was playing in the streets. It was perfectly Pandean; consisting simply of a goat's horn with five holes for the fingers, and a small aperture at the end for the mouth. It is exceedingly difficult to produce any sound whatsoever from this small instrument but the shepherd made the air resound with its shrill notes.

Several years later, in 1814, Thomas Hughes, an English classicist, visited Derviziana outside of Ioannina. There he observed a young shepherd with a flute made from an eagle's wing bone. When Hughes quizzed the shepherd on the origin of the flute, the boy told him that an eagle had carried away several of his young lambs; he then carried his razor-sharp knife to the eagle's nest and dispatched the raptor promptly, whereupon he fashioned this flute. Hughes was "startled by the shrill sounds of the shepherd's flute." The pipe was "open at both ends, requiring great force of lungs. The airs played were "characteristically wild" and equally shrill and sweet.

What these writers—philosophers, classicists, and scholars alike—did not, nor indeed could not, comment on was how music developed in Epirus. No one can: it is a stubborn palimpsest. Documentation is sparse and disputable. Evidence is fragmented. The chill of empty space blows across whatever path once existed. This is where archaeology comes in.

The three oldest flutes found in northern Greece—in the Neolithic village of Dispilio of Kastoria—are dated to 5000 BC. Cleanly drilled holes in the shaft closely resemble parts of the "shepherd's scale," the *Nigris dromos* of the *skaros*. Less than fifty miles from Dispilio in Kremasti, four additional flutes were found, fashioned from human bone. They were played around 4500–4000 BC. Some form of instrumental music on the shepherd's *floyera* entered Epirus between 5000 and 4000 BC.

Humans have inhabited Epirus since at least the Greek Paleolithic era, 20,000 to 12,000 years ago, if not earlier.[20] Starting in the 1960s, the pioneering archaeologist Eric Sidney Higgs devoted his life to excavating, mapping, and interpreting the Paleolithic cave sites like Kokkinopilos and Asprochaliko in the Louros Valley and the Kastritsa Cave on Lake Pamvotis of Ioannina.

Higgs concluded from his fieldwork in the 1960s that these rocky shelters in Epirus were used mainly by families rather than by isolated hunter-gatherers. The locations of these temporary settlements (and the hunting routes) correspond almost perfectly with the staging areas and migratory trails of the Sarakatsani. In other words, there has been continuous nomadic human habitation—from hunter-gatherer to shepherd—in this part of Epirus for thousands of years.

Higgs's research also suggests that nomads adapted their behavior to the changing environment, modifying their movements seasonally to exploit resources. By learning the rhythms of nature and weather—along with the patterns of animal migration—people in this region acquired valuable tools and strategies for survival. What he found in physical artifacts is similar to what I've found in the musical artifacts: that the seen and unseen world of Epirus shapes the people who live here, not the other way around.

The domestication of sheep for wool began around 6000 BC. Near Eastern people—those from ancient Mesopotamia—bred sheep for milk and wool. Nomads and traders drove these flocks across Asia Minor, Thrace, and Macedonia, entering the western part of

northern Greece. Domesticated sheep and goats represented innovation and security: sustenance, warmth and the raw materials
for survival. It was around this time that sheep were introduced
to Europe from Mesopotamia. One entry point to Europe was a
Balkan route through northern Greece. This is only one thousand
years before flutes were played in Kastoria, a fluttering of an eye as
far as the timeline of human habitation is concerned.

Under this narrative of animal husbandry and human migration, we conjoin a fundamental truth: all people at all times have
produced music. Those hunter-gatherers living in Epirus around
5,000 years ago sang songs and made music. So did their ancestors.
Likewise, those who introduced flocks of goats and sheep carried
with them their own musical ideas. We will never know their voice
or their sound. I'll never stumble across late Ice Age or Paleolithic
Victor 78 rpm discs.* But early inhabitants of Epirus did communicate with one another through language, music, and art.

Between 6000 and 5000 BC there was a convergence of herders and hunters in northwestern Greece. Here the shepherds may
have exchanged two ideas with the aboriginal hunters: replace
hunting and gathering with shepherding and play music not only
for yourselves but also for your flock. These two groups could have
observed that people and animals were somehow guided by music.

I think what occurred here was a culturally induced expansion
of tonal awareness. Others have suggested a similar transition.
Describing the flutes of the Neolithic era, Warren Anderson in
Music and Musicians in Ancient Greece says the "appearance of holed
flutes could not signify more obviously an evolving tonal system."

---

* Christ, I wish I could junk a box of Ice Age Victors in a cave in Epirus—
phonograph records etched in stone with a flint stylus—that captured the
ancient tones of the bone flute playing a *skaros*. But such artifacts are nonexistent: there are no fossilized remains of music. We can only take the evidence
that we have and infer that such music must have been played in an earlier time
and contextualize the circumstances and reasons for its existence.

His Master's Voice: Sheep "played into" by shepherd's tszamara.

There was a shift in lifestyle and expression in northwestern Greece by 5000 BC. When the shepherds comingled with the hunters these notions of musicality and herding synchronized. One modification to the musical environment may have been a notion of controlling a flock through the notes of the flute.

Along with herds of sheep and goats, it is probable that some germ of music was carried to the region of northwestern Greece like a spark in a crude tinderbox. A process of exchange or assimilation of ideas may have occurred simply because there was a need. This is how music and language work—they follow opportunistic paths, flourishing because they are necessary. Religion functions similarly. We slowly yet continually discover new ways of interpreting the prehistoric record containing these traits and traces of humanity.

On that icy November night in Vitsa I looked over at Stratos Harisis as he rested his flute from playing. The *skaros* he played had an arch continuous, surviving the ravages of Time and the Fates.

Takis and I left the Harisis home much heavier than we arrived. Stratos's family had prepared neatly folded parcels of homemade cheeses and lamb for both of us. Before leaving, Stratos gave us a tour of his basement and the industries that occurred therein. Trays of salted cheeses lined the edges of the cellar. Enormous metal vats gleamed in the darkness, holding oceans of *tsipouro* and *krasi*—red wine—produced in a biblical manner. Stratos presented me with three liters of *tsipouro* and a bottle of wine: enough provisions to survive healthily inebriated for five days. In six I would return to Virginia.

Two years later an Irish-British documentary crew visited Vitsa, led by Paul Duane. They joined me while I was visiting, wishing to capture some of the complexities of Epirotic music. During the course of their filming, they had the opportunity to interview Stratos Harisis and his brother Tasos, the father of Georgos Harisis, the Greek filmmaker with whom I shared *tsipouro* during the first night of the Vitsa *panegyri*, acquiring the indelible scar that I still wear.

Shot in a field near the ancestral grazing grounds of the Sarakatsani, Stratos and Tasos surveyed the descendants of their own sheep nearly fifty years after they had ceased to be nomads.

TASOS: Let's walk to the flock now. How things used to be here, Stratos. There were shepherds, flocks, horses, cows. Where did these people go, where did they all go?

STRATOS: They're all gone, all of them, gone. Progress.

TASOS: Things used to be . . .

STRATOS: The rush meadows, the sheep. There is nothing here anymore.

8

SOME KIND OF A TOOL

Somebody made this arrowhead. It had a creator long ago. This arrowhead is the only proof of his existence. Living things can also be seen as artifacts, designed for a purpose . . . this artifact, shaped to fill a forgotten need, now has no more meaning or purpose than this arrowhead with the arrow and the bow, the arm and the eye. Or perhaps the human artifact was the creator's last card, played in an old game many light-years ago. Chill of empty space.

—WILLIAM S. BURROUGHS, *THE PLACE OF DEAD ROADS*

THE DAY BEFORE I FLEW OUT FROM IOANNINA TO RETURN TO the United States, having emptied the bottles of *tsipouro* that Stratos Harisis gave me, I sat in front of a fireplace in a dark *ouzeri*, nursing a purchased *tsipouro* and a cup of hot Greek mountain tea. Or perhaps the *tsipouro* was nursing me. I had come down with a cold from the freezing hike with Takis "The Fixer" that threatened my mortal coil.

Traditional Zagorian hearths are built with a triangular mantel forming a pyramid of steps enshrining the fireplace. Placed on the steps of this mantel in the *ouzeri* were antique notions and rusted farm implements. As I crowded closer to the fire, I saw a familiar shape—a long cylinder made of wood with holes channeled across the top, but with a charred, blackened end. I asked the waitress, "*Ti einai afto?*"—"What is this?"

She replied while picking it up. "*Afto einai ena ergaleio.*"—"This is a tool."

Crouching by the fire, she blew through the stem of the shepherd's flute into the coals. This musical instrument had been retasked as a mouth-blown pipette for quickening the embers of the hearth. The holes along the shaft had been plugged and patched with glue. My mind, numbed by *tsipouro*, witnessed some kind of arcane transubstantiation—one object transformed into another object, their distinct purposes blurred yet ancient and elemental.

I asked for another *tsipouro*.

The simple shepherd's flute is the foundation of the complex instrumental music of Epirus. Music's preeminent purpose in northwestern Greece is deceptively simple: it heals. The musical "laying on of hands" is therapeutic and curative to the individual and the village. The *mirologi* produces catharsis while the *skaros* has calmative effects. Like some intricate web, the keening vocals, the shepherd's flute, the *mirologi* and the *skaros*, are interconnected, threaded through one another and everything else—a primordial, musical-cultural feedback loop.

Holding this flute in my feverish hand in the *ouzeri*, I felt as if I had brushed up against something linking me with the creation of music—the genesis of humanly organized sound. This connection with the past here implies a disconnection with music elsewhere: outside of this fragile biosphere something was lost, broken.

❧❧❧

Artifacts are objects, beings, and behaviors that leave traces— things that linger—offering evidence of their existence at one time. But, in the words of friend, philosopher of science, and fellow traveler to Epirus Gary Hardcastle, most objects or artifacts "do not wear their function on their sleeve." We know—or think we know—their purpose through continued use. Some things leave a trail behind, others do not.

The purpose of a thing or a behavior is sewn up tightly within the fabric of one's culture. The familiarity accompanying our engagement with an object causes us to ignore the possibility that at a different time this thing may have served quite a different role.

There are at least three challenges to consider when we connect an object, such as a musical instrument, with its original purpose. First, things may change so radically over time that we simply don't recognize them. Second, things can be mistakenly interpreted based on a series of earlier flawed assumptions. Third, things may have wider and deeper connections within a culture than contemporary analogies will allow. All of these pitfalls are relevant to the origin and function of music and all three challenges are subtly interconnected. Let's start with the problem of recognition and change.

In the 1958 noir crime thriller *Touch of Evil*, the once cherub-faced, elocute, and dashing Orson Welles appears as a grotesque, slurring ogre Hank Quinlan. He is a corrupt cop working the Mexican-U.S. border. When we meet him in the film, he is tasked with investigating a murder. He goes across the border into Mexico, following the trail of a suspect. Visiting a bordello, Quinlan encounters Tanya, the owner of the house of ill repute, played by Marlene Dietrich. He recognizes her as a past love; she does not recognize him at all. His physical form has changed: he has gained hundreds of pounds, acquired a limp, and aged beyond repair. But this is not all. Once ethically sterling, he is now morally bankrupt—a man vindictive, bigoted, and paid off by the Mexican cartels. Quinlan is unrecognizable to the woman who once knew him intimately.

Fast forward to the end. It's not pretty: Quinlan has framed, extorted, and murdered until the very end, when he is shot dead. He floats down the Rio Grande like a fleshy barge. Above, on a bridge, stands Tanya, surveying this funerary barque passing downriver. Her soliloquy, his epitaph, "He was *some kind of a man*."

The passage of time altered Hank Quinlan so much externally and internally as to render him unknowable, unrecognizable. He became simply *some kind of a man*. When I saw the shepherd's flute in the *ouzeri* transmogrified into a fire-making tool, I still recognized it by its form. Its function—a tool for a deeper purpose—is where we plumb mysteries, wading into unsteady waters.

We have similarly struggled to recognize the original purpose of music because its subsequent use has changed. As an analogy, think of fire. The ability to create and control fire was a skill that fundamentally enhanced every aspect of early human existence—this achievement changed everything. Fire was a tool for survival that skirted between magical and practical. Nowadays, there is no magic. Lighters, matches, and burners have demystified—and altered—our once crucial quest for fire.

Early hominids had other tools besides fire. Indeed, their fabricated stones formed elaborate toolkits. Scholars of archaeology compare how other proximal unmodernized cultures use a similar tool and infer a similar function for previous societies. But what should we make of musical artifacts?

Suppose for a moment that we could witness the sounds and sights of an ancient flute being played in a settlement perched above Lake Pamvotis in Epirus five thousand years ago. Now imagine witnessing a shepherd playing the flute two thousand years ago. And again, two hundred years ago. Would we recognize all these activities as music? Or is it another type of behavior, one so alien as to require a different name?

Perhaps we have a problem with first principles. We have lived, for a few hundred years at least, with relatively static ideas about music and its functions. But do these static ideas blind us to other potential origins of humanly organized sound? This is the second challenge, then: we may have mistaken notions based on historic and faulty assumptions.

❧ ❧ ❧

Marcellin Boule was a French paleontologist who examined the nearly complete remains of a Neanderthal. When he published his findings, starting in 1911, Boule characterized the Neanderthal as primitive, with toes opposable like those of a gorilla and a spine bent like that of an ape. To Boule, this skeleton was from a being with "functions of a purely vegetative or bestial kind." This was one of his kinder remarks. Boule's depiction shapes our imagination today. When we think of a Neanderthal, we conjure a hairy ogre with anthropomorphic qualities.*

But Boule was mistaken with both his analysis and his conclusions. In 1957, fifteen years after Boule's death, a closer evaluation of this Neanderthal revealed crippling arthritis in his feet and a host of injuries—including those to his spine—mangling his poorly healed bones. This specimen had been altered irrevocably by time and disease. Other Neanderthal fossils were found later showing a species of hominid physically quite similar to ourselves. Yet this perception of Neanderthals as clumsy, stooped brutes remains pervasive.

Boule's portrayal of this "bestial kind" of a being—not even a *bestial kind of a man*—also stymied paleoanthropology. There was a reluctance to consider Neanderthals capable of "higher" human behavior. Boule's interpretations were also a reaction to Darwinism: Boule wanted to distance humans from this savage beast. For decades after Boule's first publications we too resisted the notion that Neanderthals could reason, fabricate structures, or see spiritual things. And all of this was based upon Boule's false reckoning of Neanderthal's nature.†

Now we have warmed to the notion that Neanderthals were more human, not less—excellent news concerning my own unsavory genetic makeup. But this shift in understanding and acceptance is not so much due to new evidence. Rather, we've come to a place where we can imagine more inclusive categories of reasoning, fabrication, and spirituality.

---

* In my mind, like a hirsute, hunchbacked, and age-ravaged Orson Welles.

† As the man-beast creations of Dr. Moreau from the 1932 film *Island of Lost Souls* constantly intoned: "Are we not men?!"

Neanderthals did not change, nor did their fossil record. Our interpretations changed: they became more nuanced, forming wider circles of inference and yielding deeper connections. Or, as archaeologist Tristan Carter said, "Research over the last couple of decades has perpetually shown us that all of these characters [Neanderthals and their innovations, abilities, cognitions] are more capable, more complex than we thought."

Scientists altered the ways they perceived and interpreted things. The rest of us may eventually catch up. Anthropologist John Hawks echoes the point that Neanderthals had religious capacity, "but to be honest," he writes, "I think this is not what many Americans or Europeans would recognize as religion."

We started with the faulty assumptions from Boule. These errors shaped future interpretation. We have inherited them. And now we must undo them. The burden is on us to change our perceptions about humanity and its primordial capacities.

❦❦❦

Beyond physical and spiritual misinterpretations, we also inherited a myopic notion about the purpose, or more precisely, the *purposelessness*, of prehistoric art—and music. This flawed framework emerged a little over a century ago, and it has scarcely been questioned until recently.

Our misunderstanding of prehistoric artifacts occurred in two stages. First, we were told that all art pivots on the intellect—it is a singular expression of abstract thought. Then we were told that prehistoric cultures produced art and music from rational notions similar to ours.

It started in the middle of the nineteenth century when dozens of caves in Europe surrendered their secrets. Vivid panoramic scenes of extinct animals traced with ochre and charcoal covered subterranean walls. Scattered on the floors of some caves were stone tools and curious bones with neatly formed holes, early flutes. Paintings and flutes—both composed of slowly decaying organic materials—linked modern Europeans with their heritage.

While these artifacts were being discovered, European scholars and critics, primarily Frenchmen, were forming an overarching theory to explain artistic creation. Théophile Gautier's *Art for Art's Sake,* published in 1835, is a prerequisite text for this aesthetic framework. French philosopher Jacques Rancière describes this theory and its supporters as "an aesthetic regime of art."

Part of this regime's thinking goes like this: painting and performing music—classical modes of art—require one thing and imply another. Artists require leisure time to produce a transcendent work of art, to engage fully in the aesthetic act. They need to create in peace, not in crisis or uncertainty. Conversely, the product, a painting or a piece of music, implies an expression of abstract or symbolic thought. Art is an intellectual activity and its production requires certain social structures. This was the normative understanding of art in the nineteenth century.

On this theory, Rancière writes, "Art as a notion designating a form of specific experience has only existed in the West since the end of the eighteenth century." This Eurocentric aesthetic ideal set the stage for deeper conceptual errors. Enter two more Frenchmen.

Gabriel de Mortillet (1821–1898) and Émile Cartailhac (1845–1921) espoused major parts of this aesthetic theory. They were also early, influential European prehistorians who linked the production of Neolithic and later European art with intellectual activity.[21] They did not believe earlier Paleolithic humans had the cognitive powers for advanced expression. Following their lead, many European intellectuals viewed the art-making impulse of *later* prehistoric artists as something similar to the cognitive and creative functions of their own contemporary artists.

Were the conditions for making art or making music the same in the nineteenth century as they were at the end of the last Ice Age or the Neolithic period? No, of course not. But alternative interpretations of prehistoric artifacts would not appear until ethnographers—those outside the groupthink of the "aesthetic regime of art"—proposed them. And by then, this narrowly modern notion of ancient art and music as an expression of abstract or symbolic thought had become ubiquitous.*

Underpinning Mortillet's and Cartailhac's interpretation of prehistoric art was a robust anti-religious philosophy. Staunchly anti-Catholic, they believed that religious beliefs and superstitions stemmed from weak cognitive functions. These two men interpreted evidence of religious behaviors from burials and caves as signs of a lesser intellect. Mortillet rejected the dating of artifacts if the evidence found within the stratigraphy clashed with his philosophical views.

The two French prehistorians stand in stark contrast with paleontologist Boule. Mortillet and Cartailhac wanted prehistoric hominids to be more human, less irrational; Boule wanted prehistoric hominids to be less human, more bestial. Yet the collective body of preconceptions and prejudices they held created erroneous interpretations of evidence and a stubborn legacy of poorly founded assumptions.

There is nothing to suggest that the early inhabitants of southern Europe—and specifically Epirus—engaged in art and music as an intellectual or rational activity. Conversely, everything implies that the purposes behind these behaviors were more urgent, complex, and esoteric than our current interpretations allow.

---

* This interpretation of prehistoric art and artifact is still repeated without reflection—a rote formula. The BBC, reporting in 2002 on a piece of ochre incised with geometric lines over 70,000 years old, implied that this was the oldest prehistoric art discovered to date. To our point, the reportage continues, "While the markings are suggestive, not all scientists are prepared to classify them as a form of artistic expression and abstract thought." And, in the January 2015 issue of *National Geographic* magazine, the summary line for the lead article reads, "The greatest innovation in the history of humankind was neither the stone tool nor the steel sword, but the invention of symbolic expression by the first artists."

What if music—in its raw form, primeval and prototypal—has nothing to do with abstract or symbolic expression? Hold for a moment the thought that early humans organized sounds out of an impulse neither rational nor irrational, something that either skirted between or unified these eternal binaries. What language, what structures of inquiry and organization would we use to ponder this phenomenon?

Hence our third challenge: that there may be vast, more perplexing cultural connections between an artifact and its function than contemporary analogies—and modes of understanding—will allow.

❧❧❧

Consider the Antikythera Mechanism—the ancient artifact found scattered on the seafloor of the Aegean between 1900 and 1901. Most estimates place its construction around 150 BC, possibly earlier. Showing engineering and mechanical skills that would not reemerge for another 1,500 years, the reconstructed model of the device suggests that it came from nowhere only to end nowhere—a wisp appearing without precedent or antecedent.

Nothing has been found in the archaeological record approaching the complexity of this artifact. Today, after multiple models, hundreds of scientific papers, and a slick, high-tech documentary, most scholars of technology agree that this mechanism was the first analog computer,* one that could predict the movements of stars and the moon and, by extension, the cycle of various games and competitions held in the larger towns and cities of the Hellenic world.

In 2016, the Antikythera Mechanism Research Project published a compendium describing the structure and implied function of this object through three-dimensional digital mapping. The last line of the introduction to this study—if it were divorced from its

---

* We have likened it to a goddamn first-generation smartphone.

context—would read like an icy, ominous line of dialogue from a science fiction script by Andrei Tarkovsky:

> *We currently have a fairly secure understanding of a substantial portion of the inner workings as well as the outer displays of the Mechanism.*

We comprehend the "inner workings," but what we do not know and may never know is this: what was the larger cultural context of this device? How did it function within that context? Perhaps we are far from the mark.

Maybe the Mechanism was not a stand-alone device but rather a set of works to be housed inside of a statue of Zeus—a *deus ex machina*, a "god out of machine"—to be placed in front of worshippers? Imagine an articulated deity with flesh of marble and frame of wood and iron. Those petitioning the god paid a fee. In return they asked questions to said deity. A whirligig—the Antikythera Mechanism—deep within the head of Zeus ticked off an answer that would be translated by a temple priest. Worshippers full of awe and reverence walked away light in pocket but heavy with predictions for the future.

Indeed, one of the first mainstream articles published on the Mechanism in 1959 by Derek J. de Solla Price in the *Scientific American* suggests that the device was "perhaps set in a statue and displayed as an exhibition piece."

Perhaps the Mechanism was a luxury item commissioned by a wealthy Athenian politician to impress his peers, the whole structure and purpose of this expensive device a mystery to him.

Or maybe it was a plaything for a well-heeled Greek child. Most of us can recall some toy that mystified us, containing within itself inexplicable potency and purpose just as opaque then as the conjured memories are of our youth when we summon them now.

We may never know the full purpose. What matters is that there are alternative designs, purposes, for the Mechanism's existence beyond being a tool for calculation.

Our example need not be as complex as the Antikythera Mechanism. Consider the crypto-artifact called the "7,000-year-old Enigma," 5,000 years older than the Mechanism. Like the Mechanism, the Enigma was fashioned by the Greeks. Unlike the Mechanism, the Enigma is a Neolithic artifact with uncertain provenance, likely from Macedonia or Thessaly in northern Greece. The Enigma is a stone statuette with a beak (or pointed nose), an elongated neck, and short stumps for legs. It could be a rendering of a bird or of a deity with avian characteristics.

The Enigma was carved out of hard granite during an age when metal tools were nonexistent, hence its imponderability. The fabrication of such an artifact would have required absurd amounts of labor in addition to stone-working implements of an unknown and seemingly anachronistic nature. There is no doubt that this statuette was important to the northern Greek culture that produced it. Yet we do not know—nor may we ever know—*why* it was important.

Returning to the Antikythera Mechanism, Price's suggestion that the Mechanism may have been a part of a larger whole was left to the wayside by most scientists. The focus shifted so that we could pursue an understanding of the "inner workings" of the Mechanism. In this way, we could form cogent analogies between the Mechanism and our own contemporary artifacts. The result: we think we understand the Mechanism and its purpose because we've likened the Antikythera Mechanism and its function to our own objects. In the words of archaeologist Tristan Carter, "It's all about the archaeology of ego in us." It's all about an entrenched mode of navigating the world with our modern tools, our intellectual nearsightedness born from this stubborn perspective.

In 1972 Russian brothers Arkady and Boris Strugatsky published *Roadside Picnic.* This science fiction novel was adapted and made into a movie, *Stalker*, by Andrei Tarkovsky in 1979. The theme of *Roadside Picnic* best illustrates this final challenge—that cultural connections between an artifact and its function may be inaccessible to our standard, contemporary modes of interpretation and analysis.

In this story, scientists discover a remote corner of the world that has been visited by aliens. Extraterrestrial travelers leave behind evidence of their short stay—mysterious artifacts. Some of these objects possess extraordinary powers while others only suggest powers. A large group of influential scientists believe aliens gave these things to humankind as a gift—a gesture to advance the human species.

An outsider offers an alternative—and, it turns out, accurate—explanation. What the scientists are studying is actually space rubbish, the trash left over by an alien picnic. Properties inferred from these artifacts are purely incidental and have little relationship to the theories advanced by the scientists. Myopic speculations by a powerful thought-collective about design and purpose do not capture the actual context of the objects.

Our inquiry into the origins of music and its function discloses a similar problem. Our perceptions of artifacts and their purpose are limited to our own preconceptions of object and function—they are embedded in our contextualized understanding of *similar objects* and *similar functions* fixed within our own time. We find an artifact from the distant past and, after identifying a formal relationship with an object from the present, we assume that the functions are identical or at least similar.

I believe that although an artifact from the past, such as a flute, may be similar to an object in the present and both may be used to produce music, the actual function of music in the past might be quite different from the function of music in the present.

Music has a teleological flow like any artifact, like the Antikythera Mechanism, the 7,000-year-old Enigma, or the litter left by aliens in *Roadside Picnic*. But this flow, the trail documenting music's creation and its reason for being, is fragmented at crucial points where the story develops, hidden because of what the passage of time annihilates or warps.

Musicologist Curt Sachs wrote in 1948, "not even the earliest civilizations that have left their traces in the depths of the earth are old enough to betray the secrets of the origins of music." True enough. But what if the origins of music are not a secret but merely obscured, hiding in isolated places?

These collective failures of the human imagination open the possibility that there is an alternative explanation, a different narrative for humanly organized sound. I believe part of this story can be found in the music of Epirus.

ᖡᖡᖡ

Through my travels to northwestern Greece I've discovered that music is not just an aspect of culture; it *is* culture. It is humanity's most visceral asset. By its nature, it is both universal to all people at all times and—at least in Epirus—it is necessary. In order to understand a folk music, you must attempt to understand the folk. If you appreciate the phenomenon of music as an Epirote would, then you would connect the music with the circuits surrounding it. In this case the circuits would include (but not be limited to) religion, history, shepherding, village life, *panegyria*, and, for some, *tsipouro*. Underneath these connections, you will perceive customs—the often unspoken and subtle acts of the people—completing the circuit, illuminating the whole.[22]

If we suspend a belief that most Westerners have held for centuries—that music is something that we engage in with our intellect—and then place ourselves within a context where ancient music still exists, such as Epirus, we might begin to see the original, practical purpose of music: that it was a tool for survival.

The music of Epirus has transformed over time but has not mutated or degraded to the cacophonous ear torture I confront every day in the wasteland outside northwestern Greece. When I exit the comfortable sanctuary of my record room—or when I leave Epirus—and confront the sounds around me, it is as if music has devolved into some unrecognizable, sickly chimera. What I hear outside of Epirus lacks purpose.

There was a paradigm shift in the function of music: not only in what music has become but also an alteration in what we expect of music. If we expect nothing, then we get nothing. In effect, music has shed its purpose because we no longer believe that we need it.

The Greeks have a word, *stochevmenos,* meaning "purposeful" or "targeted." Epirotic music is *stochevmeni mousiki,* purposeful music—it is some kind of a tool. Tools address need: we believe tools fix problems.

I wish that I could have met and talked with Richard and Eva Blum. Richard, a sociologist, and Eva, a psychologist, lived in rural Greece between 1957 and 1962. They traveled mainly through Epirus and as far as Thessaloniki. The couple interviewed hundreds of villagers, nomadic shepherds, and Roma with the purpose of collecting testimony on the relationship between health and belief.

During this period northern Greece was in flux. Economic displacement, mass emptying of villages, and the sedentation of nomadic shepherds transformed most of rural Greece forever. The Blums were witness to a time when the ordinary perceptions of the Greek villager shifted, from locally informed beliefs to scientifically informed beliefs. Some would say that the movement was from behaviors based on superstition—folkloric understanding—to behaviors based on reality—scientific fact. But the Blums would have resisted this simplistic reduction.

Richard and Eva coauthored two books based on their extensive fieldwork in northern Greece: *Health and Healing in Rural Greece* (1965) and *The Dangerous Hour* (1970). They presented the notion that beliefs in extrasensory, incorporeal beings and their powers guided the day-to-day decisions of most rural Greeks. These beliefs—and subsequent behaviors—intensified when villagers encounter disease, death, crisis, and a host of anxieties associated with rural existence. Greeks interviewed by the Blums confronted what humankind has dealt with for millennia: the unknown and the unkind forces existing inside and outside of us.

Customs and behaviors among the Greek countryside dwellers—whether we call these beliefs extra-religious or pre-Christian—are sourced from two impulses: a need to explain the unseen world and a desire to protect oneself (and others) against invisible dangers. Much of the Blums' research focuses on *xotika*, unseen malevolent entities responsible for harming humans, and the villager's strategies for protecting themselves from the forces of *xotika*.

"We are all demons ourselves, which is why we cannot see the *xotika*," said one informant to the Blums.

In the Greek countryside, there were a variety of cures and spells to mediate and treat psychological and physical ailments. To the Greeks of this time and place, diseases were rooted in the intangible, sometimes hostile, spiritual realm.

A central insight gleaned from Richard and Eva's research is the notion that certain practices have traditionally been used to treat trauma in rural Greece. Although the Blums do not address it directly, music making (and listening) is one such ancient practice that addresses pain, fear, and anxiety. Likewise, there is ample evidence that for the Greeks, music has always contained the potential for effecting psychological or physical change.

In the second century AD, Sextus Empiricus, in his treatise *Against the Musicians*, tells the story of Pythagoras calming the rage of a young man by summoning a Phrygian pipe player:

Pythagoras, when he once observed how lads who had been filled with Bacchic frenzy by alcoholic drink differed not at all from madmen, exhorted the *aulete* [aulos-player] who was joining them in the carousal to play his *aulos* for them in the spondaic *melos*. When he thus did what was ordered, they suddenly changed and were given discretion as if they had been sober even at the beginning.

Humanly organized sounds also heal physical ailments. The writer Athenaeus recorded in his *Sophists at Dinner*:

The Homeric Achilles calmed himself with his *kithara*, which was the only thing Homer grants to him out of his booty taken from Eëtion, and which had the power of allaying his fiery nature. He, at least, is the only one in the *Iliad* who plays this kind of music. That music can also heal diseases Theophrastus has recorded in his work *On Inspiration*: he says that persons subject to sciatica would always be free from attacks if one played the flute [*aulos*] in the Phrygian mode [*harmonia*] over the part affected.

We know that most ancient Greek texts did not survive the erosion of time. But some of the extramusical theories articulated by Arabic and Persian scholars probably derived from Greek writings—or commentary on such writings—that were not passed down to us directly. The notion that certain *makams* or *dromoi* imparted psychological effects may have traveled from the ancient Greeks to the Arabs and back again to the Greeks via the Ottomans: yet another musical-cultural feedback loop.

That music had a palliative role in ancient Greece is perhaps not as surprising as the revelation that this function still exists in Epirus. Commenting on this continuity, John Lawson said, "Among that still living people it is possible not only to observe acts and usages, but to enquire also their significance: and though some customs will undoubtedly be found either to be mere survivals of which the meaning has long been forgotten, . . . yet others . . . may be vital documents of ancient Greek life and thought."

In northwestern Greece, music still exists as a vehicle for healing. When I attend *panegyria*, I often hear a phrase right before someone is "played into." Villagers will say to the clarinetist, *"phtiakse mas."* This means, "fix me" or "heal me," "make me feel better," or by extension of the circumstances, "let your music work into me." It is simultaneously an expression of praise or encouragement like "take me higher" and also a desperate request, "make me feel whole."

෨෨෨

There was a time when music functioned both mystically and practically, like the creation of fire. Music was intended to heal as if it contained within itself potency, a spiritual utility. But something happened. The mystical and the practical were displaced and music's function reassigned.

Evidence of this ineffable purpose of music is still here in Epirus. It might be said that as an outsider and a Westerner, I am romanticizing or even exoticizing what I cannot explain. But the fact remains that the sounds move me. That my response to the sounds seems to mirror that of the villagers of Epirus may be incidental, or may result from an imponderable set of circumstances. I cannot say which.

The strongest critique of my description of this phenomenon of music is this: claims for the curative merits of this music clash violently with scientific fact—with what we know, or think we know, about disease. How can I be sure of the efficacy of this music as a tool for healing? Are these effects real or imagined?

Before outside forces of modernity penetrated the vast countryside of rural Greece, villages were universes. These settlements represented the known world to many. Perceptions were local and taught. Notions of causality lay in unseen things. Just as the icy environment of the Arctic informed the Inuit's thoughts, so too did the often harsh and hostile landscape of northwestern Greece shape the Epirote's beliefs. Richard and Eva Blum summarize:

> There is, then, no point in debating which [beliefs of the village vs. scientific observation or fact] is more real . . . each is real if it is perceived as part of the immediate world in which the peasant lives, a world with characteristics agreed upon, at least in major ways, by many in the village. Because beliefs about what is real influence behavior, guiding future actions as well as accounting for past ones, the observer who would wish to understand better the forces which influence the peasant's conduct is well advised to attend to the latter's articles of belief fully as much as to the characteristics of his physical and social environment.

On the last night or the last morning or the last stretch of time marking the end of the *panegyri* in Vitsa, you ought not sleep. I don't. There is a reward in this.

Here is what happens. From nine o'clock at night till nine in the morning (or thereabouts) you should inhabit every moment. Fortifying yourself with *souvlakia* and *kokoretsi*, you ought to also enhance everything with *tsipouro*. As I do, you should alternate between dancing and communing. Because this is Vitsa, the last day of the *panegyri* is for the local villagers, the Vitsanians. Between three and four in the morning the seldom-heard local dances are called and a rare atmosphere descends on the courtyard along with the early morning fog. Here is when a natural (or nearly natural) altered state of consciousness develops.

Intricate, minute movements of the feet characterize the dances of central Zagori. During the repeated choreography, much stress—both tension and release—is placed on the lower leg, particularly between the soleus muscle deep in the calf and the plantar fascia of the heel. Because I'm an American by birth, there is an impulse to reduce all phenomena to their empirical fundamentals. Because I'm a Vitsanian by adoption, there is an impulse to reject scientific observation and focus more on the effect.*

The alchemy of repetitive physical contortions mixes with the elixir of *tsipouro*. A lack of sleep results in an increased attention to what is seen and a proportional decrease in inhibition to what you would like to see. You no longer hear the music with the ears but rather with the ligatures of the body.

There is opacity just outside the courtyard—an insular barrier— yet everything within the confines of the courtyard takes on a crystalline clarity. You notice curvature in things where such curvature did not exist before. Sound is refracted as light and shadows rearrange the shapes of the objects that cast them.

You may see what I have seen, or perhaps the music will shape parts of you differently, since we carry within ourselves disparate maps of experience and history.

What I have described persists until you dance the musicians out of the village with all of your friends who have now become your family.

When you wake up the next day, you feel as if you have been made whole.

---

* The Greeks, of course, have a word for this. *Psychosynthesis*—a notion richer than simple mentality—describes how some Greeks feel and do things without a need to explain the impulse or phenomenon prompting the emotion or the action.

ON FOSSILS, MEMORY

My darling child, my grief for thee where shall I cast it?
If I cast it on the mountains, the little birds will pick it,
If I cast it into the sea, the little fishes will eat it,
If I cast it on the highway, the passers-by will trample it under foot.
Oh, let me cast it into my own heart, which swells with many sorrows.

    —A *MIROLOGI*

WITHIN THE SAME YEAR THAT I FOUND THE 78 DISC THAT WOULD change my life, "Dark Was the Night, Cold Was the Ground," I acquired something else, something subtle but no less profound. As Voyager 1 plunged ever further into deep space carrying with it an everlasting sign of deathless remembrance, and long after the smoke drifted from the incinerated shack that once held a box of prewar recordings, a mobile science unit was visiting my school in rural Virginia.

At that time, I did not care for science. I relished the simple act of discovery, not the more complex task of explanation.

Two student volunteers from the nearest city, Roanoke, brought an assortment of fossils into the classroom where I sat. Spread out like baffling puzzle pieces, these rocks etched with faint impressions spoke to me. And I in turn spoke to the young scientists standing behind the fossils—a young man looking vaguely like John Denver and a young woman resembling a *Prime Cut*–era Sissy Spacek.

I told them that I had seen similar fossils on the side of a creek running behind my brother's house nearby. Intrigued, the two volunteers arranged to meet my father and me a few days later near a bridge that ran over Big Back Creek. That night my mother sewed a special pair of sky-blue shorts, to which she fashioned side zippers, hooks, and all manner of pockets for my expedition. I left the house a fledgling archaeologist.

We walked underneath the bridge that spanned the creek. A little way up we saw flecked charcoal from an ancient campfire. Further on my father picked up a broken arrowhead encrusted in silt, useless now but razor sharp and full of purpose when it was first fashioned. And then I saw an outcropping of rocks containing the evidence of life and death, a struggle that had ended millions of years ago, its history now embossed in stone. These fossils were piled next to an embankment resembling two toppled black monoliths.

The young man from the science museum eagerly turned these fossils over in his hands, scribbling details on a pad of paper before placing each rock in a labeled plastic bag and then thrusting it inside of his knapsack. We walked on.

Spread before us on this creek bank was a record of life extinguished and of tools used.

"Wait. You should see this." The young woman reached and gingerly picked up a rock slightly larger than her fist. Her blonde ponytail flicked like a mare's mane. She withdrew a small pickaxe from her multifaceted shorts, a garment vastly superior to my homemade pair, and lightly tapped at a fissure running along the side of the rock.

She opened it.

In the cleaved rock that she held in both of her hands like an open book were mirrored impressions of a prehistoric leaf. Delicate tendrils and stems told a wordless story that had been encased and forgotten for millions of years. Yet she knew what secrets lay within such an artifact fabricated by nature.

She handed this fossil to me and explained what was held within.

Nearly thirty years later I was in a *kafeneio* in Ioannina, a place called Petrino. The space was small, intimate: it felt more like an old-fashioned gentlemen's club than a modern *kafeneio*. I was having the first of three *tsipouro*.

With me were my friends Costas Zissis and Demetris Dallas. Sitting across from me was Michalis Oikonomides, a friend of Demetris's from the village of Elaphotopos. His lips were turning crimson from a glass of red wine. Michalis had studied art history and sculpture at the Sorbonne in the late sixties and early seventies. We communicated in French. His French was impeccable, mine was deplorable.

I asked him, "How do you feel when you hear a perfectly played *mirologi*?"

His reply, sourced from some involuntary place belonging to prophets or seers, left his lips more like breath than a string of words.

He said, "I understand the limits between life and death: the unavoidable harshness of reality, the futility of earthy and transient things."

What the young scientist gave me was not some relic from the Eocene epoch. What Michalis told me was not some contrived talking point. Rather, they both unwittingly imparted a fundamental lesson. They had shared secret knowledge with someone curious. The kindest of all human reflexes is this selfless act of sharing—giving to one person some kernel of knowledge or wisdom.

The people of Epirus have imparted to me an understanding of music. This simple act of sharing transcends hospitality and courtesy. It, like the rare music of this region, transforms us and makes us whole.

ACKNOWLEDGMENTS

Tom Mayer, my editor *par excellence* at W. W. Norton, deserves the highest praise. He advocated for my work at every stage. His trenchant criticism and commentary caused me to view the process of writing in a new light. I am fortunate to have an editor to work with who is so keen, curious, and knowledgeable about music. Many others at W. W. Norton helped bring the book into this world, including Vice President and Executive Art Director Ingsu Liu and her design team, and Jodi Beder, Emma Hitchcock, Rebecca Homiski, and Beth Steidle.

I'm grateful to have a friend like Ben "Dutch" Bruton. His tireless reading of drafts, acquisition of rare research materials, and concern for the integrity of my work were necessary for this book. I would have suffered without his honesty, commitment, and unflinching friendship.

Jim and Maria Potts graciously invited us to Vitsa, Zagori, in the first place. Their sustained support and friendship and Jim's feedback on earlier versions of the chapters strengthened this book. I am especially humbled by their intellectual generosity, their translations of texts, and their endless supply of source material for research and travels. I cannot thank them enough.

I am profoundly indebted to my friend Demetris P. Dallas, not only for his exceptional poetic translations of all the difficult lyrics included in this book but also for his advance reading and patient, insightful commentary on earlier drafts of the manuscript. I have learned a great deal about Epirotic culture and history from Demetris, and I've also gained humility through his sage words.

My friend Costas Zissis of Aristi helped me locate vintage photos of *panegyria*, gave me nuanced advice concerning the customs and music of Zagori, and lent constant support both during and after my research. His kindred spirit enriched mine. A true artist, he also provided two of the photographs used in this book.

Gary Hardcastle, a friend and mentor for over twenty years, helped me shape some of the ideas in this book. He and his wife Steva traveled with me to Epirus and sometimes experienced what I experienced. Gary added thoughtful direction to my search after reading some earlier chapters. Without Gary, the intellectual foundations of this book would be weaker.

Vassilis Georganos's enthusiasm for Epirotic and blues 78s formed an arch spanning the Atlantic. Our travels together dissolved whatever illusory barrier there was between the music of rural Greece and the southern United States. His friendship made many things possible that would have been unthinkable otherwise.

The vibrant musicians who last performed nearly one hundred years ago are fully and miraculously alive in the artwork that graces this book. With some strange alchemy, Robert Crumb rendered photographs into portraits containing multiple dimensions, including the ever-elusive personality of the subject. I'm deeply grateful not only for his artistry but also for the years of correspondence we've exchanged regarding this old music that we both love.

Friend and writer Ramona Stout has given me invaluable insight into how *panegyria* exist outside of Epirus and especially in the Cyclades. She also reinforced many of my perceptions on how music functions on an emotional and sensory level. I am grateful for her friendship and her intellectual engagement.

I'm fortunate to have had the art historian Vasso Petsa read my manuscript at a late stage. Her commentary reinforced (and corrected) many crucial perceptions.

Nikos Petsios and his lovely wife Effie Giannopoulos helped me in innumerable ways—including hosting my writing at their gorgeous Zagori Suites—during my trips to Epirus.

Infinite thanks to Alexis Papachristos and to Aphrodite Psina and her father Pavlos Psinas for facilitating my first meeting with the Zoumbas brothers.

Amanda Petrusich, friend and writer, traveled with me to Epirus. She has encouraged my obsession with the music of Epirus and my writing efforts. I am very grateful.

I thank Sherry Mayrent, who has been very supportive of my work and my writing. She is indeed one of the unsung heroes of traditional music preservation.

Takimi, an ensemble consisting of Tasos Daflos, George Gouvas, Thomas Haliyiannis, Kostas Karapanos, Fotis Papazikos, gave me priceless, first-hand experience with the traditional music of Zagori. I am especially grateful to Kostas Karapanos, my violin teacher, who explained many of the subtleties of Epirotic playing.

Gregoris Kapsalis, Michalis Zoumbas, and Napoleon Zoumbas— three outstanding musicians from the old school—gave me a schooling in the largely unspoken and undocumented relationship between the musician and his village. These three men are precious gems and among the best of their generation.

Yiannis Chaldoupis, his wife Nellie Kramer, and his group Moukliomos gave me valuable insight into the music of Pogoni.

Caitlin Rose—first at the *Oxford American* and then at the *Paris Review*—has given me sustained friendship and insight.

My friend George Charisis took beautiful photographs of Michalis and Napoleon Zoumbas and helped me indirectly to acquire an indelible mark during my first visit to Vitsa.

Preston Lauterbach has been a very good friend, neighbor, and counsel. His intimate knowledge of the drafting and publishing process has been extremely helpful.

I thank Menelaos Sykovelis for the moving photograph of Yiannis Chaldoupis.

I'm grateful to David and Mark Freeman for allowing ample time off from work for my travels abroad.

I've learned much from the editorial direction of and correspondence with Maxwell George of the *Oxford American*.

My friend Phillip Gregory Sougles contributed additional translations and commentary and hosted me in his spacious apartment in Athens. I thank him profusely.

Spending a few days in Athens with my friend Dimitris Kampourakis taught me a great deal about Cretan hospitality but also about overcoming my fear of motorcycles.

I'm thankful to the ethnomusicologist George Kokkonis for all of his help and scholarly work.

Stephanie Larson of Bucknell University took an early interest in my work and contributed translations and commentary.

I am humbled by the encouragement for my work shown by my friends at the *Paris Review*, including Dan Pipenbring, Lorin Stein, and John Jeremiah Sullivan.

Julia Olin and Blaine Wade of the National Council for the Traditional Arts who, along with the Association of Performing Arts Presenters and the Andrew W. Mellon Foundation, helped fund and coordinate a field recording session in Epirus.

I am grateful for the assistance of Vangelis Giannakos, the chairman of the Saracatsani Brotherhood; Basilis Salmas, president of the Fraternity of Saracatsans from Epirus in Athens; Vassilis Katsoupas, chairman of the ZEN association; the Zagori Cultural Association; and the Rizarios Foundation.

For their hospitality, lodging, and excellent food, I thank Kostas and Anna Vasdekis of En Hora Vizitsa, Demetrios "Takis" Karagiannis and Maria of Selini, Alekos and Maria Vatavalis of Filira, and Yiannis and Anthoula Tsapounis of Kafe-Ouzeri Artozis.

Many friends on both sides of the Atlantic have helped me in my writing, my travels, and my engagement with this music. I wish to thank the following: Elli Alexiou, Patroula Anagnostaki, Susan Archie, Pierre Authier, Daniel Bachman, Ben Blackwell, Chris Bopst, Jen Bopst, Ben Briggs, Caleb Briggs, Demetris "Takis" Chantzaropoulos, John Cohen, Anna Davis, Paul Duane, Eric Ederer, Robert Elsie, Nick Franco, Nick Gage, Denise Gill, Nikos Gogos, Stuart Gunter, Gottfried Hagen, John Haley, Kiki Harisis, Stratos Harisis, Tasos Harisis, Vassilis Harisis, Bryan Hoffa, Charles Howard, George Johann, Paddy Jordan, Giorgos Karagiannis, Polyvios Karras, Charalambos "Babis" Karvounis, Takis Kefalas, Marty Key, Evi Kita, George Kokkonis, Chris Leva, Kostas Lolis, Nicki Maher, Vicky Michopoulou, Philip J. Murphy Jr., Rich Nevins, Michalis Oikonomides, Thanasis Paliatsos, Christos Papachristos, Vangelis Papachristos, Dan Peck, Jesse Poe, John Reiser, Alexandros Spyrou, Ekaterina Spyrou, Spiros Spyrou, Kalliopi Stara, Panayiotis Tellis, Tom Tierney, John Tsaparis, Elektra Vasdeki, Stathis Vasdekis, John Williams, Maria Zoumbas.

Ultimately, without the love and support of my wife Charmagne, our children Riley and Caleb, and my mom Anna, this book would not have been written. They have been infinitely patient with my efforts, sacrificing their own time and happiness so that I might have the opportunity to research and write. Charmagne in particular spent many long days reading drafts and offering suggestions, insights, and commentary that would otherwise have escaped me. My wife has shown me that nothing is ever completely lost. My children have shown me the wonderment contained within each note of music that we produce. My mother gave me the breath of life, a continuous supply of books, and inspiration. I owe my deepest gratitude to them.

NOTES

1. I understand the concept of *folk* as a positive and negative binary. A positive definition is a set of behaviors, norms, and beliefs accepted by members who see their cultural identity as distinct from other groups. The negative definition is that members value a resistance to assimilation to *the other*: other ethnic groups, other linguistic groups, and other religious groups. People belonging to a particular folk tradition almost always identify themselves as originating from a specific location. If they relocate to a different location, they tend to form their own enclaves.

2. My rendering of Greek words into Latin character transliterations is largely an approximation based on what I hear in the villages of Epirus. That being said, I've rendered πανηγύρι as *panegyri*. This is the standard transliteration based on convention and established orthography.

3. This and all other song translations are by Demetris P. Dallas.

4. Where we were heading, the village of Vitsa in Zagori, was one of few regions that had operated semi-autonomously and reasonably free of Ottoman control. In 1430, a treaty was signed between the Ottoman Sinan Pasha (a Greek agent of the Ottomans) and leaders of Zagori establishing special privileges for Zagorians. It was a classic example of a protection racket—security and freedom for the Zagorians in exchange for compliance and a steady flow of revenue for the Ottomans.

5. One conduit of wealth collection central to the Turkish revenue machine was the janissary. In its best light it was a "forced draft" of a village's best and brightest. Young Greek men given to the local *bey* would be sent to Constantinople for an education in the Turkish language. Afterwards, the men would enter specialized fields needed for the empire: military or

naval training, bookkeeping, and governmental occupations of all sorts. These conscripted servants created a "closed loop system" for revenue collection. The most fortunate janissaries returned to their home region, thereby insuring some degree of favoritism or wealth for their ancestral village. This is one reason why some regions of Epirus—central Zagori for instance—were more prosperous and stable than others. However, the darkest light cast on this system reveals that it was nothing more than slavery, particularly when women and children were "collected" for the empire.

6. To this day there are many Greek villages in Albania but no Albanian villages in Greece. At the end of the Greek Civil War, Albanians living in northwestern Greece—called Chams—were expelled to Albania for having aided the fascists during World War II and for supporting the Communists seeking to "liberate" Greece.

7. The music of Epirus does not draw deeply from microtonal or quarter-tone scales—they are not part of the original musical biosphere. However, songs and dances from Asia Minor are nowadays performed at *panegyria* in Epirus. Music of Asia Minor and other parts of Greece draw from traditions that do not exclusively divide a scale into whole and half steps, but incrementally into quarter tones or other "microtones."

8. It has long been assumed that music theory was uniform throughout the Greek-speaking world. Certainly there is no direct evidence of asymmetric developments between music in the city and in the village. How could there be? No one wrote about the music and musicians that existed outside of cosmopolitan areas such as Athens. "History is normally written by and for the elites," says American archaeologist Jane Buikstra discussing the Archaic period of ancient Greece. Ancient Greek music, at least up until the third century BC, is understood largely through the lens of philosophy and literature written in the cities. But we do know a few things that suggest music theory was not uniform across Greek territories.

    Greece at this time, and earlier, was not a homogeneous, unified culture. Outside of the cities—out in the country—culture was sometimes divided along tribal, social, and linguistic lines. The Dorians, the Ionians, the Phrygians, and the Lydians (to name a few) were tribes with their own dialects, their own customs, and their own concepts of melody—*harmonia*, or octave species. Philosophical and musicological writings associated the tribal name with the indigenous *harmonia*. This implies that from a scalar or tonal perspective, the Greek tribes had an understanding of music that differed from educated city dwellers.

    By analogy, we can assume that music was different in the rural villages simply because life and culture in the cities diverged from life in the country. Robert Guisepi, writing about economics in classical Greece, says that

Peasants shared beliefs in the gods and goddesses about which the playwrights wrote, but their religious celebrations were largely separate from those of the upper classes. At times Greek peasants showed their interest in some of the more emotional religious practices imported from the Middle East, which provided more color than the official ceremonies of the Greek pantheon and spiced the demanding routines of work.

And to this, the text *Ancient Greece: A Political, Social and Cultural History* clarifies,

A considerable degree of social and cultural segregation was inherent in the demography of the Hellenistic kingdoms. As Greek settlement was predominately urban, the countryside inevitably was largely cut off from Greek influence.

If there were cultural, economic, and religious differences between upper-class urban Greeks and peasants from the countryside, it follows that there were differences in their music.

Dissimilarities between cosmopolitan and rural music making in ancient Greece are manifested indirectly in the contemporary historical record. For instance, by the eighteenth century, certain regions of rural Greece possessed specific types of aerophones to the exclusion of others: the shrill folk oboe, the *zourna*, was found in the Peloponnese, the *tszamara* concentrated in northwestern Greece, the *gaida* or bagpipe in Macedonia and Thrace, and the *tsabouna* or droneless bagpipe on certain islands and Asia Minor. Each type of wind instrument implied scales and techniques that could not be wholly transferred to another wind instrument. Similarly, different configurations of bowed string instruments—*lyra*—developed in isolated pockets across Asia Minor, the Aegean Islands, and the mainland. The scalar approach of one string instrument cannot be readily adapted to the next, despite their outward similarities.

We are not sure what explains this diversity of folk instruments and their internal melodic language, but I think that the proliferation of various indigenous instruments implied a native understanding of music unique to each region. Disparate musical sensibilities led to tribal (and regional) specialization of instruments.

9. Between 1922 and 1923 the Greek-speaking natives of Asia Minor were expelled to mainland Greece.

10. The Turks kept most Greeks illiterate during the Ottoman occupation. Education did take place—sometimes in secret—but literacy was not general in Greece until it became a modern, independent nation. From the time of the Roman conquest of Greece (and before) until the decline of the Byzantine Empire, most literature was composed by and for the elite in

urban areas and for use within the religious orders. Prior to the liberation of Greece from the Ottomans, the best educated were those living abroad or working for the Turkish administration. Therefore accounts of common village activities—such as *panegyria*—were either not recorded or simply vanished.

11. Inhabiting this region in what is now southwestern Albania and north-western Epirus was another tribe, the Chaonians. Like other Greek-speaking peoples of Epirus, they entered into a confederacy around 320 BC with the Molossian. It would not be unreasonable to assume that the Chaonians developed their own particular fixation on Pan, since much of their livelihood depended upon shepherding. Pausanias himself wrote of seeing sites sacred to Pan when he traveled through these parts.

12. In Epirus, the words Τσιγγάνος, Gypsy, and Ρομά, Roma, are interchangeable. Both non-Roma Greeks and Roma Greeks use these words. There are other words used for "Gypsy." It should be stressed that people of Roma or Gypsy descent see themselves as Greek.

13. *Tsarouchia* are stiff leather shoes with pom-poms on the toes. They were traditionally worn for dancing.

14. Though abuses have not been as systemic as the institution of slavery in the antebellum southern United States nor as brutal as the rash of lynching experienced in the Jim Crow era, there are parallels between certain social conditions of the lives of the Roma in northwestern Greece and the lives of African Americans in the southern United States.

15. There is a singular goal in crafting these bells. Each batch of *koudounia* must possess a tone similar to the collective whole. The shepherd needs to identify his flock by this uniquely pitched note. The shepherd also needs his flock to be, in the words of Arthur Foss, "naturally gathered"—he wants to exploit his sheep's biological predisposition "to follow a leader" to make his onerous job slightly easier. Foss, a late-twentieth-century travelogue writer of Epirus, states, "The chief ram in the herd had a special deep-toned bell with which all the others harmonized and followed."

16. Earlier, many villages had three *mousikes kompanies*, musical groups. Before the use of amplification, it was not unusual for a village like Vitsa to have three different bands playing in various locations so that everyone had the opportunity to be in the midst of the music. Electricity, amplification, and mass media would not reach Epirus until the late 1960s.

17. John Lawson, Lucy Garnett, and John Stuart-Glennie saw clear connections between ancient Greek popular religion and the beliefs of Greek peasants in the nineteenth and early twentieth century. Other scholars argued that only classical literature could access the ancient Greek mind and that contemporary Greeks were far removed from their ancestors. A deeper

critique, and one that is more pervasive nowadays, reduces the beliefs of ancient Greeks and their descendants to simple folklore—stories and beliefs unconnected to meaningful spiritual expression. But this notion smacks of myopic and contemporary ethnocentrism, a perspective that dismisses spiritual beliefs that stand outside of organized religion. This same criticism would reduce the stories and practices of Inuit and other Native Americans to folktales, rejecting the religious dimension of their beliefs. It is crucial to remember that the veneration of Greek gods and the participation in mystery cults was a deeply felt religious activity before the rise of Christianity. When Pan died, thousands mourned.

18. There is little documentation linking the *Anastenaria* directly to a *specific* pre-Christian rite, but there are strong similarities between this ceremony and the *general* characteristics of Dionysian rituals and rites associated with various mystery cults. Dimitris Xygalatas offers an effective critique of the historiography surrounding the *Anastenaria*, arguing instead that political agendas—namely Greek nationalism and Philhellenism—drove the narrative to explain this ceremony as a revenant of Dionysian religion. What Xygalatas does not offer, though, is an alternative theory of the origin of the ritual. In other words, even if the historical methodology is flawed, the *Anastenaria* may still be a ceremony with a pagan foundation or elements of pre-Christian belief.

19. A similar ritual was conducted in Kapesovo centuries ago when the plague-epidemic was in the area, with a procession guided by the Greek-Orthodox Metropolitan of Ioannina.

20. In the mid-1980s, Boila, Klithi, and Megalakkos, three caves on the northern bank of the Voidomatis River near the village of Kleidonia, surrendered a wealth of tools and bones dating within this range of prehistory.

21. Mortillet coined terms such as *Mousterian* and *Solutrean* and founded the first journal dedicated to prehistory, *Les matériaux pour l'histoire positive et philosophique de l'homme* in 1864. Cartailhac became the editor of this journal in 1868.

22. There are some who have described how to extract oneself from the stubborn perspective of one's culture. In part, I've taken my cue from them during this odyssey.

Philosopher of science Thomas Kuhn (1922–1996) articulated an idea first advanced by Pierre Duhem and Willard Van Orman Quine called "epistemic holism." Kuhn argued that if you wanted to understand the function of a thing, you needed to understand its connection to everything else. In order to do this, you must assume a different, incommensurable point of view—removing yourself as much as you can from your own historical and cultural context.

Anthropologist Gregory Bateson spoke of a similar strategy, naming it "system theory." Bateson said, "If you want to understand some phenomenon or appearance, you must consider that phenomenon within the context of all completed circuits which are relevant to it." In this narrative, culture is this context of completed circuits.

BIBLIOGRAPHY

Abbott, G. F. *Macedonian Folklore*. Cambridge: Cambridge University Press, 1903.

Alexiou, Margaret. *Ritual Lament in Greek Tradition*. Cambridge: Cambridge University Press, 1974.

Anderson, Warren. *Music and Musicians in Ancient Greece*. Ithaca, NY: Cornell University Press, 1994.

Aravantinos, Panagiotis [Αραβαντινός, Π.]. *Epirotika Tragoudia* [Ηπειρωτικά Τραγούδια]. Athens: Damianos, 1996. Reprinted from the 1880 edition.

Athenaeus. *The Deipnosophists*, vol. 3, books 6–7. Trans. by Charles Burton Gulick. Cambridge: Cambridge University Press, 1929.

Barker, Andrew, ed. *Greek Musical Writings*, vol. 1: *The Musician and His Art*. Cambridge: Cambridge University Press, 1984.

Bateson, Gregory. *A Sacred Unity: Further Steps to an Ecology of Mind*. New York: Harper Collins, 1991.

Beaton, Roderick. *Folk Poetry of Modern Greece*. Cambridge: Cambridge University Press, 1980.

Becker, Judith. *Deep Listeners: Music, Emotion and Trancing*. Bloomington: Indiana University Press, 2004.

Blacking, John. *How Musical Is Man?* Seattle: University of Washington Press, 1973.

Blum, Richard, and Eva Blum. *The Dangerous Hour: The Lore and Culture of Crisis and Mystery in Rural Greece*. New York: Charles Scribner's Sons, 1970.

Blum, Richard, and Eva Blum. *Health and Healing in Rural Greece*. Stanford, CA: Stanford University Press, 1965.

Bowden, William. *Epirus Vetus: The Archeology of Late Antiquity*. London: Bristol Classical Press, 2003.

Brewer, David. *Greece, the Hidden Centuries: Turkish Rule from the Fall of Constantinople to Greek Independence.* London: I. B. Tauris & Co., 2010.

Brondsted, Peter Oluf. *Interviews with Ali Pacha of Joanina.* Edited by Jacob Isager. Aarhus: Aarhus University Press, 1999.

Buikstra, Jane. "American School of Classical Studies Investigating Deviant Burials at Faliro." Interview by Sakis Ioannidis. ekathimerini.com, 2016.

Calt, Stephen. *I'd Rather Be the Devil: Skip James and the Blues.* Chicago, IL: Chicago Review Press, 1994.

Campbell, J. K. *Honor, Family and Patronage: A Study of Institutions and Moral Values in a Greek Mountain Community.* Oxford: Clarendon Press, 1964.

Carter, Tristan. "Neanderthals in a Boat?" Interviewed by Kate Allen. thestar.com, December 27, 2016.

Clarke, Edward Daniel. *Travels in Various Countries of Europe, Asia and Africa.* London: printed for T. Cadell and W. Davies, 1816.

Clogg, Richard (editor). *Minorities in Greece: Aspects of a Plural Society.* London: C. Hurst & Co., 2002.

Cowan, Jane. *Dance and the Body Politic in Northern Greece.* Princeton, NJ: Princeton University Press, 1990.

Cross, Geoffrey Neale. *Epirus: A Study in Greek Constitutional Development.* Cambridge: Cambridge University Press, 1932.

Dalven, Rae. *The Jews of Ioannina.* Philadelphia: Cadmus Press, 1990.

Danforth, Loring, and Alexander Tsiaras. *The Death Rituals of Rural Greece.* Princeton, NJ: Princeton University Press, 1982.

Davenport, R. A. *The Life of Ali Pasha of Tepeleni.* London: Thomas Tegg & Son, 1837 (originally published 1822).

Demos, John, [Δήμου, Γιάννης], ed. *Zagorision Vios* [Ζαγορισίων Βίος]. Athens: Rizarios Foundation, 2003. With English translation by Demetris P. Dallas.

Dodds, E. R. *The Greeks and the Irrational.* Berkeley and Los Angeles: University of California Press, 1968.

Fermor, Patrick Leigh. *Roumeli: Travels in Northern Greece.* New York Review of Books, 1966.

Finkel, Caroline. *Osman's Dream: The History of the Ottoman Empire.* New York: Basic Books, 2005.

Foss, Arthur. *Epirus.* London: Faber, 1978.

Fox, Robin Lane. *Pagans and Christians.* New York: Harper & Row, 1988.

Fromm, Annette. *We Are Few: Folklore and Ethnic Identity of the Jewish Community of Ioannina, Greece.* Lanham, MD: Lexington Books, 2007.

Gage, Nicholas. *Eleni.* New York: Ballantine, 1996.

Garland, Robert. *The Greek Way of Death.* Ithaca, NY: Cornell University Press, 1985.

Garnett, L. M. J. *Greek Folk Songs.* London: Elliot Stock, 1885.

Garnett, L. M. J., and J. S. Stuart-Glennie. *Greek Folk Poesy.* 2 vols. London: Billing & Sons, 1896.

Greene, William Chase. *Moira: Fate, Good and Evil in Greek Thought.* New York: Harper Torchbooks, 1963.

Guisepi, Robert. "Economy and Society in Classical Greece." academia.edu, n.d.

Hammond, N. G. L. *Epirus: The Geography, the Ancient Remains, the History and the Topography of Epirus and Adjacent Areas.* Oxford: Oxford Press, 1967.

Hawks, John. "Were Neanderthals Religious?" Interview by Barbara J. King. NPR, *Cosmos and Culture*, December 7, 2016.

Hesiod. *Homeric Hymns and Homerica.* Trans. by Hugh G. Evelyn-White. Cambridge: Cambridge University Press, 1914.

Higgs, E. S., and D. Webley. "Further Information Concerning the Environment of Palaeolithic Man in Epirus." *Proceedings of the Prehistoric Society* 37 (1971), pp. 367–80.

Holland, Henry. *Travels in the Ionian Isles, Albania, Thessaly, Macedonia during the Years 1812 and 1813.* London: Longman, Hurst, Rees, Orme, and Brown, 1815.

Holst-Warhaft, Gail. *Dangerous Voices: Women's Laments and Greek Literature.* London and New York: Routledge, 1992.

Hourani, Albert. *A History of the Arab Peoples.* New York: MJF Books, 1991.

Hughes, Thomas Smart. *Travels in Sicily, Greece and Albania.* London: J. Mawman, 1820.

Kaplan, Robert. *Balkan Ghosts: A Journey through History.* New York: St. Martin's Press, 1993.

Kavakopoulos, Pantelis [Καβακόπουλος, Παντελής]. *Tragoudi, Mousiki, kai Horos stin Epiro* [Τραγούδι, μουσική και χορός στην Ήπειρο]. Ioannina, 2016.

Katsenos, Demetrios [Κάτσενος, Δημήτριος], ed. *Sarakatsanaioi, Poreia ston Topo kai sto Hrono* [Σαρακατσαναίοι, Πορεία στον Τόπο και στο Χρόνο]. Athens: Sarakatsan Fraternity of Athens, 2012.

Kokkonis, Yiorgos [Κοκκώνης, Γιώργος], ed. *Mousiki apo tin Epiro* [Μουσική από την Ήπειρο]. Athens: Hellenic Parliament Foundation, 2008.

Krystallis, Kostas [Κρυστάλλης, Κώστας]. *Pezographimata* [Πεζογραφήματα]. Athens, 1894.

Kubler, George. *The Shape of Time: Remarks on the History of Things.* New Haven, CT: Yale University Press, 1962.

Kuhn, Thomas. *The Structure of Scientific Revolutions.* 3rd ed. Chicago: University of Chicago Press, 1996.

Lawson, John Cuthbert. *Modern Greek Folklore and Ancient Greek Religion: A Study in Survivals.* Cambridge: Cambridge University Press, 1910.

Lazaridis, Kostas [Λαζαρίδης, Κώστας]. *Zagori kai Demotiki Mousa* [Ζαγόρι και Δημοτική Μούσα]. Ioannina, 1973.

Leake, William. *Travels in Northern Greece*, vol. 1. Boston: Adamant, 2001.

Levi, Peter. *The Hill of Kronos*. New York: E. P. Dutton, 1981.

Levin, Flora R. *Greek Reflections On the Nature of Music*. Cambridge: Cambridge University Press, 2009.

Lolis, Kostas [Λώλης, Κώστας]. *Mirologi kai Skaros* [Μοιρολόϊ και Σκάρος]. Ioannina, 2003.

Lowery, Heath. *The Shaping of the Ottoman Balkans, 1350–1550: The Conquest, Settlement and Infrastructural Development of Northern Greece*. Istanbul: Bahcesehir University, 2008.

Michaelides, Solon. *Music of Ancient Greece: An Encyclopaedia*. London: Faber & Faber, 1978.

Mithen, Steven. *After the Ice: A Global Human History 20,000–5000 BC*. Cambridge, MA: Harvard University Press, 2006.

Nachman, Eftihia. *Yannina: A Journey to the Past*. New York: Bloch Publishing Company, 2004.

Nilsson, Martin. *Greek Popular Religion*. New York: Columbia University Press, 1940.

Plomer, William. *The Diamond of Jannina: Ali Pasha, 1741–1822*. New York: Taplinger Publishing, 1970.

Pomeroy, Sarah, Stanley Burstein, Walter Donlan, and Jennifer Roberts. *Ancient Greece: A Political, Social, and Cultural History*. New York: Oxford University Press, 1999.

Potts, Jim. "Epirote Folk Music." *Anglo-Hellenic Review*, Spring 2006.

Potts, Jim. *The Ionian Islands and Epirus: A Cultural History*. Oxford: Oxford University Press, 2010.

Price, Derek J. de Solla. "An Ancient Greek Computer." *Scientific American*, June 1, 1959, pp. 60-67.

Psaroudakis, Stelios [Ψαρουδάκης, Στέλιος]. "Protogeni Aerophona kai i Avevaie Martiria tou Dispiliou" [Πρωτογενή αερόφωνα και η αβέβαιη μαρτυρία του Δισπηλιού]. Polyphonia, Tefchos 2, Anixi. 2003, pp. 7–20.

Racy, A. J. *Making Music in the Arab World: The Culture and Artistry of Tarab*. Cambridge: Cambridge University Press, 2003.

Rancière, Jacques. *Aisthesis: Scenes from the Aesthetic Regime of Art*. New York: Verso, 2013.

Romaios, K. A. "Greek Popular Dances." *Labyrinth* 1 (1973), 49–57.

Rouget, Gilbert. *Music and Trance*. Chicago: University of Chicago Press, 1985.

Sachs, Curt. *Our Musical Heritage: A Short History of World Music*. New York: Prentice-Hall. 1948.

Saunier, Guy. *To Demotiko Tragoudi tis Xenitias* [Το Δημοτικό Τραγούδι της Ξενιτιάς]. Ioannina: Hermes, 1990. Reprint of 1983 edition.

Schlesinger, Kathleen. *The Greek Aulos: A Study of Its Mechanism and Its Relation to the Modal System of Ancient Greek Music*. London: Methuen, 1939.

Sextus Empiricus. Against the Musicians. Ed. and trans. by Denise Davidson Greaves. Lincoln: University of Nebraska Press, 1986.

Sfalagakos, Panayotis. "The Role of Theory in Translating the 'Moiroloi,' or Ritual Lament, of Inner Mani." pp. 175–185. In *Thinking Translation: Perspectives from Within and Without.* Conference Proceedings, Third UEA Postgraduate Translation Symposium.

Theodosiou, Aspasia. *Authenticity, Ambiguity, Location: Gypsy Musicians on the Greek-Albanian Border.* [Germany:] VDM Verlag Dr. Muller, 2011.

Touma, Habib Hassan. *The Music of the Arabs.* Portland, OR: Amadeus Press, 1996.

Tsiaras, Anastasios [Τσιάρας, Αναστάσιος]. Laikes Kompanies–Laika Organa kai Laiki Praktiki Organopaichtes [Λαϊκές Κομπανίες–Λαϊκά Όργανα και Λαϊκοί Πρακτικοί οργανοπαίχτες]. Ioannina, 1987.

Wace, A. J. B., and M. S. Thompson. *The Nomads of the Balkans.* London: Methuen & Co., 1914.

Wiseman, James, and Konstantinos Zachos, eds. *Landscape Archaeology in Southern Epirus, Greece, 1.* Vol. 23, American School of Classical Studies at Athens, 2003.

Xygalatas, Dimitris. "Ethnography, Historiography, and the Making of History in the Tradition of the Anastenaria." *History and Anthropology* 22, no. 1 (March 2011), pp. 57–74.

Zissis, Costas. *Zagori: Images of a Greek Heritage.* Athens, 2016.

DISCOGRAPHY

Chaldoupis, Yiannis, and Moukliomos. *Parakalamos: Field Recordings from Pogoni, Epirus*. JSP Records, 2014.

Floudas, Yiorgos, and Vassilis Triantis. *Arta: Field Recordings from Arta and Preveza, Greece*. JSP Records, 2015.

Harisiadis, Kitsos. *Lament in a Deep Style, 1929–1931*. Third Man Records, 2018.

Ta Takoutsia [Τα Τακούτσια]. To Glendi tou Manthou [*Το Γλέντι του Μάνθου, Σύλλογος Νέων Αρίστης*]. Produced by Costas Zissis. Syllogos Neon Aristis Zagoriou, 1999.

Takimi of Epirus. *Vitsa: Field Recordings from Greece*. JSP Records, 2014.

[Various.] *Five Days Married and Other Laments, 1928–1958*. Angry Mom Records, 2013.

[Various.] *Why the Mountains Are Black: Primeval Greek Village Music, 1907–1960*. Third Man Records, 2016.

Zoumbas, Alexis. *A Lament for Epirus: 1926–1928*. Angry Mom Records, 2014.

ILLUSTRATION CREDITS

INDEX

Note: Page numbers in *italics* refer to illustrations.